PARTY ANIMALS

PARTY ANIMALS

SAMANTHA MAIDEN

THE SECRET HISTORY OF A
LABOR FIASCO

VIKING
an imprint of
PENGUIN BOOKS

VIKING

UK | USA | Canada | Ireland | Australia
India | New Zealand | South Africa | China

Viking is part of the Penguin Random House group of companies
whose addresses can be found at global.penguinrandomhouse.com

First published by Viking in 2020

Copyright © Samantha Maiden, 2020

The moral right of the author has been asserted.

All rights reserved. No part of this publication may be reproduced, published, performed in
public or communicated to the public in any form or by any means without prior written
permission from Penguin Random House Australia Pty Ltd or its authorised licensees.

Cover photograph by Dominic Lorrimer/*The Sydney Morning Herald*
Cover design by James Rendall © Penguin Random House Australia Pty Ltd
Typeset in Adobe Garamond Pro by Midland Typesetters, Australia

Printed and bound in Australia by Griffin Press, part of Ovato, an accredited
ISO AS/NZS 14001 Environmental Management Systems printer

 A catalogue record for this
book is available from the
National Library of Australia

ISBN 978 1 76089 315 6

penguin.com.au

For Matilda, Bill and Ned

CONTENTS

	Introduction: Risky Business	1
1	Keating and Kelty	13
2	Campaign	29
3	Mayday	41
4	The Bill Labor Couldn't Afford	53
5	Mother of All Lies	63
6	Choppergate	79
7	The Politics of Rape	95
8	Negative Gear	117
9	Retirees, Karma and the Death Tax	135
10	Blame Game	153
11	An Unexpected Week at Portsea	165
12	Silence of the Lambs	185
13	The Quiet Australians	197

14	An Act of Bastardry	209
15	Clive Palmer and Adani	231
16	Not Changing the Rules	255
17	The Ballad of Kaila Murnain	271
18	Albo's Destiny Thing	291
Acknowledgements		313

INTRODUCTION
RISKY BUSINESS

Bill Shorten had grand ambitions to become Australia's next Bob Hawke. It must have come as a rude shock to discover that he was, instead, starring in the revival of the 1993 musical *Fightback!*, faithfully retracing the steps of John Hewson. A quarter of a century separates the defeats, but both men can claim the miserable honour of losing the unlosable election. Hewson campaigned for a GST from opposition but could not explain how the new tax would apply to a birthday cake. Shorten pledged action on climate change, but could not explain how much his policies would cost the economy. Too late, the Labor leader hit on a better answer: that doing nothing would cost Australians more.

Like Hewson before him, Shorten faced a prime minister known for his arrogance, who had served as treasurer before contesting a leadership ballot, who was damaged by internal leadership wars and was written off and underestimated in the looming contest. Paul Keating and Scott Morrison were fighting elections nobody expected them to win and campaigned without the weight of great expectations beyond an honourable defeat. Instead, they ended up winning. Can these victories be explained solely by their campaign brilliance? Of course not.

Both leaders wanted to tell voters the truth about their big policy agenda. They believed voters would reward their honesty. It didn't go exactly to plan. Labor was heavily influenced by the lessons of Julia Gillard and her carbon tax 'lie', and the fate of Tony Abbott, who won the next election with promises of 'no cuts to hospitals, no cuts to schools', before he did just that in his first budget. If trust was broken between voters and politicians, Labor hoped to heal that scar on democracy with transparency.

The Labor Party's own report into the 2019 election defeat, conducted by former SA Premier Jay Weatherill and Craig Emerson, nominates multiple reasons for the fiasco. First, Labor did not settle on a persuasive strategy for winning the election. Second, there was no formal campaign committee established, a claim rejected by those who point out there was a 'strategic review group' that included Labor's Campaign Director Noah Carroll and the leadership group. It's reasonable to suggest, however, that it was not terribly effective and did not meet after the election was called.

Also highlighted by the report was the fact that Labor

didn't craft a simple narrative, and lacked a culture and structure that encouraged debate, which led to the dismissal of warnings from within the party about the campaign's direction. In addition, Labor targeted too many seats, ensuring resources were spread too thinly. Labor's election campaign did not adapt to the new Liberal leader and his reframing of the election as a choice between himself and Shorten.

The change in Liberal leadership was a fundamental shift that the review notes required careful analysis and consideration – 'but this did not occur'. The report also claimed there was 'no documented strategy that had been discussed, contested and agreed across the campaign organisation, the leadership and the wider Labor Party'. This is a finding disputed by Shorten's office, who note that the ALP reviewers Weatherill and Emerson never asked them to provide any strategy documents. But whatever the truth, few seemed to know what the strategy was.

Labor was on high alert for an early election. But Labor did not expect danger to arrive in the form of the Liberal Party dumping a sitting prime minister. This was a rupture that most believed signalled the end of the government.

Much has been written about the genius of Scott Morrison turning up in Queensland wearing a baseball cap, but surely there is more to his victory than a dress-ups box. The prime minister was aided and abetted by an opposition that had dared to awaken the sleeping giant of Australia's democracy: voters' deep, primal fear of risk.

Veteran Labor campaign strategist Peter Barron, an adviser to Hawke and Keating who travelled with Shorten during the election, hates giving interviews. He prides himself on keeping the confidences of the political and business leaders he has worked with over decades, including the late Kerry Packer. But he would agree to say this: risk was central to Labor's fate.

'The search for a simple answer is a futile search,' he said. 'But the electorate hates risk. There was an accumulation of risk factors. Policy, personality. If you had to choose one word, you would say "risk". I don't think they liked Morrison any more at the end than they did at the start. But I think they thought he was less risky.'

The report explicitly states that 'Bill Shorten's unpopularity contributed to the election loss'. The former Labor leader does not accept this characterisation. However, many of his colleagues do. The idea his popularity was a factor is supported by the Australian National University's trusted electoral study, which found Shorten was the most unpopular leader in 30 years.

The ALP's own post-mortem into the election also accepts this, but arguably overstates it as a contributor to the election loss. Shorten's supporters view the report as a transparent attempt to blame him personally for the defeat. But the intense focus on the popularity of a leader holds future risks for Anthony Albanese too. If the polls suggest he also struggles to excite voters, will the Labor Party be prepared to dump him before the next election?

Consider the evidence of federal elections in Australia's recent history – the winner is frequently the party that can paint its opponent as more risky and radical. Australian voters are risk averse, a tendency pronounced when the economy is in trouble.

In 1993, Barron's brutal advice to Keating was to run on the GST alone – not compassion, or the Asian century, or Aboriginal reconciliation. His anti-GST manual included in the tool kit this memorable line: 'If you don't understand it, don't vote for it, and if you do understand it, you'd never vote for it.' Does that sound familiar? It should, because Morrison stole it to fight Labor's franking-credit reforms at the 2019 election. The Liberal prime minister campaigned parroting the actual words Keating had used to defeat Hewson.

The fate of the referendum on an Australian republic in 1999 is another example. Again, voters demonstrated an aversion to perceived risks, rejecting an Australian head of state. The biggest backlash was in Queensland, Western Australia and Tasmania, the same states that turned on Shorten. As with the 2019 federal election, Victoria and the ACT were the ALP's greenest pastures in the republic referendum.

The winning argument was about risk. The 'No' campaigners called the direct-election model 'the politicians' republic' and claimed you can't trust politicians. One of the most effective slogans was: 'If you want to elect the president, vote No to the politicians' republic.'

The 'No' campaign won the day, based on the argument that it was too risky to abandon the status quo.

Shorten always knew this. In a speech to the Fabian Society in 2004, he said, 'In the 1999 republic referendum, [John] Howard understood that inner-suburban voters, with both

Liberal or Labor tendencies, would support a republic. The "No" vote would be found in the outer suburbs and regions where people were sceptical about the "risk" of change. These suburbs and towns have become Howard's political heartland – the PM plays directly to their aspirations, fears and prejudices.'

In 2007, Kevin Rudd and the ACTU's 'Your Rights at Work' campaign won by painting Prime Minister John Howard as the radical. They did that with the ammunition the Liberal Party gave them: WorkChoices. The industrial relations laws set off genuine concerns in the community, which Rudd surfed into government. In 2013, Tony Abbott framed former Prime Minister Julia Gillard as a liar and a radical for introducing a carbon tax. Playing 'spot the radical' at the next election, Labor argued the Turnbull Government were the radicals plotting to privatise Medicare. The history of Health Minister Peter Dutton's $7 co-payment for GP visits under Abbott underlined the threat.

The man who taught Shorten how to be a union leader in the 1990s, former ACTU Assistant Secretary Chris Walton, argues elections are always won and lost on one question. 'Who is the radical? Generally you will find whoever is able to paint the opponent as the radical wins,' he says. 'How did Keating and Bill Kelty get away with some of their radical changes? Keating's argument is you always get away with more if you put it in a frame.'

The bigger reform story provides the architecture. But the frame Scott Morrison used against Labor was simple and devastating. Every reform was reduced to a new tax. Negative-gearing reforms designed to boost housing affordability are called a housing tax, franking-credits reforms are a retiree tax. Vehicle-emissions targets? That's a car tax.

Morrison even managed to turn Labor's new target for 50 per cent electric cars by 2030 into a plot to 'end the weekend' in Australia. 'And in typical Labor fashion, they want to ram it down the necks of all Australians,' said the prime minister. 'So the cheapest car you can currently buy, as an electric vehicle, presently, my understanding is, including all on-road costs and the rest of it, is about $45,000 to $50,000 a year. That's the cheapest car Bill Shorten wants to make available to you to buy in the future, and I'll tell you what – it's not going to tow your trailer. It's not going to tow your boat. It's not going to get you out to your favourite camping spot with your family. Bill Shorten wants to end the weekend when it comes to his policy on electric vehicles where you've got Australians who love being out there in their four-wheel drives. He wants to say see you later to the SUV when it comes to the choices of Australians.'

Politicians have taken risks and won elections, but it's easier to do from government than opposition. John Howard took the GST to the 1998 election, for example – a big risk – and still won, although barely.

But instead of calming a nervous electorate on the risk question, Shorten's campaign championed change. Returning to the Blacktown hall where Whitlam had launched his 'It's Time' campaign, Shorten said, 'Never has the case for change been more clear or more urgent. Do we have the capacity to push through it?' he asked. The answer arrived a few days later on election night. 'No.'

It was galling for Labor to lose to a prime minister they regarded as a policy-free zone. As ALP frontbencher Mark Butler observed, it was a government that Morrison himself had compared with *The Muppet Show* during the leadership ballot, and when you get your 'backside handed to you by Fozzie Bear and Kermit the Frog – it's time for some serious reflection'.

The lesson is not simply that you cannot have risky policies, but that you must also paint your opponent as riskier. In 2004, Howard was expected to lose to Mark Latham but framed him as dangerous, flaky, an 'L-plate leader'. After he was filmed delivering a bone-crushing handshake to Howard during the election, it seemed he could not be trusted to shake your hand, let alone run the economy. Could a man who went AWOL during a tsunami and then shaved off his own hair, which he did, shortly before he quit as party leader in January 2005, be trusted to keep the nation relaxed and comfortable?

Latham's resignation was preceded by a meeting of the ALP national executive in Anthony Albanese's office in November 2004 that included a who's who of the Labor Party: Campaign Director Tim Gartrell, who is now Albanese's chief of staff; union leader Bill Ludwig from Queensland and a unionist called Mark Butler from South Australia, who went on to federal politics (and calling Scott Morrison a muppet); Labor pollster John Utting, and the Australian Workers' Union's national secretary, Bill Shorten.

Shorten warned at the time that the lessons of Latham's defeat were self-evident. 'The principal lesson from four federal election losses is clear,' he wrote. 'Labor has failed to establish its economic management credentials to voters in the provincial centres and outer suburbs of metropolitan Australia. Economic credibility is a gateway through which Labor must pass before it can bring its policy strengths in health and education to bear.

'In 2004, Labor failed to dent the Coalition's commanding lead as economic managers. Instead, Labor relied on its traditional strengths in health care and education, together with a dramatic appeal in environment policy. Labor underestimated the impact of the daily media cycle, looking for new issues within a day of the release of key announcements.'

Fifteen years before he lost the election, Shorten had written his own political obituary.

Before he entered parliament, Shorten had argued Labor should reject the theory that people want services rather than tax cuts. Many voters, he argued, wanted both. 'The Hawke and Keating Governments introduced seven different income tax cuts over thirteen years,' he wrote. 'Labor should support personal income tax cuts and fewer, simpler business taxes. This will send a powerful message of understanding about managing productivity in a competitive economy. The time for short-term fixes is over. Labor's supporters want us to talk dollars as well as sense.'

But it was a lesson Labor had forgotten by the time Treasurer Josh Frydenberg handed down his first budget on 2 April, in which the Liberals announced a projected surplus and tax cuts. Labor's leadership group, gathered together in a budget lock-up to run through the numbers, decided against offering greater relief to more workers beyond low-income families. In the days that followed, Tanya Plibersek, Chris Bowen and Jim Chalmers all argued against going beyond that. 'When they matched the tax cuts, people came to me and said, "Well, we can't do [bigger] tax cuts,"' Shorten said in an interview for this book.

This is not the way Labor's Treasury spokesman Chris Bowen remembers it. 'Nobody was arguing for tax cuts,' he said. Even if they had, Labor's big spending in health and education would have precluded additional tax cuts. Shorten's pet project, Labor's Medicare Plan for Cancer, didn't leave a lot of extra room. 'They matched us on tax cuts,' said Bowen. 'We just didn't have room [for more tax cuts] with health and education spending.'

Ultimately, Shorten announced on the eve of the election that Labor would offer a better deal for workers earning under $40,000 but it would not support tax cuts for high-income earners in the later years. 'We will not be signing up to the Liberals' radical, right-wing, flat-tax experiment, way off in the future, a scheme that would see a nurse on $50,000 paying the same tax rate as a surgeon on $200,000,' he said.

It is one of his biggest regrets of his time as ALP leader. 'Yes, the bracket that we targeted should be first, but for the ten million Australians who earn less than $125,000 a year, in hindsight now we needed to be offering them tax relief,' he said. 'The government was defending tax breaks for the very well off, but they were using these people as human shields and we should have taken them off the table and given them greater return and response, which is another way of stimulating expenditure as well. And if I had my time again, I should have argued the case for more.'

Delivering bigger tax cuts would not have solved all of his problems. Shorten underplays his own failure in controlling the spenders in his cabinet. In fact, he was one of them. This new spending demanded his economic team search for new policies, including franking credits, that were weaponised during the campaign. It was an election that Labor should not have lost, but the lessons go deeper than one campaign or the failure of one leader.

Shorten always believed he had been underestimated. 'The reason why is this. Everyone told me I couldn't beat Abbott. Everyone told me to vote for the 2014 budget. Everyone told me Malcolm Turnbull was unbeatable. I am constantly told we are going to fail. There were a lot of times when people have told me it's not going to happen.'

This time, Shorten was convinced it was going to happen. Not because he was arrogant or triumphant, but because, he believed, the data told him so.

In an interview for this book, Shorten later compared the 2019 election to piloting a plane without navigation instruments. 'Any pilot training to fly a plane, if you're told there's not a mountain in front of you [and] all of a sudden there is a mountain in front of you. You will take different action based on the information and data you are getting.'

Flying after the instrument panel has failed is known as 'partial panel flying'. Pilots train for it, preparing for a potential emergency. To survive, they need to first recognise that there is a failure. They need to rely on instinct. Bill Shorten had good political instincts. But when it was critical, his instincts failed him.

1
KEATING AND KELTY

Scott Morrison just casually dropped it into the last question time before he called the election on 11 April. It was a reference to an old accusation, previously investigated by police, that Bill Shorten had raped a teenage girl at a Labor youth camp in the 1980s. But it was so subtle, so artfully constructed, such a throwaway little line, that few journalists noticed it, let alone reported it. It seemed designed only for Shorten's ears.

'On Tuesday night, for the first time in 12 years, we were able to bring the budget back into surplus, back in the black!' the prime minister said as he pounded his fist on the despatch box. 'The last time the Labor Party saw a budget surplus, as we know, was in 1989.'

But suddenly, it was apparent Morrison was talking about

something else too. 'The leader of the opposition – I don't know what his hairstyle was like back then, but he was running around, I know, at those Labor vanguard conferences at the time, whipping it up with his friends at parties and goodness knows what. That was the last time that we saw a budget surplus delivered by the Labor Party.'

If you watch the video, Shorten doesn't flinch – he continues reading his notes for his budget-in-reply speech. He doesn't even look up. But he heard it. Before Morrison could continue, the Speaker, Tony Smith, intervened. 'The prime minister's time has expired,' he said. Morrison had made his point and walked out of the chamber.

The giveaway is the use of the word 'vanguard'. Anyone who followed the case closely would recall this was the name of the ALP camp where the alleged incident occurred. So, when Morrison referenced the 'vanguard conference' at 3.04 pm, on 4 April 2019, Shorten knew what he was talking about and so did the prime minister.

It landed on the other side of the chamber like unexploded ordnance. In that moment, the prime minister was telling his opponent face-to-face that he remembered the rape claim and that, perhaps, the Liberal Party might have cause to ensure voters were reminded too? For the ALP, it didn't seem like an empty threat.

The Labor leader was losing sleep over it and it was on his mind when he prepared to get some advice from two heroes of the ALP over his campaign strategy: former Prime Minister Paul Keating and Bill Kelty. Shorten told Kelty there was a 'personal issue' he was grappling with. He had confided to staff how deeply worried he was that the Liberal Party would try to use the issue against him. The fear was that the allegations would resurface in the MeToo era, despite the case being closed.

All these years later, as the pair settled down to discuss Shorten's policy speech, Kelty had some other probing questions around the Labor leader's performance in the first fortnight of the campaign. What was it that was getting under his skin and affecting his performance? He didn't seem himself.

Chris Bowen believed the rape allegation was a contributing factor in a disastrous press conference in Adelaide, complaining to colleagues that 'some idiot had told him 10 minutes before that News Corp was going to run the story. Later in the campaign, Shorten confided in Bowen his fears that the allegation would be splashed across the News Corp tabloids. 'They are going to do this,' Shorten said. But Bowen had urged him to put it out of his mind. 'They either will or they won't,' he said. When a controversy blew up over Shorten's late mother during the campaign, the ALP believed the criticism that News Corp had gone too far stopped them from reheating the rape allegation.

Keating's advice to Bill Shorten was blunt. It was delivered over a speakerphone, in the middle of the election campaign, as Shorten sat in a 32nd-floor suite at the Grand Hyatt in Melbourne, finalising his speech for a Sunday rally. 'Remember this: they can't beat you, Bill, only you can beat yourself,' he said. 'If you campaign well, you can't lose. But you've got to have a structure.'

Like a trainer preparing a boxer for a prize fight, he was supposed to be giving the Labor leader a pep talk before the next televised debate. Keating later told MPs he thought Shorten was campaigning badly and that he told him so. But he still believed Labor could turn things around.

Keating's old friend, the former union leader Bill Kelty, was with Shorten in the $2000-a-night suite as the former PM offered his advice. Kelty listened as well, although he hardly needed to – he knew it off by heart. They still spoke regularly, sometimes calling each other on a daily basis.

But there were deeper disagreements left unspoken. 'We both had a real concern about [Shorten's] tax strategy to have tax reform without tax cuts,' said Kelty. 'Paul Keating and I had many conversations. He had them with Chris Bowen and I had them with Bill Shorten.'

Labor was offering tax cuts, but not at the level Kelty and Keating believed was required. Labor planned to hit high-income earners with an effective top tax rate of 49 per cent. That was when Labor's proposed deficit levy and the Medicare levy were added to the base of 45 per cent. It was simply too high.

Keating and Kelty's own philosophy was simple. They did not believe in a small-target strategy. Kelty believed it was proper to pursue reforms, including the removal of tax concessions for negative gearing for investment properties. He was also consulted by Shorten over the plan to abolish franking-credit refunds for shares, an idea the Liberal Party turbocharged by calling it the 'retiree tax'. But there was an important caveat. Kelty believed the proceeds should be devoted to delivering substantial income tax cuts, not simply new spending. Keating agreed with Kelty. The pair, intertwined forever by their shared history in the Hawke Government, were on a unity ticket.

Shorten listened, but he didn't always act on that advice in the lead-up to the 2019 campaign. And if the truth is told, Kelty wasn't always convinced he should. Keating provided plenty of advice to Bowen and Shorten on how to develop killer lines and hone their argument, but it didn't mean that the economic agenda adopted by Labor was the agenda he would have chosen.

In their frequent conversations, Keating and Kelty would discuss that, perhaps, the world had changed and the old rules no longer applied? 'Bill and Chris were convinced the tide had turned on priorities, so tax reform could be used for expenditure,' said Kelty. 'Paul and I thought the world had passed us by.'

The spenders in Labor's shadow cabinet, who were loading up the promises that required the tax increases, were another focus for Kelty's concern. 'These people are murdering you,' Kelty had warned Shorten before the campaign even started. 'You are going to an election with something that's untenable.'

Kelty was also concerned there were too many policies. 'It was like Phar Lap trying to have a jockey with 15 stone on him. You do sit there and think, "If you give another promise, you'll be handing out free toothbrushes to every child, and free toilet paper to incontinent Australians. Christ, mate, there's so many." They appeal to the audience and then, 20 minutes later, people can't remember what the promises were.'

In another life, the Prime Minister, Scott Morrison, had been the architect of the Lara Bingle 'Where the Bloody Hell Are You?' tourism ads. Kelty didn't think much of him as a politician. 'He's an advertising man. The way you beat an advertising man is just go straight for the jugular. Just look at him and say, "You're the highest taxing government in history, you've got an economy growing at 1.5 per cent, personal debt has increased, government debt has increased under your watch, living standards are falling, you've got no health policy, you've got no wages policy. This election will be about you, because you are the worst, incompetent government." And they are. "You've got no energy policy, no climate-change policy and yet you pretend to be a government. You're not a government – you're not a government's arsehole."'

When concerns were raised, the old guard was reassured that Labor was winning in the opinion polls. 'Bill and Chris Bowen were convinced that the tide had turned on priorities,' said Kelty, 'so tax cuts could be used for expenditure. They both told us there was a growing community acceptance of the need to increase expenditure.'

An old guard of Labor greats was advising Shorten in his quest to become prime minister. Keating was 75 and Kelty 71. But Bob Hawke, 89, was dying and would succumb to old age in the final days of the campaign. Hawke was unwell, but still concerned that Labor did not have this election in the bag. He was never a fan of 'the bad language' of Shorten describing big business as the 'top end of town', complaining it made Labor look anti-business.

Kelty was a hero to Shorten and the Labor leader had cultivated him as a mentor. They'd first met when Shorten was in his 20s and had sought Kelty's blessing for a career in the unions. Later, when an opportunity arose for Shorten to enter state politics and he had to choose between becoming a Victorian MP or running the Australian Workers' Union, he went to see Kelty again. 'State politics?' Kelty asked. His tone betrayed his disapproval. It was a better apprenticeship to serve workers in the real world as a union leader, he advised, and set your sights on federal politics.

As a younger man, Kelty had also sought out mentors. Hawke was his own political inspiration. The union leader earned the nickname 'the sorcerer's apprentice'. But he was also Keating's trusted friend. When Hawke and Keating signed the 1988 Kirribilli Pact – the agreement to hand over the leadership after the 1990 election – it was Kelty who witnessed the signing of the document. In Keating's version, he wanted a mutually trusted member of the Labor caucus to witness the deal. Hawke refused and suggested the businessman Sir Peter Abeles. Keating asked for the ACTU Secretary, Kelty. Hawke would later abandon the succession pact after Keating's 'Placido Domingo' speech, in which he suggested that Australia had never had a great leader.

'People say be nice to everybody,' said Kelty. 'Hawke wasn't nice. They weren't nice people – they were brutal. Even with me. Keating and Hawke didn't say, "Oh, Bill, thanks for all your hard work and the ACTU, this is great, it's a really nice document." They would say, "I've never seen so much shit in all my life, throw it in the bin,"' he laughed.

But on this Saturday night in April, Keating and Kelty were fretting over the 2019 election result. They could see the real prospect that Shorten might lose, even as the polls insisted otherwise. The purpose of this meeting was to provide some input into a major speech that Shorten would deliver the next morning to announce new policies on childcare and a dental-health plan for pensioners. But as the two men tried to help Shorten hone his lines, the truth was that Labor's tax narrative was not a story Keating and Kelty completely believed in.

Shorten improved during the campaign and was beating Morrison in the debates. The Labor leader was quite focused on that too, although how many swinging voters are terribly engaged in televised debates is another question.

'He did do a lot better after that. Labor's strategy was not clear [but] at least he tried to structure the argument,' said Kelty. 'He had reasonable criticisms of the government. You've got to have a policy framework. But you sit there and you do start to think, "How do we win with this?"'

Kelty believed that Labor's tax policy could have been pitched in a similar way to the super reforms in the 1990s. You should give people a choice and ensure they're not worse off, not create an army of losers. That might involve grandfathering it or phasing it in more cautiously.

By Easter, Labor knew the campaign was in trouble. It had been a rough start with some unforced errors at press conferences and clashes with reporters over climate-change policy and superannuation that flared into 24-hour stories. The ferocity of the news coverage and the press pack should not have come as a surprise, but it did. Shorten was winning the televised debates but still getting smashed in the media on a daily basis. For years he had avoided tougher interviews – now he was getting savaged daily by a snarling media pack keen to put Australia's next prime minister under scrutiny. If journalists had sometimes failed to apply the blowtorch to Labor in the past, seduced by the bloody travails of the Liberal Party's leadership-coup culture, a massive overcorrection was in full force.

By the weekend of 27 April, when Kelty visited Shorten at the Grand Hyatt, the campaign was scrambling to change course and address problems. Shorten wasn't convinced there was a strategy to close the final fortnight. He feared that his hand-picked Campaign Director Noah Carroll had shut the door to his office and was too often incommunicado. There were Labor staffers working at the campaign HQ in Parramatta with Carroll who complained they had never had a conversation with him. Sharon McCrohan – a trusted ally and political consultant paid for by the ALP, who worked out of Shorten's office – was deployed to HQ to try to fix the problem. Her job – staff would later wryly observe – was to patrol the campaign headquarters and politely inquire if there was a strategy.

McCrohan also wanted to provide some back-up to the media team that felt they were drowning in the daily task of responding to hit jobs in the tabloids. On the campaign bus, there were problems as well. Shorten was getting muddled by too many advisers briefing him before press conferences with too much detail. In a change of practice, his Chief of Staff, Ryan Liddell, started preparing him for press conferences instead.

Liddell's previous job was running Shorten's media office and he was good at cutting out the clutter and briefing Shorten on exactly what he needed to know. It was hoped the changes would put the Labor leader back in his comfort zone. His Press Secretary Fiona Sugden was sent to manage the travelling journalists, who the ALP regarded as increasingly feral. All of these changes were swirling the same weekend that Shorten bunkered down in a hotel room with the former union leader and prime minister to prepare for the next debate.

Kelty was privately scathing of the Labor frontbenchers demanding more funding for their fantasy portfolios. 'They're nice people,' he would tell Shorten, before ripping into them. The hardest political opponents were not bad people doing bad things, he warned, but nice people doing expensive things that cost you an election. 'It is good people trying to do unsustainable things. Big spenders have always been a great danger to Labor.'

Some of those good people, including Labor frontbencher Jenny Macklin, were the subject of internal criticism from colleagues for backing spending measures and opposing the savings proposals, including negative gearing. Macklin was initially cautious of the negative-gearing reforms when first proposed by Bowen in 2015, and about the franking credits.

But Macklin was also a wise head with a deep understanding of Australia's tax and transfer system and welfare payments. When it emerged that Bowen had dangerously underestimated the number of pensioners impacted by the franking-credit policies, Macklin was brought in to try to fix the mess. At the time, a year out from the election, Keating was also concerned, warning Shorten, 'You've got to protect the bloody pensioners.' After a swift backlash, Labor exempted pensioners from the franking-credit reforms.

Tanya Plibersek's big spend on schools was another area of concern. As deputy leader she had enormous authority to secure her preferred policies and a huge spending envelope. But how effective was that spending after the Liberal Party largely neutralised complaints it had gutted schools spending under changes announced by Malcolm Turnbull?

'I doubt whether we won many votes on education, although we were spending billions more over the decade,' said Kelty.

Bowen had tried and failed to get shadow cabinet to consider simply matching Turnbull's Gonski 2.0 schools package or to trim their own policies to keep costs under control, but he didn't win that debate. The spenders had another victory.

After the election, some Labor frontbenchers would concede there was a sense that policies needed to be locked in and announced before the election to guarantee they were 'on the books' after the win. Lobby groups too were 'banking the win', focusing on what Labor would guarantee to implement rather than campaigning to win government.

There was clearly a division of responsibilities when mentoring Shorten and Bowen. Kelty steered clear of Labor's Treasury spokesman. He complained he could barely understand a word Bowen was saying. 'Chris Bowen is really smart but I have never been able to communicate with him,' Kelty admitted. 'That may say something about both of us. I did say to Bill on a number of occasions that I could not understand Chris Bowen's strategy on tax. I was happy with tax reform and said that he should follow what we did on super.'

But Kelty's view that Bowen was largely to blame for the position Labor found itself in reflects his closeness to Shorten. Bowen and Labor's Finance spokesman Jim Chalmers had been trying to rein in the spenders for years. But Shorten was ambitious to have a big agenda as prime minister. He didn't want to simply coast into government on a negative campaign. He was also conflict averse and wanted to keep his frontbenchers happy. More than that, he was mindful of keeping Anthony Albanese's leadership ambitions in check and that meant keeping his supporters happy in shadow cabinet.

For a long time Labor did have more generous income tax cuts than the Coalition for low-income earners, right up until the 2 April budget. 'Keating, obviously, I respect,' said Bowen. 'But we did have bigger tax cuts. That's my answer to that. Keating never liked the deficit levy but he never said, "You need more tax cuts."' Labor had planned to reintroduce the deficit levy for high-income earners that would have delivered an effective marginal tax rate of 49 per cent, when the impact of the 2 per cent Medicare levy was included. This was an outcome Keating had publicly criticised for years.

Keating and Kelty understood that delivering a bigger surplus than the Liberals was important to Bowen, but were not convinced that would help Shorten win an election. Bowen had decided that the big failure of the 2016 election, when the ALP came close to an upset win, was getting hammered in the final week over his economic statement. Labor had admitted in the dying days of that campaign that its policies would cause a $16.5 billion blowout in the budget deficit over the next four years. Labor had included $5 billion in savings from the Coalition's superannuation reforms it was campaigning against. The budget bottom line would not improve for three federal elections.

Bowen's view fuelled the Labor economic team's frantic search for new savings measures in the lead-up to the 2019 election – new tax crackdowns beyond negative gearing. 'I knew that he was keen to have a greater surplus than the government,' said Kelty, 'and get a gold star from the Parliamentary Budget Office, or even a row of gold stars. There was a case for a bigger surplus, but a much bigger surplus, to say we are building a huge national future fund to protect us from impending disasters. But a bigger surplus and even bigger expenditure could only mean one thing with our miserable growth performance – higher taxation.'

However, Bowen believed that if the budget bottom line was better, they might have even won in 2016. This was an assessment completely at odds with Labor's own polling, which showed the party surged in the final week off the back of the 'Medi-scare' campaign. In 2016, it had been the risk the Liberals posed to Medicare – and false claims Turnbull planned to privatise it – that swung votes to Labor in the final weeks. If Bowen's thesis was correct, the controversy over Labor's books should have seen the ALP's vote go down, not up.

The 'evidence' that the Liberals wanted to privatise Medicare was flimsy. It was largely based on publicly available information that it was considering outsourcing some back-office operations. There was no suggestion of a privatised Medicare. As Health Minister Sussan Ley explained at the time, she was talking about new technology like 'tap-and-go' payment systems and apps.

But scare campaigns are potent when they reinforce an existing belief, in this case that the Liberal Party cannot be trusted on Medicare. Turnbull conceded as much when he was forced to dump the outsourcing project and admitted there was 'fertile ground in which that grotesque lie could be sown'.

History repeated at the next election. Labor's franking-credit policy was the reform that gave birth to a scare campaign on a 'retiree tax' and a death tax that didn't exist.

The election defeat brought clarity. 'We did not reconcile tax reform with tax cuts, the climate-change policy did not have a transitional map and the comprehensive became the complex,' said Kelty.

But he doesn't pretend that clarity was present at the time. 'The sad part was that Bowen and Shorten did all the hard work on tax reform but lost it all in expenditure increases.

To be fair to Shorten, he had great qualities. He worked hard, was a genuine moderate. He was closer to us than Albanese ever was. Albanese used to be one of the people in the NSW Labor Party who was always hopping into Keating all the time. Shorten was pragmatic. He is a good person.'

After the election, the Treasurer, Josh Frydenberg, observed it would have been nice to hear from Kelty during the federal election campaign about Labor's tax and spend agenda. 'It's interesting that Bill Kelty is saying this after the election, because we didn't hear that from Labor or senior people like Bill Kelty before the election.'

He was wrong about that. In fact, Shorten heard it from Kelty all the time. But it was a fair question: why didn't Keating and Kelty say it more publicly before the election? Perhaps it would have made a difference and helped Labor to change course? Kelty has thought about it. But hindsight was a luxury that simply wasn't available to them at the time. 'We never pretended we were practitioners,' Kelty said. 'We were philosophers. And the polls showed Labor was going to win. It seemed the tribe had spoken.'

2
CAMPAIGN

The day after his conversation with Paul Keating and Bill Kelty at the Grand Hyatt, Bill Shorten and Tanya Plibersek took to the stage to reveal the childcare policy, surrounded by cheering Labor volunteers. It was one of the biggest announcements during the campaign: a $4 billion plan to deliver low-fee childcare to working families. Promising free childcare for families earning under $69,000, it had gone to shadow cabinet on 24 April. Four days later, Shorten was announcing it. This was the kind of policy Labor could have launched a big TV and radio blitz on.

There was only one problem. The policy was finalised so late, there were no TV ads prepared to tell parents the good news. The Labor Party HQ, in the midst of fighting an election campaign, didn't even know the policy was coming.

The closest it came to getting a run in any of Labor's TV commercials was some dot points in an ad about something else. It was mind-boggling.

As Labor frontbenchers would soon discover, no focus-group work or polling had been done on how to sell the childcare policy. ALP campaign chief Noah Carroll and his team were incredulous at the frontbenchers' demands for research into the new policy they had lobbed into the middle of a campaign. The normal sequence was to road-test ideas with research before you finalised policy, to work out how best to sell it to voters. How the hell could they research something they hadn't been told about?

While the finalisation of the childcare policy was late, it had not been plucked out of the air. Labor's childcare spokeswoman, Amanda Rishworth, a working mother and six months pregnant during the election campaign, had been methodically working on the policy for months, but had been repeatedly told the ALP had run out of money to pay for new spending. That all changed on 2 April, when Josh Frydenberg handed down his first federal budget and moved to match Labor's tax cuts. At the same time the Liberal Party announced a forecast surplus, the Labor Party's polling took a hit. Both the ALP and the Liberal Party's research confirms it was a turning point in the Morrison Government's fortunes.

The centrepiece of the budget was $158 billion in income tax cuts over a decade. In his budget-in-reply speech, Shorten acknowledged, 'Our opponents have finally seen the light on supporting the bigger, better and fairer tax cuts for 10 million Australians that I put forward at my last budget reply speech. And tonight I can confirm that, from 1 July, if you earn between $48,000 and $126,000 – no matter who you vote for in May – you will get the same tax refund. But the Liberal tax plan does not do enough for 2.9 million Australians who earn less than $40,000. Labor will provide a bigger tax refund than the Liberals for 3.6 million Australians.'

But the decision not to back the entire package of tax cuts sharpened discussions in Labor's leadership group that they needed to find something to counter the tax cuts. 'They were like, "Shit, we need a new cost of living measure,"' a Labor frontbencher confirmed. Shorten's office turned to Rishworth. Luckily, she was able to say she had one in the bottom drawer. It had already been costed by the Parliamentary Budget Office and sent back with revisions.

The inspiration for her policy was the US Democrats presidential candidate Elizabeth Warren. She had announced in February 2019 her plan for universal childcare for low-income Americans. But there was a curious element to Labor's fast-tracked childcare plan. The policy included a big gender-pay-gap measure – a taxpayer-funded wage increase for early educators.

This policy was great news for childcare workers. But it had not been developed by Rishworth, or even the policy unit in Shorten's office. The wage plan had been the brainchild of United Voice, the union for childcare workers and one of the ALP's biggest donors. In the run-up to the 2016 election campaign, United Voice had donated $839,028 to the party.

The Gillard Government had introduced a similar plan on the eve of the 2013 election. It proposed to give pay rises only to union-aligned childcare centres. The plan was later the subject of a parliamentary inquiry. The Auditor-General, Ian McPhee, had described the policy as 'unusual'. But the new proposal did not limit the pay rise to union-controlled centres.

Shorten and United Voice's National President, Gary Bullock, had dealt directly over the policy. After the Labor leader finalised his agreement with the unions to fast-track the wage plan for the election, Rishworth was directed by Shorten's office to take it to shadow cabinet. As soon as the policy was announced on 28 April, the Coalition attacked it. The policy was designed to deliver up to 100,000 early childcare workers a pay rise of 20 per cent over eight years, and the Liberal Party quickly linked it back to their core campaign message.

'What this staggering intervention into the labour market boils down to is higher taxes for all Australians,' the Liberals' campaign spokesman Simon Birmingham said. The Education Minister Dan Tehan went further: 'This is a fast track to a socialist, if not communist economy.'

However, if the policy was communist, Scott Morrison was Che Guevara, because the Liberals' own policy already covered close to 100 per cent of fees for some low-income families. It was all pretty overblown and stupid, but the real problem was not that the Liberal Party were accusing Labor of sending in Karl Marx to prepare morning tea for under-fives, but that the ALP couldn't get their act together to shoot an ad to sell the idea of free childcare for low-income families.

Nonetheless, the new policy for taxpayers to help fund a pay rise for childcare workers was certainly unorthodox. The involvement of the unions in both crafting the policy and bankrolling Shorten's election campaign can only give rise to questions. There was nothing arms-length about his dealings with United Voice.

The proposal sparked further controversy. When Shorten appeared to leave the door open to subsiding wage rises in other low-paid, female-dominated professions, the Coalition pounced. 'The other real question is this: what about construction workers, who are getting paid the same, men and women?' said Morrison. 'What about people working in the retail industry? What about people who are hairdressers? Is he going to subsidise their wages?'

However, childcare wasn't the only big policy crammed into the speech. Labor was also proposing to roll out a new dental-health plan for seniors, offering annual teeth checks worth up to $500.

'Friends, this is a ripper,' said Shorten. 'Our plan will provide up to $1000 every two years to help pay for dental services. If we win the election, a Labor Government will expand Medicare to cover the dental care of three million pensioners and seniors.'

When Tanya Plibersek was health minister she had introduced the Child Dental Benefits Scheme and had raised the idea of a similar scheme for pensioners for years. So it was something of a mystery why it was being announced so late.

The double announcement was, in the words of Shorten's own staff, 'nuts', because one policy was going to get drowned out. Labor frontbenchers described the strategy as akin to 'pissing up against the wall a few billion dollars', but their attempts to tell Shorten this was a bad idea were shut down. According to one Labor frontbencher, 'He thought he was losing the election and wanted a big bang to reset the debate.'

When the shadow cabinet had met on 24 April to tick off on the big childcare announcement, there were front-page reports that Shorten had misled a coal export terminal worker in Gladstone in Queensland by insinuating that Labor would consider tax cuts for high-income earners. The workers had told him that some men were earning up to $250,000 a year by working night shifts. 'Well, we're going to look at that,' Shorten said. But Labor's policy was to increase the top tax rate to 49 per cent. The worker he had spoken to stood to pay $11,500 more tax under Labor's plans.

Campaigning in Townsville the next day, Shorten had been forced to play down the prospect of tax cuts for high-income earners, telling reporters that Labor would remove the deficit levy within four years. 'We would like lower income taxes for everybody, but you've got to do it when it's sustainable,' he said. 'The other point I made to that worker is that this government's tax cuts are on the never-never. What I won't say to workers is I'll give them a tax cut and cut their hospitals and schools at the same time.'

But Morrison was quick to jump on Shorten's stumble. 'We know Bill Shorten can't manage money but we also know he can't tell the truth to people,' he said.

In the final 72 hours of the campaign, Shorten took another risk. He asked Labor colleagues if he should challenge Morrison on his religious views. Plibersek expressly warned him against it. 'Don't go there,' she said. She told Shorten there was no upside in getting into a fight with the prime minister about his spiritual beliefs. But the Labor leader couldn't help himself.

The issue had first arisen on the Monday when a journalist put the following question to Morrison: 'What's your belief: do gay people go to hell?' The prime minister had replied, 'I support the law of the country and I always don't mix my religion with politics and my faith with politics. You know, none of us are perfect, none of us are saints in that respect. We try and do what is right and we try and do what is best and that's what always sought to guide me in terms of my own personal faith. My faith is not about politics. It's about just who I am, just like it is for everyone who holds such a deep faith.'

In December 2017, Morrison had been one of the Liberal MPs who left the House of Representatives chamber rather than vote for same-sex marriage when it was legislated, joining Tony Abbott, Kevin Andrews, Andrew Hastie, Michael Sukkar, Stuart Robert, Rick Wilson and Bert van Manen.

Shorten had raised the issue of gays going to hell, unprompted. But after the journalist's question to the PM, it all looked like a bit of a set-up. It was not unknown for both the major parties to plant questions with journalists on the campaign buses.

'I cannot believe that the prime minister has not immediately said that gay people will not go to hell,' Shorten said. 'I think if you want to be prime minister of Australia, you are going to be prime minister for all people. And I just don't believe it. The nation's got to stop eating itself in this sort of madness of division and toxicity.'

In response, Morrison issued a statement accusing Shorten of a 'cheap shot'. He did not believe gays were going to hell. 'No, I do not believe that,' he said.

Shorten's 'gays going to hell' gambit was an indication he was worried. Like Plibersek, Labor's deputy Senate leader Don Farrell feared the election result would be much closer than voters or the media appeared to realise. Senator Farrell remained hopeful Western Australia would get Labor over the line. 'The West will come to our defence or aid. So it's going to be a late night. Don't start slashing your wrists too early.'

Could they actually lose? Farrell's hopes for a Labor victory had hovered around 76 or 77 seats, the bare minimum to form government. Nobody who had any access to the Labor Party's tightly held polling believed they'd win more than that. It was too close for comfort.

The other big problem was the expectation of a Labor landslide. 'I thought we would fall over the line. I still think that's the outcome. It's tightened. Queensland, which looked like it was going to deliver us a couple of seats, doesn't look like it's going to deliver it now, so we've got to pick it up around the country.'

Farrell had just returned from Proserpine in Queensland. The big pitch of local MP George Christensen was 'Standing up for the North'. The slogan appeared to extend well beyond the confines of Australia's borders, all the way to the Philippines, where he had travelled so frequently he'd earned the nickname 'The Member for Manila'. Melbourne's *Herald Sun* had driven many of the stories about Christensen, including revelations of briefings from Australian Federal Police to Malcolm Turnbull and Peter Dutton about his travel. Afterwards, Christensen suspected the leaks about his travel had come from Turnbull's office.

But Queensland's *Courier-Mail* seemed a little cooler on the story and his local community didn't appear to give a stuff. Christensen had a Filipino fiancée and if the local MP had found romance overseas, his constituents didn't seem fussed about his extraordinarily frequent travel.

'Despite all of the problems Mr Christensen has had, he's going to win,' Senator Farrell predicted. 'Herbert is too close to call. We could win it with a decent preference flow. I think we are in strife in Queensland. We might end up one ahead in NSW. Victoria, we are not doing as well as we hoped. ACT, we will pick up one.

'We are essentially on 72. In order to form government, we need two seats. So Labor could form a government by only winning two seats. I can't see us not winning two seats. But it's tightened as they've thought more about our policies. They like what we want to do with their money. They just don't like the way we want to raise it. That's the problem.'

The Labor powerbroker was one of the original faceless men who'd rolled Kevin Rudd as prime minister in 2010. Senator Farrell was a witness to a notorious 2009 temper tantrum when Rudd had delivered an expletive-laden rant directed at Labor's David Feeney. 'I don't care what you f***ers think!' Rudd said. Two of those at the meeting – Farrell and Feeney – helped organised the challenge to Rudd. Shorten and former NSW ALP Secretary Mark Arbib were the others.

Farrell recognised that Labor was taking another big gamble.

'No opposition since John Hewson in 1993 has fought an election on a platform of such magnitude and including increased or new taxes. I think at the end of the day what is really odd about this election is the number of people voting early. So there's a whole lot of people who have made up their mind.

'It was always a risky strategy, but if we were going to have any economic credibility at all we needed to explain how we were going to spend these vast amounts on health and education. Well, I think eventually [voters] will come to say, "We've had enough of this mob. They are too divided. Too dysfunctional. And we will give the other mob a go." I think that's what will happen.'

That's what Labor hoped would happen. The alternative, a late swing to the Liberals, didn't bear thinking about.

During the campaign, Labor's leadership group joined a daily 6 am phone conference call, allowing Shorten, Plibersek and Noah Carroll to compare notes, plan the messages for the day and – in theory – to identify and prevent mistakes before they were made. On Friday 17 May – the day before the election – the conference call was a subdued affair, despite the expectations around the group that they would be forming a government within days. Bob Hawke – Labor's longest-serving and most popular prime minister – had died the night before.

Some in the leadership group were trying to get clearer information on the actual polling out of Labor's head office, bypassing Carroll. They were never given hard copies of the 'track' polling, showing how individual seats were going. The poll suggested the election was very tight. It never suggested the ALP could crack more than 76 or 77 seats.

But with the published polls so consistently pointing to a Labor victory and the leader remaining confident, the leadership group put its trust in the hope that the undecideds would break their way. That day, the media was briefed that Labor was on track to win, despite the fact this was not the actual takeout from the people on the 6 am hook-up.

Shorten was preparing to ditch campaigning in Queensland marginal seats to visit Hawke's widow Blanche d'Alpuget in Sydney, and then return to Melbourne. Published polling still had Labor in front on a 51 per cent to 49 per cent two-party preferred vote. But in NSW and Queensland, fears mounted that the $60 billion dividend imputation tax grab was hurting Labor. Scott Morrison called it the 'retirees tax', despite the fact that pensioners were exempt.

As Carroll outlined the polling on Friday morning, he explained it was clearly 'patchy' and he couldn't guarantee victory. 'But can we win?' Plibersek had kept asking throughout the campaign. 'Can we win on those numbers?' Carroll would never give a straight answer. After finally getting a handle on the ALP's polling late in the campaign and realising they were not doing as well as expected, Labor Senate leader and Shadow Minister for Foreign Affairs Penny Wong was flat. 'It was depressing,' she confided to colleagues.

Shorten, for his part, remained confident. He was convinced that Victoria would come to the rescue and deliver seats. As Carroll tried to give an answer during the phone hook-up to the only question anyone wanted answered, Shorten interrupted him, insisting it was all okay.

Don Farrell remained confident Shorten could get there. 'He's never had a political setback,' he said, before adding, 'but sometimes, in politics, your luck runs out.'

3

MAYDAY

In the middle of the election campaign, Australia's newly appointed Family Court Chief Justice, William Alstergren, was driving when he received a startling phone call. The man on the end of the line was Gavan Griffith QC, a former solicitor-general, with some helpful advice. He reminded Alstergren that the Labor frontbencher Mark Dreyfus QC, the man who would soon be Australia's next attorney-general, was opposed to the Liberals' planned merger of the Family Court and Federal Circuit Court.

Ahead of the proposed changes, Alstergren had been appointed chief judge of both institutions, but, said Griffith, it would make no sense for him to continue to hold the two roles. The QC explained to Alstergren that perhaps he should consider which job he would prefer to keep. But don't quit before the election, he added, just wait until after the caretaker period.

Alstergren was well aware of Labor's opposition to the merger of the two courts. But really, a phone call to advise him when to resign seemed presumptive. He had no intention of quitting. He assumed Griffith had been put up to it by Dreyfus, a claim the Labor frontbencher denies.

However, there was no confusion over the next phone call that Alstergren's office received, in the final week of the campaign. Dreyfus' office wanted to lock in a meeting in the week after the election. It seemed clear enough that the subject was post-election employment arrangements. The chief judge naturally connected this new approach with the earlier call offering resignation advice. As both men knew, Dreyfus had no power to sack a judge – any decision would have to come down to Alstergren agreeing to relinquish one of the jobs.

Another newly appointed federal court judge's private discussions with Alstergren reinforced that view. The new Victorian judge told colleagues that Dreyfus said to him, 'Look, you will just have to get used to me being your boss.' Whether or not the remark was delivered in good humour, the message was received. It was also gossiped about in legal circles, travelling all the way to London.

Australia's High Commissioner to the UK, former Attorney-General George Brandis, had heard the story too. Funnily enough, Brandis had also discussed his employment with Gavan Griffith QC. The former solicitor-general had reassured Brandis that he had gone to see Dreyfus in Melbourne and urged Labor to 'leave Brandis alone because he is doing a very good job'. This underlined the plausibility of the idea that Griffith was acting as some sort of helpful go-between, even if it was a self-appointed role, because he clearly was in contact with Dreyfus.

Griffith denies he was acting for anyone. 'I do not "do work" for the Labor Party,' he said. 'For this millennium I have lived in and practise out of London, from whence I observed the election, and where you find me this morning.' He urged that the Brandis vignette be 'deleted' from this book, but did not deny the private conversation occurred.

Brandis regarded any attempt to sack him from his London posting as nothing more than political spite from Labor. As a public servant, Brandis had recently received a glowing performance review from the UK in his role as high commissioner. The Department of Foreign Affairs Secretary Frances Adamson had conducted the review by video conference in early 2019, around the same time chatter that Penny Wong would sack him was doing the rounds.

In his previous role as Senate leader, Brandis had double-crossed her too many times and she didn't trust him. As soon as the federal election was over, he expected to face the same fate as former Victorian Premier Steve Bracks, who was sacked from his position as Australia's consul-general in New York in 2013 by the incoming Abbott Government – before he officially started.

But Brandis' and Alstergren's heads were not the only ones on the chopping block. According to *The Australian Financial Review*, Treasury Secretary Phil Gaetjens was also on 'borrowed time'. Labor's Treasury spokesman

Chris Bowen had criticised Gaetjens after it emerged that, in his previous role as Scott Morrison's chief of staff, he had requested Treasury provide information used to attack Labor's franking-credits reforms.

'I don't have a quarrel with that,' said Bowen. 'That is the role of a political staffer. My quarrel is that this man has now been appointed the secretary of the Treasury, a role which should be entirely non-partisan – beyond reproach when it comes to partisan politics.' The implication was that Gaetjens would be walking the plank after the election.

And so it must have been with the grim fatalism of the condemned man called up from the cells for a public hanging that Gaetjens dutifully marked in his diary Bowen's specific request that the two men schedule a discussion on Sunday 19 May, the morning after Labor's presumed victory.

Shorten had also sounded out the former NSW Premier Kristina Keneally about replacing Joe Hockey as the Australian ambassador to the United States. News of these discussions leaked in April, but was buried in a gossip column in *The Sunday Telegraph*. It was serendipitous for the campaign that this did not get a bigger run, because it went straight to Labor's expectations of a win that it was already considering jobs for loyalists. The real story was that Shorten had promised the Washington gig to a former Labor foreign minister, Stephen Smith, not Keneally, but regardless of the truth it was not a good look to be canvassing the issue before the election was won.

During the campaign, Keneally played a high-profile role but was surprised to find out just how disorganised the show seemed to be, concerns she later outlined in a confidential submission to the ALP review.

Meanwhile, Shorten had written to the prime minister in February 2019, to inform him that Labor wanted to meet with public servants to ensure a 'smooth transition to power if an election results in a change of government'. He noted that pre-election guidelines stated that the opposition had a right to seek public-service briefings three months before an election. 'Opposition shadow ministers will contact departmental secretaries to begin arranging briefings in coming days,' he wrote. Morrison promptly leaked his response to the letter to highlight Labor's cockiness.

Labor's preparations to form government were intense. The leadership group had even conducted 'Transition to Government' meetings. Shorten's frontbench was carefully and methodically preparing to take office. Deputy leader Tanya Plibersek, Penny Wong and Chris Bowen were all part of the preparations, planning out how they would govern on that Sunday morning.

However, the inspiration was not hubris, frontbenchers claimed, but the belief that Australian politics was broken, that trust in politicians was at an all-time low and the way to rebuild was to govern from day one, to not break any promises, to deliver carefully-costed and constructed ALP policies. But this dream would soon prove a mirage. The election result was fermenting even as Labor carefully planned its first 100 days.

*

Since the 1950s, only three Labor leaders had won government from opposition: Gough Whitlam, Bob Hawke and Kevin Rudd. Shorten had worked hard to live down his starring role in knifing both Rudd in 2010 and Julia Gillard in the lead-up to the 2013 election. The pair had even turned up at his campaign launch.

It was a small group that joined Bill and wife Chloe Shorten in the Grand Hyatt on election night in his suite on one of the hotel's upper levels. It included his Chief of Staff, Ryan Liddell, strategist Sharon McCrohan and former Hawke Government fixer Peter Barron. Liddell was the staffer he was closest to, an intense bond that was almost a father-son relationship. Power was measured in the Shorten office by your closeness and proximity to the leader and your longevity of service. Loyalty was paramount. His speechwriter James Newton, who had started jogging with Shorten in the early days to get inside his head, was also a close friend. McCrohan was a Labor veteran and in some ways she was also the second COS in the office. Shorten trusted her completely.

Barron had advised everyone from New South Wales Premier Neville Wran to Bob Hawke to Kerry Packer. He was also one of former Labor powerbroker Graham Richardson's closest friends and the pair kept in constant contact. His daughter Helen had married Labor's Sam Dastyari, although the pair separated after Dastyari's fall from grace and departure from politics. A veteran of countless nights watching election broadcasts in hotel suites with nervy Labor leaders, Barron had been briefed on all the polling but privately fretted that there didn't seem the mood for change he had encountered at other elections.

A man who went on gut instincts, he didn't like the feeling on the ground and he didn't like the volume of policy. 'It's too complicated,' Barron had warned Shorten. As Noah Carroll would later observe, the ALP was marching into war with chainmail that weighed five times its own body weight. Barron stuck around on the campaign, but others who'd raised concerns, including ALP President Wayne Swan, were sidelined and disappeared.

As the Shorten family settled in for a big night, it became clear from the very early numbers that the anxious may have been onto something. By 7.15 pm – just over an hour after the closing of polling places on the eastern seaboard – it was clear that this election was not going to plan. First came the news that Herbert in Queensland was likely lost. Tasmania and Western Sydney were not great either. At 7.25 pm, Antony Green – the ABC's famed election-night number cruncher – observed that even though the results were very early, the pattern was 'the opposite' of what the polls had predicted would happen.

Some staff in the leader's office had been tipping 82 seats on election night: a majority government. This possibility melted away early in the evening as it emerged very clearly that Queensland was not going to yield the seats on which Labor had been counting. Victoria, too – Shorten's home state, which had recently returned the Andrews Labor state government and was consistently the most anti-Coalition state in published polls – was returning much more muted results. As the picture became clearer, Shorten's supporters tried to calculate ways in which a Labor minority government might still be possible. What if WA voted differently and returned a handful of Labor gains? It didn't.

Half an hour's drive away, at the Hyatt Place Melbourne, Essendon Fields, Labor supporters and campaigners were gathered in expectation of an historic night. They were seeing the same broadcast, however, as their leader and his advisers. The mood soured quickly to one of incredulity and bitterness. The Liberals had just spent another term tearing themselves apart. And now voters were returning that mob to run the country?

As the news turned nasty for Labor on election night, Shorten's mother-in-law, Quentin Bryce, was left in a back room waiting for what was expected to be a grand celebration. But as the results tanked, she was left forgotten for hours. When friends complained that their parents were annoyed by the retiree tax, the Labor leader had once joked that the ex-governor-general might get on the bandwagon. Labor's reforms to franking credits had clearly alarmed retirees and, it would appear, even MPs' mothers-in-law.

The Victorian plumbers' union boss, Earl Setches, who had walked the Kokoda Track with Shorten, headed for the Grand Hyatt. The pair had known each other for years, since they'd emerged as young union leaders. It was Setches who had once described Shorten in a newspaper profile as having 'Phar Lap's heart beating in the body of an aardvark'. It was supposed to be a joke about his athleticism.

Setches arrived at Shorten's hotel suite around 8.30 pm. From the moment he entered the room, it was clear it was over. 'It was a shit sandwich in there. They had their back to the telly,' Setches said. Bill looked up. 'G'day, digger,' said Shorten.

With his back still to the television and with a raise of the eyebrows, Shorten made it clear the election was lost. 'Mate, not our night,' Shorten said. 'I've let people down.' The atmosphere in the room was heavy. 'It was like a death, it was that quiet,' said Setches.

Chloe gained a reputation for being highly strung during the 2016 election, when, underwhelmed at her husband disappearing from the family once again to lock himself in a room at another hotel to write his election-night speech, she had briefly suggested she might not turn up for the event. Shorten's Chief of Staff, Cameron Milner, was forced to momentarily pause proceedings while Mrs Shorten was assured by the Labor leader he'd be returning to the family's side as soon as possible.

But when the news was bad – and the news on election night was as bad as it gets – Chloe could generally be relied upon to be the calmest and most reassuring voice in the room. While all around were losing their cool, she knew how to handle herself in a crisis. Daughters Clementine and Gigi were with their parents on election night. For the couple's youngest child, Clemmie, getting asked to go and watch television while the adults digested the news was too much. 'Daddy's lost, hasn't he?' she asked Setches.

Before they left the hotel, Shorten made it clear he would stand down as Labor leader. 'Time to spend some time with my kids. My family has missed so much.' The reality was that after losing a second election there was no prospect of staying on.

Shorten travelled by car to the hotel at Essendon Fields after 10 pm. While he was on his way, Anthony Albanese was already calling for an overhaul of Labor's policy. 'I have been someone who has never put myself before the Labor Party as a whole,' he said. 'And as part of that team I must accept, as we must collectively, responsibility for the fact the many people who rely on us will be disappointed that the outcome tonight is uncertain.' Albanese's remark about not putting himself before the party as a whole was a reminder that he had not challenged after the 2016 election result. It was a clear signal to the Labor Party: it's my turn now.

When he arrived, Shorten went straight into a huddle with Ryan Liddell and speechwriter James Newton. They had prepared three speeches for election night. 'One where we won, one where we didn't know and one where we lost,' said Shorten. 'I remember saying around 7.30 pm, "Let's get speech Number 3 out." I felt for volunteers, for my staff, for my MP colleagues who had worked so hard. There were millions of people who did vote for us – but not enough clearly. It's not just your own disappointment – it's also other people's disappointment.'

'It is obvious that Labor will not be able to form the next government,' he told the crowd. 'And so, in the national interest, a short time ago I called Scott Morrison to congratulate him. I wish Jenny and their daughters all the very best, and, above all, I wish Scott Morrison good fortune and good courage in the service of our great nation.

'Now that the contest is over, all of us have a responsibility to respect the result, respect the wishes of the Australian people and to bring our nation together. However, that task will be one for the next leader of the Labor Party, because while I intend to continue to serve as the member for Maribyrnong, I will not be a candidate in the next leadership ballot.'

Shorten acknowledged Labor's supporters, the trade union movement, and particularly Bob Hawke. 'It was not to be. Labor's next victory will belong to our next leader, and I'm confident that victory will come at the next election. I leave the stage tonight, but I encourage all Australians, particularly young Australians, never lose faith in the power of individuals to make a difference. Never give up. Never give up aiming for better.'

Shorten headed back to the Grand Hyatt after conceding defeat. There he was joined by AustralianSuper boss Ian Silk who had also walked the Kokoda Track with Shorten and Setches. There were some attempts at gallows humour to lighten the mood, with the assembled regaled with tales of 'Silky' falling over in the wilds of Papua New Guinea during the trek while answering the call of nature.

Shorten didn't spend much time talking about what had gone wrong, although that conversation would be had in the week that followed. It was over. Friends stayed to drink and chat and commiserate until Shorten was urged to go to bed by Chloe. She told him he had a big day tomorrow, and put him to bed.

There were no bones to be made about the result. It was not an error, or one of those close results in which a party wins the popular vote but loses the election. Labor lost both, decisively. And as the celebratory drinks went flat at the Hyatt Essendon Fields, the autopsy began. What had they done so disastrously wrong? What warning signs had they missed?

4
THE BILL LABOR COULDN'T AFFORD

The most successful social-media clip the Liberal Party released during the election campaign, titled *Ladies and Gentlemen: Bill Shorten,* is a three-minute showreel of awkward, embarrassing videos of the Labor leader. It begins with images of him stroking his own face with his hands clenched into little paws, like a marsupial performing a grooming ritual. A man in a high-vis vest refuses to shake his hand. He tells a cow, 'You're very handsome,' while his wife, Chloe, smiles. There's a clip of him telling Arnold Schwarzenegger, 'I'm going to be Australia's next prime minister.' The movie star gives him a funny look. The hero image of the clip is him dancing in a Kiribati headdress, twirling around with a goofy, frozen smile. But it is only as he begins to run for television cameras, and picks up the pace as he swings down a hill, his arms pumping and his baggy t-shirt flying in the breeze, that the Benny Hill soundtrack cranks up.

Months after the election, when asked why Labor lost, conservative columnist Andrew Bolt nominates 'his funny running style' as among his top three concerns. During the election, Shorten admitted that voters had taken to hurling insults, in person. 'Some old bloke, I don't think he's ever voted Labor since 1920, he rolls down the window as I'm jogging by and says, "And ya can't even run!" I said to him, "You're welcome to join me."'

Could it really be that even the Labor leader's jogging style was electoral poison? But Bolt is deadly serious. 'That went to the inauthenticity of Bill Shorten,' he explains. 'You might recall, in particular, one tape of him accelerating down a bridge, with the flip-flop feet. And I just think, for many people, he would have looked a fake. And to many tradies he would have looked not very strong. I don't think Bill Shorten will ever be running in public again, if his media people have any brains.'

The idea that Shorten was unelectable, whether or not the core issue was his deportment during physical exercise, is not one that the man himself is willing to concede. 'If I was so unpopular, why did we almost knock off Malcolm Turnbull?' he said in an interview for this book. 'If I was unpopular, why did we win Longman? If I was unpopular, why did we win Braddon? [Labor won both seats during the Super Saturday by-elections in July 2018, but the seats were lost in the federal election that followed] Plus the others, but they were the two kind of make or breaks.'

But while he disputes the idea he was unpopular, the ANU's election study disagrees. According to the survey of 2000 voters, Shorten was the least popular leader of any major political party since 1990. Scott Morrison was the most popular leader since Rudd led Labor to the 2007 election.

And therein lies the terrible dilemma that faced the ALP. While there was consistent evidence that Shorten was an unpopular opposition leader, he was set many tests that he passed with flying colours. Each time, whether it was the ascension of Malcolm Turnbull, the 2016 election, the royal commission into trade unions, or the Super Saturday by-elections after the citizenship fiasco, he rose to the task. And hadn't the Labor Party learned the hard way about the transactional costs of changing leaders?

As prime minister, Turnbull painted Shorten as a snivelling sycophant to billionaires. In 2017, he launched a memorable tirade. 'There was never a union leader in Melbourne that tucked his knees under more billionaires' tables than the leader of the opposition,' he began. 'He was such a sycophant, a social-climbing sycophant if ever there was one. There has never been a more sycophantic leader of the Labor Party than this one and he comes here and poses as a tribune of the people. Harbourside mansions – he is yearning for one! He is yearning to get into Kirribilli House. You know why? Because somebody else pays for it. Just like he loved knocking back [billionaire businessman] Dick Pratt's Cristal, just as he looked forward to living in luxury at the expense of the taxpayer. This man is a parasite.'

But when Morrison took control, he quickly framed the choice for voters as a personal one between the two leaders. 'You vote for me, you get me. You vote for Bill Shorten, you get Bill Shorten,' he said.

Penny Wong admitted, 'I don't think we were prepared for the assault on him personally when it came and we should have been. I didn't think we were collectively serving him well and that involved various things.'

But Shorten had formed the strong view that he had been underestimated. It was Shorten who insisted, against the advice of his Treasury spokesman Chris Bowen, that Labor oppose huge chunks of the budget cuts in the Abbott Government's first budget. Labor vowed to oppose the shift in the pension age to 70, the tightening of Family Tax Benefit Part B eligibility, the move to restore twice yearly indexation to fuel excise, the planned $7 per visit charge to see a GP and the plan to kick some young unemployed off Newstart. It was a decision that proved a political masterstroke that laid the ground for Labor's success in the 2016 election. For Shorten's supporters, it was evidence that when he listened to his own political instincts, they were good.

Over the years, Shorten weathered the storm over the allegation that he got his union, the Australian Workers' Union, to bankroll his bid to enter federal politics. A former national secretary of the ALP, Bob Hogg, called on him to resign over those revelations after it emerged Shorten had failed to reveal that a labour hire company had paid the salary of his campaign director during the 2007 election campaign.

THE BILL LABOR COULDN'T AFFORD

The secret was kept for nearly a decade. At the time of the deal, the company had been involved in negotiations with the AWU for a new enterprise bargaining agreement, although Shorten maintained he was not directly involved in the arrangement.

Hogg believed that the idea the revelations that had emerged during the royal commission didn't damage Shorten was a joke. He wrote an open letter that began, 'Dear Bill – is the concept of conflict of interest beyond your understanding? His campaign director was paid for by a company whose employees were covered by Bill's AWU, and therefore, as union members, deserved their interest to be protected to the maximum. The payment wasn't declared until Bill was reminded eight years later: a real lapse of memory, sloppy book-keeping or a hope no-one would notice. Take your pick.'

Before the election Labor powerbroker Graham Richardson claimed that 'even God' had given up on the Liberals and Labor was a sure bet to win the election. After 18 May, he said it was no surprise they lost.

'Australians were never going to vote to make Bill Shorten prime minister,' he said. 'Labor persisted with him and the "unlosable" election was lost. Plenty of senior Labor people, including myself, shirked our duty to the party. Like the 600, we rode headlong into the valley of political death. It wasn't a shock to me and while it may have achieved little or nothing, I should have spoken out.'

In fact, even the Labor leader's wife, Chloe, was so concerned with his popularity that she asked the party to consider commissioning a serious piece of research into why voters did not see the man her family and friends knew and loved. According to ALP officials, this was a proposal Noah Carroll put on the backburner in the lead-up to the 2019 election. There were subsequent claims Shorten asked for help with softening his image during the election, but this, surely, was too little, too late.

Opposition leaders are rarely popular. After all, how many times had it been said about Tony Abbott that he was unelectable? Even John Howard was once lampooned for his low approval ratings on the front page of *The Bulletin* when he was opposition leader. The headline was: 'Why Does This Man Bother?' He went on to govern for 11 years.

There's one big problem with the theory that Labor would have won the election with a different leader. Although it's true that Shorten consistently lagged behind Scott Morrison, and before that Malcolm Turnbull, as preferred prime minister, it is a fact that the party's primary vote has fallen in every single election since Rudd was elected in 2007.

'Bill Shorten shouldn't carry the can on his own for our collective failures at the last election,' Labor frontbencher Jim Chalmers observed on the eve of the November 2019 release of the ALP election review. 'We simply couldn't build a big enough constituency for our agenda. Our problems in the campaign did go beyond one leader or one election; there is a structural problem with our primary vote.'

But the doubts about Shorten were there from the beginning. Certainly, there was no great enthusiasm to anoint him as Labor leader when his big moment arrived. The evening of Rudd's federal election campaign launch in Brisbane on 1 September 2013, some MPs and officials gathered on the back deck of Wayne Swan's home, overlooking the pool. There was Victoria's Stephen Conroy, the Queensland ALP State Secretary Anthony Chisholm, union leader Paul Howes, SA Labor's Don Farrell and NSW ALP Secretary Jamie Clements. All assumed Rudd was heading for defeat.

There was a reason the men went to his house, apart from being keen to catch up. It was because Swan, who had once described Rudd's treatment of people as 'extraordinarily vindictive and juvenile', was boycotting the ALP campaign launch.

Swan was not exactly wildly enthused at the prospect of Bill Shorten's leadership either. Not after Shorten's role in removing Rudd and Gillard. However, Swan would never have voted for Anthony Albanese.

In 2012, Albanese had sobbed when he announced he'd vote for Rudd in the leadership ballot against Gillard and tendered his resignation as manager of government business. Gillard refused to accept it and after Rudd's first run failed, they continued to work well with each other. Rudd reclaimed the leadership in 2013, after which Swan was dumped as deputy prime minister. Swan was unconvinced by Albanese's claims that he was some sort of innocent bystander to the plotting against Gillard. For the next five years, he didn't speak to Albanese.

Anyone who gives an old friend the silent treatment for that long is seriously pissed off. Eventually, Jim Chalmers, who was close to both men, tried to organise a reconciliation over beers. The evening later sparked rumours he was shifting to the Albanese camp. In fact, he was simply trying to bring to an end one of the greatest frosts in the Labor Party since former NSW Labor MP Belinda Neal was accused of chopping up the names of her enemies and sticking them in the freezer.

The evening of the drinks at Swan's family home was the first and last visit of Jamie Clements. As a result of his NSW Right faction's involvement in Gillard's removal, Swan cannot have been thrilled to have him drinking beers in his house.

According to Clements, it was Stephen Conroy who was most disparaging of Shorten's prospects. 'I am the only person to have been at his 18th, 21st, wedding and 40th, and I still don't consider him a friend,' he claims he said.

Clements, in his role as a faction operative, had canvassed Chris Bowen and other NSW MPs. 'They were like, "Yeah, it's got to be Bill,"' he said. 'But Sam Dastyari was still behind the scenes encouraging Albanese. The reason why I think Sam did it was because of the direct election of leaders. He picked up the idea and ran with it. He believed the best way to lock it in was to have a proper ballot. Everyone agreed Bill was best placed to beat Albo, and they were afraid Albo would reform the party. Everyone basically came to the view that Bill was going to have to become leader at some stage, that we had no chance at the next election, so we should let him get it out of his system.'

As history tells us, Shorten proved remarkably persistent. Getting him out of Labor's system took around six years.

5

MOTHER OF ALL LIES

Kevin Rudd was a man on a mission during the 2019 election and it was a project that involved frantic activity criticising Rupert Murdoch's News Corp tabloids and badgering Bill Shorten to finally subject those 'fuckers' who worked for them to a royal commission into media ownership. He ended his election campaign commentary the way he began – with a no-holds-barred evisceration of the media mogul.

When *The Daily Telegraph* decided to splash the Labor leader's dead mother, Ann Shorten, all over the front page during the campaign, accusing her son of lying about her life story, the former prime minister sprung into action on the texts. 'Gidday,' his message to Bill Shorten on 8 May had begun. 'Don't let the News Corp fuckers get you down. They massively overreached today.'

As was his practice, Rudd then proceeded to outline to Shorten, a man fighting a national election campaign, his personal Twitter analytics detailing how many people had scrolled past his latest musings on the social media website. Rudd reported he had been religiously tweeting attacks on News Corp every day. 'Each tweet getting up to 100,000 impressions. And I'm told, it's actually starting to drive their editors nuts. I will start naming their editors next week. Not working for them quite like it used to. KR.' By the end of the election he was boasting that during the campaign he had reached 3.2 million people 'through my daily Twitter and Facebook assaults on Murdoch media bias'.

Rudd had been at it for months, texting Shorten over summer to press home his big idea. 'Gidday. Wanted to discuss your thinking on the Royal Commission on Media Ownership,' he said. 'Including abuse of monopoly power in killing the National Broadband Network at a massive financial cost.'

A royal commission was Rudd's idea, described by Malcolm Turnbull as 'a conspiracy theory' that Murdoch conspired with the Liberals to kill Labor's original fibre optic to the premises National Broadband Network model to protect his own business interests, including Foxtel.

'The conspiracy theory is itself insane,' Turnbull said. 'Pay TV services, like Foxtel, have been smashed everywhere by over-the-top streaming services like Netflix. Labor's approach would have taken six to eight years longer to complete and would have cost upwards of $30 billion more – leading to even more expensive broadband. So in summary, by ensuring NBN is completed sooner and at lower cost, the disruption of Foxtel's business model occurred sooner than it otherwise would have done.'

As a politician, Rudd had actively courted the News Corp newspapers on his rise to the top, but if the friendship was strained after he blamed the media mogul for contributing to the prime ministerial 'coup culture' in 2010, it was terminated when he contested the next election. *The Daily Telegraph* had kicked off the 2013 campaign with a full-page photograph of Rudd and the headline: 'Finally, you now have the chance to KICK THIS MOB OUT.'

The Daily Telegraph's call to boot Rudd from office was followed up by a photoshopped image of Anthony Albanese and Labor MP Craig Thomson in Nazi uniforms. The entire story was based on the fact that Albanese had apparently caught up with the disgraced MP Thomson for a beer.

Rudd's thesis was that News Corp did not conduct themselves as a news organisation, but as a political party. 'That's why the Murdoch media has become such a cancer on the wider cause of democracy,' he wrote in an opinion piece the summer before the 2019 election. 'We often ponder why democracy has been in such a mess across the Anglosphere. While Murdoch cannot be blamed for the lot, he's been a big part of the equation. By contrast, the Canadian democracy has been in reasonable shape. Interesting that there is negligible Murdoch presence there.'

He pointed to News Corp's decision to despatch his 'leading henchman' from the *New York Post*, the newspaper's editor-in-chief Col Allan, to Sydney during the 2013 election to ensure Tony Abbott was elected. 'Murdoch's henchmen say this is all the stuff of conspiracy,' he wrote. 'They should read the compulsory filings by News Corp on the New York Stock Exchange in 2013 warning explicitly of the threat to Murdoch's television interests represented by internet-based competitors.'

Allan, a former *Daily Telegraph* and *Sunday Telegraph* editor, was the same person Rudd had accompanied to a New York strip club, Scores, in September 2003. At the time, Allan had delivered the immortal line 'Yes, it was a gentleman's club and Mr Rudd behaved like a perfect gentleman', after claims surfaced the Labor leader may have gotten handsy with female performers. Rudd had been in New York to attend United Nations meetings as the opposition Foreign Affairs spokesman. Rudd admitted he was drunk and the evening was hazy, a disclosure that only seemed to improve his bookish image ahead of the 2007 election.

Allan was famous for being News Corp's longest-serving editor, for unforgettable front pages, and for urinating in the sink of his Holt Street office in Australia. Staff claimed that during news conferences he would sometimes relieve himself in his office, rather than walk across the newsroom floor to the men's toilets. His nickname was Col Pot. After the online news site Crikey profiled him with a feature titled 'Pissing In The Sink', Allan confirmed the story, while insisting it didn't happen very often. Whatever the truth, in Rudd's estimations Allan had clearly gone from being a buddy to enjoy a boozy night out with at a strip club in New York, to a threat to democracy, all in the space of a decade. Life moves fast.

Just days before Rudd texted Shorten in January 2019, the Labor leader had publicly announced he would not join the trail of Australian political leaders who called on Rupert Murdoch when in New York. Shorten revealed he had been given an open invitation to meet with Murdoch whenever he was in the United States – but rejected the offer.

'I will deal with the Australian representatives of every media company,' Shorten told the ABC's *7.30*. 'News Limited and Mr Murdoch shouldn't take that as any view on him in particular. I'll deal with their local management just as I deal with the local management of the ABC.'

In the interview, Shorten suggested he wasn't taken with the idea of a taxpayer-funded inquiry into News Corp. 'Who owns a particular newspaper – that's not something I can change or affect,' he said. 'Some elements of the media are very aggressive critics of Labor, but I'm not going to whinge about that.'

But the ferocity of the press pack early in the campaign, after a string of negative stories about electric cars and Labor's climate-change policies, clearly prompted a change of heart. In Darwin on 18 April, he accused media outlets of running a 'malicious and stupid scare campaign'.

Asked about a report in *The Australian* that businesses might be forced to spend $25 billion on international carbon credits to meet Labor's emissions reduction targets, Shorten went on the attack. 'It is a nonsense claim and it is built upon the back of a big lie. It says somehow that using international offsets to help abate carbon is a bad thing. Well, if it's a bad thing, why don't they go to Josh Frydenberg, the current treasurer, who used to believe it didn't matter where you cut the carbon from, as long as you were cutting the carbon? The News Corp climate-change deniers, and their ally, the prime minister – a coal-wielding, climate-denying cave-dweller on this issue – they all say, "Look at the cost," but never mention the cost of extreme weather events, do they?'

This was the build-up to Shorten's appearance on the ABC's *Q&A* program on 6 May, when he was asked by a woman in the audience, Kathryn Watt, 'What will your leadership culture be? How will your government guide all of us as a community in relation to our culture in being a decent and caring country to live in?'

'I'm not going to be a messiah,' he replied. His answer then turned to his late mother, Ann Shorten, who had worked at Monash University, where the show was being filmed.

'She was the first in our family to ever go to university. She wanted to be a lawyer, but she was the eldest in the family and needed to take the teacher scholarship to look after the rest of the kids. My mum was a brilliant woman. She wasn't bitter. She worked here for 35 years. But I know if she had other opportunities she could have done anything. I can't make it right for my mum. And she wouldn't want me to. But my point is this, what motivates me, if you really want to know who Bill Shorten is, I can't make it right for my mum but I can make it right for everyone else.'

In an election campaign that seemed devoid of authenticity, his personal confession about what drives him as a politician started to get a lot of traction on social media that Monday night. The next morning, Neil McMahon in *The Sydney Morning Herald* hailed his performance as 'powerful', 'personal', 'genuine', and a rare 'moment' in a lacklustre campaign.

However, *The Daily Telegraph*'s Tim Blair was up early at his Sydney home to read the newspapers online. At 7.19 am, the columnist promptly published his response to the *SMH* piece on his blog. 'Sob story sells Mother Short' was the headline. 'For the average viewer, it was perhaps the most powerful and personal sentence uttered in the campaign,' Blair wrote. 'But for any viewers with an awareness of Ann Shorten's many and considerable accomplishments, it was perhaps just Bill being Bill. Dr Ann Shorten not only wanted to become a lawyer; she did become a lawyer. And she achieved a great deal else besides, as her Victorian Bar Association obituary makes clear.'

Scraping the internet for any mention of Mrs Shorten, Blair dismissed the 'moment' as a confected story. 'At 74, Ann Shorten lived alone with a friendly corgi called Barney and several thousand books in a comfortably cluttered house in Chadstone,' he wrote, quoting from an article by Melbourne journalist Andrew Rule. The article noted that the 'luminous intellect that led a teacher to become an historian and then a barrister in late middle age shone through everything she said'. Blair declared Shorten's log-cabin story about his mother rubbish. 'It doesn't sound as though his mother needed Bill Shorten to make anything right for her. She appears to have taken care of that entirely by herself,' he concluded.

Despite the popularity of Blair's blog on *The Daily Telegraph*'s website, nobody seemed to take great offence or even notice it for an entire day on the election campaign trail – apart from the newspaper's editor, Ben English. In fifteen sentences, Blair had laid out the entirety of the research material that would appear as a news story on the website at 11 pm that night.

Conspiracy theories would later abound that the Liberal Party dirt unit had given the story to *The Daily Telegraph* – a claim the Liberals furiously denied. It would appear, however, it was the gift of Tim Blair, via a Google search.

The holy grail of a great tabloid editor is an election front page that is unforgettable and has a high impact. English, a veteran newspaper editor who was relatively new to the top job at *The Daily Telegraph*, decided that Blair's sharp observations on Shorten's 'sob story' would make a fantastic splash. That afternoon, he would be seen excitedly pacing the newsroom floor, trying to get people to come into his office and look at the front page.

The next morning, on the front page of the newspaper it was trumpeted under the headline 'Mother Of Invention – Revealed: Shorten's Heartfelt Tale Missing Vital Fact'.

Some of the draft versions were even stronger. One option featured a giant photograph of Bill Shorten and his dead mother – mercifully, the final product kept the image of the late Ann Shorten off the front page. The original headline options included something even more incendiary about Shorten's mother, including the headline 'Mother Of All Lies'.

At 10.24 pm on 7 May, Ben English put the front page up on Twitter and all hell broke loose. 'I worked for the *Tele* twice in the '70s and '80s,' journalist Peter Logue responded. 'It had some great editors. They'd be embarrassed at this fetid, mean, partisan trash and they wouldn't even give you a job as a copy boy.' A social media user known as Baroness the Lady Bucket wrote, 'We were warned that the level of scum produced by the Liberal Party and their curs in the next two weeks would be particularly vile. The warning was understated.' Sam McLean, a former GetUp director who had subsequently joined Bill Shorten's office, posted a video of a punch-drunk prize fighter accidentally punching his own face.

But one newspaper in the News Corp stable had refused to run the story: Melbourne's *Herald Sun*. The decision was made by editor Damon Johnston, who had led the newspaper for seven years. A veteran of News Corp, he had been burned by Sydney's 'exclusives' before, most notably when, in 2009, *The Sunday Telegraph* had published near-nude pictures from the 1970s of a woman they believed to be Pauline Hanson. Unfortunately, the woman, featuring pubic hair that was more landscaped than was generally the norm in that decade, was not Pauline Hanson. News Corp was believed to have paid a huge sum to the One Nation leader in a defamation settlement. Against his initial instincts, Johnston had published the Hanson story in the *Sunday Herald Sun* and was then forced to issue a grovelling apology.

Culturally, the 'Pauline Hanson nudes' saga had a big impact on the *Herald Sun* being sceptical of Sydney stories and wanting to put a magnifying glass over them. The

Herald Sun was a more conservative publication in tone, and had a more experienced and forensic news desk, than most of the tabloids interstate. But it also took risks when required, including breaking the news that Victoria Police were secretly investigating Cardinal George Pell over allegations of the sexual abuse of boys.

The Melbourne newspaper sells more copies than *The Daily Telegraph*, a fact that tends to be forgotten or ignored in Sydney's Holt Street offices. When *The Daily Telegraph* ran the 'King Leer' front page, including claims about Geoffrey Rush's conduct towards a co-star, the *Herald Sun* didn't touch the story. Later, that helped protect Melbourne's bottom-line from the record damages payout that followed. (*The Daily Telegraph* has since appealed against the decision.)

In terms of the internal News Corp politics, it was a big call for the *Herald Sun* to reject Sydney's 'Mother of Invention' story, particularly given the controversy that followed. The *Herald Sun*'s powerful and influential columnist Andrew Bolt supported the stance. 'Shorten spoke truly when he said his mother sacrificed her dream to be a lawyer, taking up teaching to help her siblings,' he wrote. Bolt's support for the decision of his masthead to reject the story, given his power within the company and the widespread belief he was anti-Labor, was a bombshell. It would be accurate to say that Ben English was furious.

The *Daily Telegraph* front-page story claimed that 'Bill Shorten's live TV monologue about how his mother's ambitions to be a lawyer were thwarted by her working-class roots has been hailed as an election-winning moment, but omitted the fact that she went on to enjoy an illustrious career as a barrister after a midlife occupation change.' The reporter was promptly savaged online, perhaps unfairly given Tim Blair was clearly the research brains behind the operation.

The Daily Telegraph had emailed Labor's HQ the afternoon after Blair's blog was published with some seemingly innocuous questions about Shorten's mother, which immediately rang alarm bells. Dealing with the bombardment of negative stories on Labor during the campaign from News Corp became a full-time job. They felt they were drowning and no attempts to respond or carefully frame a rebuttal got them anywhere.

When Labor's Communications Director Gerard Richardson got a tip from a friendly News Corp journalist that *The Daily Telegraph* was about to 'dump a bucket of shit' all over the front page in the morning, he dialled in the news to Shorten directly to warn him it involved his mum. At first, Shorten seemed calm. 'Fuck, they will stop at nothing,' he said. But his anger started rising the more he thought about it and by 9 pm he had posted a lengthy response on Twitter.

The next morning, Shorten was in Nowra, NSW, with the Health spokeswoman Catherine King, touring a private medical centre. Things seemed relatively calm. There was only one question journalists wanted answered. 'Mr Shorten,' one of them began, 'there was a story in the newspapers this morning about your mother. Is this campaign dirtier than the last one you fought?'

'Well, I'm going to take a little bit of time on this answer and I thank you for asking it,' he replied. 'My mum suffered a catastrophic heart attack in her sleep . . . sometime on the night of Saturday the 5th of April, the 6th of April 2014. So she never woke up. So, it's been about five years to last month when she passed away. I miss her every day. I sometimes . . . get a sense of how she would react to things, because she was such a strong and clever woman. But I'm glad she wasn't here today to read that rubbish . . .

'Let's go through why this is an issue. On Monday night in *Q&A* I was again asked about my leadership style and what drives you. I think that's a very fair question. But as part of my answer, I spoke about my mother. Now I've actually spoken about my mum before.'

This was true. He'd outlined her life story in more detail during the campaign, a fact that was pointed out to *The Daily Telegraph* before publication.

'But one thing I did say about my mum and I started to explain her story. She was born in Victoria, grew up in North Melbourne, 1935, peak of the Depression. Her mum was a bookbinder. Her dad was a printer. They've even got ancestors in their family tree who were convicts. Now, I'm waiting for that to come out in *The Telegraph*. She came from very modest circumstances. She topped her school. She went to a Catholic convent school, the family were Irish Catholic. She got the best marks. But no-one in my family had ever gone to university. She was very keen to do Law. She had a great brain. But family of four, she was the oldest. They didn't have the money to pay for her tuition to go to university, so she had to take a teacher's scholarship.

'I come from a great family. Mum, you know she was very brave. When she got her teacher's scholarship, I remember her youngest brother, my surviving uncle George, telling me the story. They'd go down to Station Pier, because my mum wanted to see the world. So they'd have the streamers. You know when you see the pictures of the old shipping liners setting off in the '50s? The reason why they held the streamers is the people on the wharf would hold one end of the streamer and their family on the boat. And then eventually as the ship sailed, it would break.'

It was the streamer story that set him off. He was clearly emotional, live on national television. The press conference felt claustrophobic, with journalists crammed shoulder to shoulder and next to Shorten as his eyes filled with tears. Some of his staff started to quietly cry as he spoke.

'And I remember my uncle telling me as I was preparing the eulogy for my mum five years ago that he thought that she was the bravest woman he'd ever met. Do you know in the 1970s while she was raising us she did a PhD full-time? She raised us, she worked full-time and she did a PhD. Then in the 1980s, when we're still at school, Mum enrolled in Law school in her late 40s.'

Shorten had attended university with his mother, who had topped her classes in her 50s. 'She got a Supreme Court prize, which is the highest award you can get. She couldn't get articles at a law firm because you know what, as much as we love law firms, when you are an older woman in your 50s, you don't sort of look young and jazzy and you're doing your work. I just wish some newspaper outlets would do some of their homework beyond that. She got about nine briefs in her time. It was actually a bit dispiriting. She'd wanted to do law when she was 17.

'But, she discovered in her mid-50s that sometimes you're just too old. And you shouldn't be too old, but you discovered the discrimination against older women. And so she eventually, while she kept her name on the bar roll for a number of years, she came back and she did other things. Who do some people in News Corp or some . . . and it's not all the journalists, I make that very clear . . . who do some of these lazy people think they are that because they think that I explained myself at *Q&A* on a Monday night that they play gotcha shit about your life story? More importantly my mum's.

'I choose to give you that last bit of the battle of her time at the bar, because my mum would want me to say to older women in Australia that just because you've got grey hair, just because you didn't go to a special private school, just because you don't go to the right clubs, just because you're not part of some backslapping boys' club, doesn't mean you should give up. What I said at *Q&A* is what drives me.'

His full answer was 1656 words long.

Prime Minister Scott Morrison sought to distance himself from *The Daily Telegraph*, an unusual occurrence, describing it as an 'upsetting story' and insisting the election should remain focused on the policies. 'Bill lost his mother five years ago and I can understand that would have upset him a great deal. I would only extend my best wishes to him.'

In the aftermath, there was a general view that the newspaper had gone too far and that the story was tasteless and omitted relevant facts. As a result, there was great speculation on the campaign trail that *The Daily Telegraph* would pay a high price for the front page if Shorten was elected.

The ACTU commissioned polling to assess whether the issue was having an impact with undecided voters. There were great hopes in Labor ranks that this 'moment' on Shorten's deep love and admiration for his mother could be a turning point in the campaign.

It is fair to say *The Daily Telegraph* remained displeased with the star columnist's repudiation of the story, a fact Andrew Bolt confirms. 'Oh look, people got cranky. Did I change my mind? No. Did Ben English change his mind? No. That's called a debate.'

Bolt insists it was evidence of diversity within the News Corp stable. In an interview for this book, Bolt confirmed Shorten personally called during the election to thank him for his stance on the story about his mother.

'I criticised Bill Shorten very strongly for his policies. I know I had calls from him, thanking me for playing it fair,' Bolt said. 'I am not one that takes an axe to someone gratuitously. I've only probably got a dozen phone calls from him in my life – it's not like it was a constant flow of information. He thanked me for what I did when the police were investigating him for rape charges. He thanked me for doing the decent thing.'

While the Labor Party's relationship with News Corp was sometimes testy, when pointed in the right direction the tabloid press could have its uses. It was just a matter of finding the right material. The scandal over the Speaker

Bronwyn Bishop's helicopter ride in November 2014 was perhaps the greatest example. Faced with hostile coverage, Shorten's office had hooked into the one thing that the media – struggling with budget cuts, fewer reporters and a 24/7 news cycle – desperately needed that they could give them: stories.

6

CHOPPERGATE

It was a dramatic entrance, even by Bronwyn Bishop's standards. Descending from the skies in a helicopter to a Liberal fundraiser, she landed on a golf course in Geelong. But it was an ill-fated journey, which crash-landed her career. Extracting her from the wreckage and securing her resignation proved a crisis for the Abbott Government. Her career ended in a bonfire of scandal and ridicule. Tony Abbott, who once bragged he was the 'political love child' of Bronwyn Bishop and John Howard, did not emerge unscathed. He was removed as prime minister and replaced by Malcolm Turnbull just weeks after her helicopter ride was revealed.

For Shorten, the 'Choppergate' scandal swept away the rolling coverage of his appearance at a royal commission into trade unions as yesterday's news. He had been rebuked by the Commissioner, Dyson Heydon AC QC, over his 'non-responsive' answers at the commission just a week before. Shorten was also trying to head off a brawl at the ALP national conference over boat turn-backs and same-sex marriage.

So, this scandal was perfectly timed, but no accident. A political veteran, Bishop was not simply foolish to charter a helicopter to travel the short distance from Melbourne to Geelong, she was unlucky to have found herself under the microscope of the Labor operatives who engineered a political crisis.

The Speaker had landed on the lawns of the Clifton Springs Golf Club on 5 November 2014 in the style of a US president returning to the White House. But news of her unorthodox manner of arrival took a while to get out. The headline in July 2015 in the *Herald Sun*, the newspaper that broke the story, was 'Hair Force One'. It featured a photoshopped image of Bishop, complete with her signature beehive, disembarking from a presidential plane.

On the day the story appeared, the official travel records were silent on the helicopter, simply referring to a $5000 charter flight. But in the weeks that followed, journalists piled on, poring over photographs of her 'spectacular' helicopter arrival, overseas travel records, her flights and her chauffeur-driven car trips to the theatre. No document was left unexamined, no angle left unexplored. It was a journalistic feeding frenzy. Talkback radio was alive with outrage and readers devoured stories online.

Despite all this forensic examination, in her final speech

to the House of Representatives Bishop hinted at secrets that remained unearthed about her career-ending helicopter trip.

Bill Shorten, who was in the chamber to listen to Bishop's final speech after she lost her preselection, knew one. Choppergate was a political scandal that had been written, authorised and engineered by a group of young Labor staffers in his office.

For six years, Labor was running one of the most methodical, relentless and successful investigative journalism units in Australia – only it wasn't staffed by journalists. It was staffed by political researchers. As the ranks of newspaper journalists in the Canberra press gallery shrank and the demands for scoops and 24/7 coverage grew, it would prove a mutually beneficial arrangement. Traditional journalistic rounds, including economics, defence, health and education, had been abandoned. But a political scandal? Now that can still sell newspapers.

The Labor staffer who spotted the Bishop helicopter ride was Ben Foster. He was a big, ginger-bearded Hawthorn Football Club supporter whose Facebook account consists largely of photographs of him drinking beer and going to the footy. Later, he went to work for Victorian Premier Dan Andrews. After Bishop lost her preselection and left parliament, Foster posed standing next to Bishop's official photograph as Speaker in Parliament House, raising his eyebrows and clutching a box of champagne. In his own modest way, he started a bushfire that helped topple Tony Abbott. Later, he came up with a grandiose title to take the piss out of Labor's research unit. He dubbed it the 'Democracy Empowerment Unit'.

When the parliamentary travel records came in, Foster needed to be methodical. Go through the documents, find the stories. When he spotted Bishop's $5000 trip from Melbourne to Geelong, it struck him immediately as unusual. He emailed the office at 6.46 pm on Thursday, 25 June 2015. Subject: Bronnie got a charter from Melbourne to GEELONG.

'An hour's drive. I wonder if Marlesy ever jags a charter?' he asked.

'Marlesy' was Richard Marles, the Labor MP. His federal electorate included Geelong, but there was no chance he had ever used a helicopter to get there. Another staffer, Shawn Lambert, replied three minutes later. 'You've got to be fucking kidding me.'

Ryan Liddell, Shorten's then press secretary, knew a story when he saw one. 'That is ripe for the papers thank you very much,' he replied.

From there, it was a matter of pulling the story together in a way that would work for the tabloid newspapers. Another Labor staffer, Victor Violante, pointed out in an email that it was an 80-minute drive versus a 35-minute flight. 'That's $116 a minute. And that's not counting all the time that would be wasted on take-off and landing. Still can't get my head around this one.'

The discussion quickly turned to the likelihood the event had been a political fundraiser. That was something Shorten's office could chase in Victoria, or get a journalist to hunt down with the Liberals as a follow-up to the story.

But the story didn't immediately take off. In fact, it kept getting spiked, overlooked and rejected by various newspapers. But when it made its way into the *Herald Sun*, it had found its perfect vehicle. A Melbourne newspaper, with a daily beat to keep up the pressure, and a journalist with the local contacts to chase down the fundraiser angle.

The morning after the first story was published, Andrew Moore, a Labor staffer in the media unit, sent around the clips of 'Hair Force One' to outbreaks of spontaneous joy in the office. 'Yarn going off on Herald Sun Facebook page and website!' Shawn Lambert emailed. 'Real good gear,' Ben Foster said, who was most admiring of the sub-editor's 'Hair Force One' headline.

But there was no time to waste basking in the glory. It was all hands on deck to provide a strong follow-up to the story. Stephen Spencer, a former journalist who had run the media unit under Simon Crean's leadership but now worked for Penny Wong, was busy trawling Twitter for evidence of Bishop's trip to Geelong. He found it, spotting photographs of her arrival at the Geelong golf course.

However, she wasn't on a plane as the early reports had assumed. It was a helicopter! The photos were gold. Labor was on a roll. Labor MP Rob Mitchell also spotted the images and tipped off the media.

Choppergate was born. The revelation that the Speaker had arrived by helicopter, and there were the photos to prove it, was truly a gift for Labor from the heavens.

Foster wanted to know if Labor could lodge a Freedom of Information request for Bishop's diary for the day. Was this a job for 'Deloris'? Deloris Van Cartier was the pseudonym Lambert had created for the Shorten office's FOI requests.

This was the job of Andrew Anson, a 26-year-old researcher. If his first request was denied, he was adept at launching appeals and a complaints process. Miss Van Cartier was a very busy lady.

Anson had joined the Labor Party in his teens and still looked barely out of high school, but his political research skills were freakish, although useless in this instance. 'Alas Speaker not captured by FOI so she is beyond Deloris' reach!' Anson replied.

The trick on the first day when the story dropped was not to leave any Labor fingerprints on it. Ideally, a Labor Party spokesperson should not be quoted. The idea was to make the breaking news look organic rather than an ALP 'drop' to the newspapers. But once it was unleashed, Labor's talking heads could pile on, creating a media storm. They had a day of media planned around it.

It was a strategy the media unit would deploy repeatedly. Pretending the ALP was an innocent bystander to the scandal, as shocked as any other reader of the newspaper, was all part of the parlour game. Sometimes, it was a game not even shared with newspaper editors, who might be loath to take a 'drop' from the Labor Party. It was another smart way that Labor manipulated a sometimes hostile media landscape. A journalist might not always tell an editor where a story came from, leaving a mystery around who provided the original tip-off. Dropping the stories was also about building relationships in the press gallery.

Within 24 hours of Choppergate breaking, the Labor Party was pumping out the 'Ride of the Valkyries' soundtrack from the film *Apocalypse Now* in attack ads featuring fleets of helicopters. The ads noted that Bishop's trip to Geelong, given the short distance, was more expensive per kilometre than NASA's mission to Pluto. Destroying enemies' ministerial careers was hard work, but it wasn't always this much fun.

Shorten, surrounded by fresh lettuces in a Melbourne supermarket for his daily press conference, was soon wheeled out to express his profound shock and dismay. He looked genuinely surprised. It was an Oscar-worthy performance.

'We have Mrs Bishop, who thinks she is so important that she can't even be bothered getting a car between Melbourne and Geelong, a one-hour car trip. It is such a colossally arrogant thing to do.'

The Speaker's short trip from Melbourne to Geelong for a Liberal Party fundraiser had cost taxpayers $5,227.27. Treasurer Joe Hockey would later admit it 'didn't pass the sniff test'. It was a comical extravagance for a 75-kilometre journey that thousands of daily commuters would complete in their cars.

The Choppergate story would become a monster. It soon spread to national mastheads, dominating the headlines for weeks in a saga that drained the life out of the Abbott Government.

Closing a year of anger over Abbott's austere first budget and his plans for a $7 GP co-payment, a deficit levy and cuts to health and education, it was the final insult.

It was the first of many quiet successes for the Shorten office, which helped to topple Tony Abbott and build a mythology within Labor that played into a growing sense of invincibility in the lead-up to the 2019 election. For Shorten, the scandal also proved to be a circuit breaker. Forced to give evidence at the royal commission into trade unions in July 2015, there was more than just his credibility on the line.

All was forgotten, though, as Bronwyn Bishop's helicopter came over the horizon, and Shorten was no longer the story. The pressure he was under had been weighing on his staffers' minds when they'd gone looking for the distraction that Choppergate provided. Saving Private Bill Shorten from the scrutiny of a royal commission, slaying the speaker of the House of Representatives and helping topple Abbott was all in a busy day's work for the leader's office.

Before long, there was an opportunity to return fire to Dyson Heydon. Just a month after Choppergate broke, Marcus Priest, a lawyer, former journalist and Labor adviser, had heard that the royal commissioner was billed as the guest speaker at the Sir Garfield Barwick lecture. On 12 August, Priest rang the NSW Bar Association requesting a copy of the invitation, and asked whether the group knew it was an event associated with the Liberal Party. The invitation was duly sent to Priest, but after doing so, the association's publications manager Chris Winslow became alarmed that a story might appear in the media. He decided he should alert the royal commission and emailed the counsel assisting the royal commission, Jeremy Stoljar SC: 'Re the Barwick lecture: does he know this is connected to the Liberal Party?'

The next day *The Sydney Morning Herald* broke the story. The revelation scored a Walkley Award nomination, another win for the tireless Shorten office.

The news sparked calls from Labor, the Greens and unions for the government to shut down the royal commission. Once again, Shorten expressed his shock. 'If it is true that a royal commissioner investigating Tony Abbott's political opponents is now attending a Liberal Party fundraiser, that is incredibly serious, incredibly concerning.'

Ultimately, Heydon did not stand down but the affair helped to bolster Labor's arguments that the commission was a political witch-hunt, providing some protection in the event of any findings against Shorten.

By 2016, Labor had turned its attention to the Greens. They discovered that Greens leader Richard Di Natale had failed for over a year to declare the family farm in Victoria's Otway Ranges. Labor staffer Mat Jose then googled the maiden name of Di Natale's wife, Lucy Quarterman. What came up was a cached ad of her searching for an au pair.

The ad suggested the family was paying an au pair just $150 a week including free rent and board. Sharing the love with Fairfax this time around, the story was duly farmed out to the *The Age* and *SMH*. The newspaper article was later the subject of a Press Council complaint because it claimed that, based on a 40-hour week, the au pair was earning $3.75 an hour. Au pairs rarely work such long hours, but equally the $150 stipend was hardly generous by au pair standards.

The next big hit was Health Minister Sussan Ley in the summer of 2017. The lazy days of January are a time most political journalists disappear to the beach and a skeleton staff covers the rosters. The annual migration of bogong moths invades Parliament House, with reporters arriving at work to find the carpet littered with large, dying insects. If you're lucky, a cleaner might be encountered hoovering up the dead. Stories are scarce, but if they're good the media impact is huge. Desperate radio newsrooms and television reporters can generally be relied on to regurgitate any front-page news.

Once again the 'Democracy Empowerment Unit' in Shorten's office played a starring role. The story begins, however, in Ley's office at the end of 2016. On 1 December, a staffer alerted the minister to an incoming Freedom of Information request. 'FYI I've just been notified that the attached VIP manifests are going to be released under FOI tomorrow,' the email to Ley warned. The 'VIP' or 'very important person' flights are for RAAF charter flights for MPs that are organised by the Defence Department.

The email explained that the material to be released related to the period around the end of the autumn sitting in March, when parliament was extended and a number of flights were organised by the Prime Minister's Office to get MPs and senators home to Perth, Brisbane and Newcastle. The documents also included 'a couple of other trips in this period that the health minister and DPM [deputy prime minister] took which may also prompt questions'. In fact, Ley's constant work trips to the Gold Coast had already been raised as a potential problem in her office.

But here was the mysterious part. The Freedom of Information request was lodged under a fake name. 'The FoI was submitted under a pseudonym – so not clear if the information is going to a journalist/opposition/random,' the email stated.

It was 33 days after those documents were returned to the mystery applicant that the story wound up in the *Herald Sun* on 3 January. 'Exclusive: Taxpayers have forked out more than $12,000 for Health Minister Sussan Ley to charter a VIP jet to the Gold Coast for an afternoon meeting,' the report revealed. 'Documents released under Freedom of Information laws reveal Ms Ley and an adviser took the RAAF plane from Canberra to attend a Pharmacy Guild conference in Queensland in March. Ms Ley and her adviser departed Canberra on the private plane at 11.45 am and returned shortly after 6 pm, spending about 3½ hours in the air.'

The real story was that Ley was sick and had cancelled her appearance and trip to the Gold Coast. At the last minute, Prime Minister Malcolm Turnbull's office had intervened and insisted she attend, necessitating the chartering of a RAAF flight to transport the virus-ridden Ley to the conference.

The irony was not lost on Ley's office when the $12,000 charter flight exploded into a crisis. Turnbull had remained furious with Ley after the 'Medi-scare' campaign during the 2016 election and she was out of favour. The fact that she and her office had repeatedly begged to respond to Labor's claims, compiling huge dossiers of material – only to be rebuffed by Turnbull's team and even his pollster Mark Textor – didn't seem to matter.

In the weeks that followed, speculation would even swirl inside Liberal Party ranks that it was an inside job, lodged by a factional powerbroker to target Marise Payne's travel, but instead capturing Ley. However, the real problems started when Shorten's Democracy Empowerment Unit got on the job.

Miss Deloris Van Cartier – AKA Andrew Anson – was lying in bed in Adelaide on the morning of 3 August, reading about Sussan Ley charging taxpayers $12,000 for charter flights to the Gold Coast.

Neither his alter ego, nor anyone else in the Labor Party, had been involved in this FoI request, but he was happy to assist in a potential follow-up to the story. Anson decided to fire up the Shorten office's subscription to RP Data.

The property data firm allowed members, at a price, to have access to ownership data across Australia. It was an expensive but invaluable tool in tracking down addresses about property holdings. In political terms it was a Willy Wonka factory of useful information, spitting out the home addresses and property history of anyone in Australia.

The Shorten office had requested an RP Data subscription after the debacle involving former Victorian Labor frontbencher David Feeney. One of the original faceless men who tapped colleagues to roll Kevin Rudd and install Julia Gillard, Feeney was an old friend of Shorten's. He'd sparked controversy before the 2016 election when it was revealed he'd failed to disclose a $2 million investment property in Northcote, which he claimed he'd forgotten he owned. Feeney resigned from parliament in February 2018 when he was unable to produce evidence he had renounced his citizenship. Paperwork was clearly not his strong suit.

But Feeney's painful experience unwittingly led Labor

to claim Sussan Ley's ministerial scalp. In the wake of the Feeney fiasco, ALP Secretary George Wright had signed off on the RP Data subscription to ensure the Labor Party knew what houses their MPs owned.

Simply by punching 'Sussan Penelope Ley' into the database, the fact that she had bought a property on the Gold Coast immediately came up, including the sale date. From there, it was a matter of checking MPs' travel records to examine whether she was on any taxpayer-funded flights on the day she bought the property. Bingo. The dates matched.

By lunchtime on 3 January, Shorten's Press Secretary, Sarah Michael, was emailing *Herald Sun* journalist Annika Smethurst, breaking down the extensive findings of the Shorten office research.

'RP Data records show Sussan Ley bought a property on Main Beach in Queensland on 9 May 2015,' she wrote. 'On 9 May 2015 she claimed travel allowance for her and her husband in Main Beach, Queensland under the guise of "minister – official business".' The total cost to fly her and her husband to buy the property was $3,949.15.

Labor's dossier on Ley ran to 27 pages. In just a few hours, the Shorten team had forensically broken down the travel allowance she had claimed – page 7; every flight she had taken to the Gold Coast – page 11; and the COMCAR usage on those days – page 17. There were media stories for days. The Turnbull Government's next ministerial scandal was good to go.

But once again, it took a while to get the story up. On 5 January, Shorten's office got the good news just before 9 am.

It was two days after Michael had sent the Ley dossier through. 'Ok I think I'll finally have a good space for this tomorrow,' Smethurst emailed. 'I love it.'

Later in the day, Shorten's office discussed whether or not to provide a comment from a Labor spokesman in the story.

'This story will splash across all the states,' Michael wrote. 'Front pages all round so well done! One caveat they just got word which could be bull that a prominent AFL star may have overdosed in hospital in which case they'll hold coz they want it on the front page. If it's not true it'll run tomorrow in the Tele, courier, Hun [*Herald Sun*] etc on the front page.'

Gerard Richardson, Shorten's senior press secretary, again stressed the importance of no Labor quotes in the first story so it didn't look like an ALP stitch-up. 'Let's leave it but word up Keogh for tomorrow,' he said.

The *Herald Sun* published the Sussan Ley story at 8 pm on the newspaper's website. It revealed that she had 'charged taxpayers thousands of dollars for a trip to Queensland with her husband during which she bought a $795,000 Gold Coast investment property'. 'Government documents reveal in May 2015, after announcing at Brisbane's Wesley Hospital $1.3 billion in funding to list new medicines and vaccines, Ms Ley went to the affluent suburb of Main Beach.

'She billed taxpayers $370 on her travel allowance to stay the night on the Gold Coast with her partner, on the same day she bought the ocean-view apartment,' the report stated.

Inside Ley's office, her staff were in meltdown over the story. Just before Christmas, her longstanding press secretary and adviser Troy Bilsborough had left the office. Bilsborough was a good operative. The staff left behind had no idea how to handle the unfolding crisis and were panicking.

Ley's spokeswoman said the couple had travelled to the Gold Coast because the minister had 'stakeholders to meet with'. But once the scale of her travel was revealed, it did seem excessive. Why was she spending so much time in Queensland? One reason was her media strategy to roll out the 'good news' in her portfolio every Sunday. She needed to be somewhere on the weekends where she could do a press conference for the 6 pm TV news. Clearly, some perusal of the local real-estate offerings had also occurred.

Unhelpfully, Brownyn Bishop agreed to give journalists fresh quotes on the Ley scandal, assisting voters to connect the dots to Choppergate. People attacking Ley were 'behaving like a pack of dogs', she said.

'I do know there are socialists out there who want to attack free enterprise. Socialists, like alcoholics, will blame anyone but themselves. Whereas alcoholics can damage their own family, socialists can destroy the whole country.'

Turnbull soon released a statement announcing the health minister would stand aside until the investigation was complete into her travel claims. As the pressure continued, she quit as health minister before a report into the matter was finalised. 'Australians expect the government to deal with these serious matters very thoroughly and in accordance with the Statement of Ministerial Standards,' said Turnbull. After her resignation, he also announced a new compliance body to oversee parliamentary expenses.

It had taken just four days to destroy her political career. The health minister apologised to her cabinet colleagues for the 'distraction' she had caused. 'I'm very confident that the investigations will demonstrate that no rules were broken whatsoever,' she said. 'But I also recognise, as you describe it, the pub test, and I recognise that for people who live in my electorate, who work hard, who understand about living on fixed incomes and have experienced a life I've experienced in the past, this has a look that, you know, that I don't understand those issues and I don't recognise them, and in fact the opposite is the case.'

Ley never made it back.

In March, the findings of the inquiry concluded she had breached the rules just once. The sole breach was using a COMCAR to take her from her hotel to the $800,000 apartment she purchased, a five-minute journey. Claims she broke the rules by visiting the Gold Coast on New Year's Eve and piloting a plane were dismissed on the grounds she could prove official business on those days.

'I simply table the outcome of the investigation, as I said I would, and in doing so allow people to draw their own conclusions,' Ley told parliament. 'Regardless of these facts, the public impression was cast.'

Ley remained on the backbench for years, until Scott Morrison restored her to a more junior ministry after the 2019 election. Just like Bronwyn Bishop before her, Ley voted to dump the prime minister who had dumped her. When the petition was circulated for a leadership ballot against Turnbull in August 2018, she was among the first to sign.

7

THE POLITICS OF RAPE

In the last question time before he called the election, Scott Morrison had alluded – subtly, but unambiguously – to the allegation that Bill Shorten had raped a young woman at a Labor vanguard camp in the 1980s. It had set off alarm bells within the ALP.

In the weeks leading up to the prime minister's question-time barb, the party had received information from a businessman with previous links to Morrison. He claimed to have inside intelligence: that the rape allegation was going to 'blow up' Labor's campaign.

The Labor leader tasked his Chief of Staff Ryan Liddell and ALP consultant Sharon McCrohan to deal with it, and engaged lawyers, including Arnold Bloch Leibler, a leading commercial law firm with offices in Melbourne and Sydney, and a Victorian silk, Neil Clelland QC. Shorten advised his staff to deal with it so he could focus on fighting the election.

Clelland, who specialised in defamation, worked on legal arguments to present to News Corp if it tried to publish during the election campaign. Given there was nothing new in the allegation, it could give rise to criminal defamation. A simple reference to the fact that the account of the alleged victim had been investigated and dropped by police would not necessarily protect the media from a massive defamation claim.

Lawyers also examined whether it could amount to an attempt to interfere with an election. They investigated whether 'bots' were pushing the story on social media and whether this might represent a breach of foreign interference laws. They also raised concerns with Facebook in Australia over the sharing of the old rape allegations.

Morrison's decision to use a rape claim in question time to psych out an opponent was a tactic Shorten regarded as 'disgusting' and beneath the office of prime minister. His reading was that it was a sign Morrison was under pressure and desperate.

Shorten's personal lawyer, Leon Zwier of Arnold Bloch Leibler, opened a file and every contact with the businessman was carefully diarised and recorded. Zwier had also represented Shorten without charge at the royal commission into trade unions. The Labor leader would later thank Zwier – twice – in both his concession speech on election night and his address to the ALP's caucus, for the lawyer's 'incomparable' wisdom as a counsellor and adviser.

The file notes prepared by the law firm do not name the prime minister's friend who was feeding the Labor Party the information, although everyone involved knew who he was.

He is referred to somewhat dramatically throughout the legal file notes as 'Deep Throat', the same pseudonym given to the secret informant who provided information during the Watergate scandal.

His claims that *The Daily Telegraph* was planning a story, and that he was meeting with the journalist who was preparing it, were particularly concerning. Deep Throat told his ALP handlers that he had access to two documents that could only have come from Kathy Sherriff, the victim of the alleged rape, or police. It was her statutory declaration and a receipt from NSW police of lodgement. The man claimed he had been 'helping' the prime minister with background on the rape claim, but that now he had 'played him' he was happy to hand it over to the ALP. He provided no documentary evidence to support his claim of discussions with the PM, it was simply a claim he made to the Labor Party and there was no way of verifying it.

On 24 April, he told his Labor handler that *The Daily Telegraph* planned to publish a story reigniting the rape claims five days later. In an attempt to caution the Liberals against using the material, the Labor operative dealing with him raised a range of legal consequences that might follow if lawyers acting for Sherriff chose to pursue a private prosecution so close to an election. For example, it might give rise to allegations of a criminal conspiracy or an attempt to pervert the course of justice.

When challenged on the veracity of the story, the businessman provided screenshots on his phone of the questions a journalist had sent to Victoria Police. But Deep Throat had even taller tales that alarmed the ALP. He claimed to have inside information that approval for the story had been sought from Lachlan Murdoch, the co-chairman of News Corp.

This claim is entirely false according to News Corp journalists, who insist it was nowhere near publishable. But Shorten's office didn't know that at the time. His legal team believed that, if true, this 'green light' from Murdoch implied the media empire would be prepared to take the risk of publishing a defamatory story.

Other Labor sources within News Corp were feeding the party contradictory advice. One Sky News host told the ALP that News Corp management were putting pressure on journalists not to run the story, fearing that, if Labor won, it would be used to call a royal commission into Rupert Murdoch's empire.

There were two scenarios that might explain Deep Throat's curious behaviour. The first was that he was trying to recycle insider Liberal gossip to barter for favours and influence with the incoming government. The alternative scenario was that he was just running a little psych-out session for the Liberals to freak Labor out. Whatever the motivation, Labor regarded his information seriously.

Privately, friends of Shorten complained about 'Scott Morrison's prayer circle of Satan' trying to mess with the Labor leader's head over the rape claim. 'They are into it up to their devil-worshipping eyeballs,' one of them said. At first, it had all seemed a little paranoid.

Fittingly, given the role it would later play, Sherriff's allegations first surfaced on social media. She emerged for the first time when Shorten stood as a candidate for the Labor leadership. 'You probably get crazy messages all the time, but I need help,' she posted on Kevin Rudd's Facebook page in 2013. She said Shorten had 'done things' to her without permission.

It was the beginning of a nightmare for Shorten, and a publishing dilemma for Australian media outlets, many of whom were aware of her claim, but were also acutely conscious of how prejudicial it was and legally risky to report. 'In '86, I went to a Young Labor camp down near Geelong,' she said on Facebook. 'I was alone. At about 4 am, there was a knock at my door. It was him at the door. He pushed me into a bathroom, up against a towel rail, pulled down my pants and raped me.'

Shorten, who had never heard of the allegations until he nominated for the leadership, said it had simply never occurred. The police probe that followed was a trauma that left deep scars on all of the participants. Given the high profile of the accused, the police were careful to investigate the case in a painstaking way to ensure they were not accused of bowing to political pressure. Finally, police sought advice from the Office of Public Prosecutions, which advised that 'there was no reasonable prospect of conviction'. No charges were laid.

'The police have now concluded the investigation,' said Shorten. 'The decision speaks for itself. It is over.'

But in the age of the internet, stories never die. And while 50 years ago such allegations would have faded into history relatively quickly, for Shorten the claims were kept alive. For his loyal staff and a team of lawyers, who spent years trying to contain the issue, it was the great phantom menace of the campaign.

The fear of a public confrontation with Sherriff was so elevated during the election that there was discussion in Shorten's office about whether Australian Federal Police officers travelling with him needed a description of her to prepare for the event, should it occur. It's part and parcel of life for any prime minister or opposition leader, the police being alert to individuals who might have a reason to show up and cause a confrontation or an incident.

There were also fears the tabloids would interview his accuser and the issue would detonate during the campaign. Those fears about how to handle the issue consumed the Shorten campaign. Labor staff talked about the constant threat of exposure of the rape allegations which they felt was 'very real'. And they were told there were political forces behind it.

It was *The Australian* that had first published the allegation five years earlier. Editor Clive Mathieson asked the paper's crime reporter Dan Box to look into the rumours, but to proceed with extreme caution. A separate team of reporters was set up to poke holes in what Box found, to ensure the story was not only cautious but watertight.

The story's headline, published on 14 November 2013, was 'ALP Figure Faces '80s Rape Claim'. It revealed the following:

'A senior Labor figure is under investigation by Victoria Police after it was alleged he raped a teenager at an event organised by the party's youth wing in the 1980s.' Bizarrely, the revelations coincided with Kevin Rudd's resignation from parliament, forcing the newspaper to rule him out as a suspect, lest readers 'join the dots' and presume it was Rudd who'd been accused. 'Despite the timing of Kevin Rudd's resignation from parliament last night, *The Australian* can confirm the man is not the former prime minister,' the report said.

A lawyer for the unnamed MP, Leon Zwier, said the rape claim had never previously been raised by his client in the intervening three decades. 'The unsubstantiated claims are absolutely without foundation and are distressing for his family and for him,' the statement said.

It was only after the investigation was dropped nine months later that the 'senior Labor figure' chose to reveal his identity. 'The allegations were untrue and abhorrent,' Shorten said. 'This has been deeply distressing for my family. I'm thankful for the love and support of Chloe and the support of my staff and parliamentary colleagues.'

Denied her day in court, his accuser turned to Channel Seven's *Sunday Night* program for justice. They dubbed the investigation 'Project X'. Kathy Sherriff was put up in five-star hotels and flown to Sydney for a three-camera interview with Seven's award-winning journalist Steve Pennells. Soon after police dropped the case they met at Fratelli Fresh in Alexandria for lunch.

'Obviously, as you can imagine, it would have been the story of the year,' Pennells recalled. An exclusive interview with the woman accusing a Labor leader of rape was guaranteed to create a media firestorm. But only if it could be broadcast. The group headed to Seven's studios where they recorded a marathon three-hour interview. To conduct such a long interview was highly unusual, but it was one of Pennells' first assignments for *Sunday Night* and it was a highly sensitive subject. 'In the interview she was emotional. It was a powerful, gut-wrenching interview, but nothing matched up.'

For months, the producers kept hunting for witnesses to back up her story. Pennells' role in Project X over, he was blissfully unaware that Sherriff had flown to Melbourne after his interview to assist *Sunday Night* obtain more vision for the investigation. They hoped to visit the site of the vanguard camp, and the program had Sherriff draw a map, which she described in great detail. But there was more. The current affairs program also asked her to wear a concealed microphone during a discussion with the Victoria Police detectives who'd dropped the case.

In the spring of 2014, Sherriff walked into a Melbourne police station with a recording device in her bra. A novice in the dark arts of tabloid TV, the woman was keen to do her best for the producers. 'Testing, testing,' she whispered down her top as she entered the premises. Outside, a TV cameraman and producer were parked nearby and keeping her under surveillance.

'It was a Zoom recorder, so we didn't realise until we got the transcript,' said the producer. 'She's saying "Testing, testing" in the police station. I was just thinking, "Holy fuck – the police are going to realise they are being recorded."'

Against the odds, though, the police didn't seem to realise. This was lucky, because what Sherriff was not told by her new tabloid TV friends was this: it's illegal in Victoria to tape someone without their knowledge, let alone inside a cop shop.

But the project languished during a period of management upheaval at *Sunday Night*. Executive Producer Mark Llewellyn had departed, and the new EP, Steve Taylor, and supervising EP, Suzanne Smith, who arrived some months later, were both ex-ABC – an organisation known for a more genteel culture. But the pair did prove inquisitive. When they discovered what Project X was, and that it had involved a covert recording inside a police station, they freaked out and alerted Channel Seven's legal team. Management was horrified and wanted the recording destroyed. Smith was horrified and told the producer so. 'What on earth did you plan to do with that – it's an illegal recording.'

So, despite the three-hour studio interview with Sherriff, the police station audio, the five-star hotels and the flights, the story never went to air. Seven abandoned Project X in early 2015. Sherriff was furious and believed she had been dudded by the Seven Network.

'But as I explained to her, which she couldn't really understand,' said Pennells, 'we couldn't verify anything in her story. You've got to have the proof.'

As would emerge as a pattern, she attacked Pennells in social media posts and accused the TV producer of being 'a drunk' who could not be trusted. But the pressure on Seven was coming from all directions. The female producer who researched Project X was left shaken after a Victorian union figure approached her at a Melbourne pub to introduce himself and urged her to stop digging into the rape claims. He claimed to know where her parents lived.

'What's a pretty little girl like you doing poking her nose where it isn't wanted?' he asked. Channel Seven offered the woman security checks at home after the incident. She did stop digging. And for a long time, nobody did poke around in it – until the 2019 election.

After losing a few nights' sleep over it early in the campaign, Shorten stressed he had compartmentalised it. His staff and lawyers were dealing with the issue. However, rumours swirled regardless. Labor's Treasury spokesman Chris Bowen would later claim that 'some idiot' had told Shorten that News Corp was about to run the rape claim 10 minutes before the disastrous press conference on 17 April, when he clashed with Ten Network reporter Jonathan Lea over the cost of his climate-change policies.

Meanwhile, the rape story was getting pushed around on social media through all the extreme right-wing channels. Liberal Party strategists at HQ in Brisbane were counting tens of thousands of views for the Facebook pages being shared by white supremacist groups. Because of that, the social media giant was tagging it as extremist material. As a result, the Liberal strategists believed, Facebook was limiting access to the news stories they were sharing.

'One day without Facebook analytics would probably send news outlets bankrupt,' a Liberal staffer said. 'So no-one wanted to touch it, because it was a story being put around by extremist elements of the Right.'

Around this time, a political consultant working for the Liberal Party's negative research unit at its headquarters in Brisbane decided it was time to take a closer look at the story. Someone had to 'pony up' and make the call, he said, so he phoned Kathy Sherriff. The pair spoke for 20 minutes. His strategy was simple – he told her the truth.

'You can't lie. Because she's just as likely to record the conversation and put it on Facebook,' he said. 'I had members volunteering to talk to her. Let's just say usual suspects from Queensland.'

The research unit spent a week looking into the Sherriff saga but was concerned it would backfire if it was raised. The research unit even had a pitch: it proposed to use feminist Clementine Ford's book *Boys Will Be Boys* on why women are not believed as the hook. It was some hook. But Australia's punitive defamation laws and the fact that white supremacists were pushing Sherriff's story on Facebook were both huge problems in getting a mainstream media outlet to touch it.

Eventually, Liberal Party Director Andrew Hirst expressly told the research unit to stop pursuing the rape angle. Later, word went out to some candidates and staffers not to touch it with a bargepole. This was deemed necessary after several Liberal MPs, including – according to the consultant – Queensland's George Christensen, offered to speak directly to Sherriff. The MP, who was under attack from Labor's own dirt unit over his frequent trips to the Philippines to visit his fiancée, had perhaps decided that what was good for the goose was good for the gander.

Labor remained on high alert for any mention of rape in connection with Shorten. On 2 May, the Liberal Party put out a press release about a Labor candidate, Luke Creasey, who was in strife over old Facebook posts. A junior staffer in the prime minister's office seconded to the negative research unit had found that Creasey had made jokes about rape. After days of pressure, he resigned. The Liberal Party's press release noted that victims rarely lie about being sexually assaulted and that 'false reports on this are incredibly rare. Yet, Shorten chose to stand by his candidate this morning, with full knowledge and awareness of these comments.'

To Shorten's team, hypersensitive to any mention of 'rape' and 'Bill Shorten' in the same sentence, it sounded like deliberate word association. Morrison kept referring to the ALP leader using the 'young man's defence', which Labor read as another game of using words with hidden meanings.

The next day, during the second televised debate, one of the first questions was about rape, prompting the Shorten team to flinch as it was asked. The following morning, Morrison was talking about rape again. The question was: 'Prime Minister, if you were to win the next election, what would you do in the first 50 to 100 days of your next government?' Morrison commenced his answer by saying it was tax relief, before adding, unprompted, a reference to sexual assault. 'I mean, we had many questions last night. We had one of the early questions on rape and women being raped and the lack of reporting. It's important that their stories are believed and that they know that if they come forward, their stories will be believed. As I said, my father was a police officer and you can only pursue the crimes when they're reported often, so the women, in those circumstances, I think should have a greater sense of confidence that if they tell their stories, they'll be believed.'

Labor duly noted the prime minister's latest musings on rape. Even Liberal staffers at HQ confirm they watched the clip and suspected that Morrison simply couldn't help himself. It was a signature Morrison move, the kind of cryptic comment that involved plausible deniability that he was alluding to the Shorten allegations.

After one of the debates between Shorten and Morrison, Labor strategist Sharon McCrohan noticed that the rape claims were being shared from an old article in *The Advertiser*. It was a *Herald Sun* story, but it was not behind the paywall on *The Advertiser* website – perfect if someone wanted to push it on social media. McCrohan spoke to colleagues who concluded there wasn't much they could do if it was being orchestrated by Labor's political opponents – short of getting the story removed from the internet.

Labor's Communications Director Gerard Richardson spent hours on the phone to News Corp editors, trying to resolve the issue. Eventually, they agreed to take the story down. If you search for it today, it comes up as a 404 – a broken link.

Around this time, a *Herald Sun* reporter, Rob Harris, spoke to West Australian Liberal MP Ben Morton. The story that subsequently did the rounds in the Labor Party was that Morton had rung Harris wanting to know why the rape story had been taken down. It took nearly four months for Morton to respond to my texts after the election, but when he did he said he doesn't remember this exchange at all. 'Who is Kathy Sherriff?' he asked. 'I don't know anything much about this. I actually can't really remember it. I don't recall that, at all.' A day later he called back. The exchange did occur, he said, but he insisted it was the journalist contacting him.

Morton is a big bloke who likes to underline his everyman credentials by listing his old job as a bus driver on his CV. A former WA Liberal Party director, he is respected in the party. He is also a trusted member of Scott Morrison's inner circle. In the week of 'madness' in August 2018 that ended the prime ministership of Malcolm Turnbull, Morton organised Morrison's numbers and ensured that he – and not Peter Dutton or Julie Bishop – emerged victorious. During the election campaign, Morton was a constant presence by Morrison's side, travelling most days on the PM's RAAF jet, providing a sounding board and strategic advice. He insists the Labor Party story that he was asking for information was completely wrong. The reporter sent him the link to the rape story, not the other way around.

As the election continued, Sherriff became more agitated about wanting to get the story out. Supporters of Sherriff had sent texts to journalists that she was 'ready to talk' and asking them to fly interstate to speak to her. *The Daily Telegraph*'s political editor, Sharri Markson, who was at home on maternity leave, was repeatedly contacted by supporters of Sherriff to interview her. Rather than the newspaper chasing the story, it was Sherriff's own supporters pushing it.

'Kathy is waiting to speak to you, sorry to add to the pressure,' one text said. Meanwhile, friends of Sherriff were sharing emails claiming that she was being hounded by the tabloid that was declining to run the story.

Finally, on the evening of Tuesday, 14 May 2019 – four days out from the election – Kathy Sherriff broke cover. Rebuffed by journalists, she posted on her Facebook page that she had formally requested that Victoria Police re-examine her allegations against Shorten.

'We call for my case to be reopened. I have done this on my own accord without the assistance of the media or the many friends and supporters who have tried to help me in the past or in recent months. This is my journey alone. I know that many people will criticise the timing of my actions – but my right to justice and the rights of rape victims everywhere, is more important than politics.'

From the moment she posted on Facebook, containment of the story moved to a minute-by-minute operation inside the Shorten camp. There were multiple calls from journalists. Labor's press team pushed the case that there was nothing new in the claims at all, other than a trip down to a police station. The entire team was braced for the story to hit a mainstream outlet or for one of the journalists on the campaign bus to ask a question. The next morning, an eerie silence prevailed. No News Corp or Nine newspaper reported her remarks, or the possibility of new evidence. Neither did any other paper, or any of the breakfast shows on TV or radio.

The only mainstream outfit to touch it was 2GB's Ben Fordham, who interviewed her lawyer, Melbourne QC

Peter Faris, on his afternoon radio show on 15 May. 'Well, three days out from the federal election, rape allegations have resurfaced against the Labor Party leader Bill Shorten,' Fordham began. He appeared to be reading from a script drafted by lawyers. 'We need to make clear these allegations are being vigorously denied by Mr Shorten and I want to add as well that police did not press charges when the matter was investigated back in 2014.'

Fordham revealed that Sherriff had visited the Spencer Street police station and requested that detectives reopen the case. Fordham also recounted that he was contacted by 'a friend of Kathy's who arranged for me to speak with her today, which I have done'.

In his communication with Faris, Fordham said the QC had explained that he was 'currently not acting for Kathy because he was retired', but had attended the police station with her.

'I did act for her, briefly, in 2014 and since then I've retired,' Faris said. 'No doubt as a result of that, I was approached two days ago to give her some assistance, particularly with regard to going to the police station and dealing with the evidence. My assessment of her is she is a very intelligent, bright woman and I think she would make a great witness.'

Former radio broadcaster turned blogger Michael Smith also interviewed Sherriff on 17 May – the day before the election – for his website. News Corp, Nine newspapers, the ABC and *Guardian Australia* didn't touch it.

But on Facebook – the sleeping and unaccountable giant of news – the story was enthusiastically shared. It didn't matter that the news media chose to ignore the re-emergence of Sherriff – the story spread anyway. This was Shorten's nightmare – conservatives, bloggers and Facebook would drive the rape claims back into view during the campaign. And it was coming true. The real battle, however, was in his head, and there's no doubt the constant pressure left him shaken. Some wondered if it was even a factor in his tearful breakdown over *The Daily Telegraph*'s front-page story about his mother.

After the election, hardly anyone noticed when, on 19 July, Sherriff provided the following update on Facebook. 'I have been in discussion with the authorities both in Melbourne & elsewhere constantly,' she said. 'I have also been able to harness more important information. As we all know, I have been waiting decades, the wheels of justice turn slowly, and I am confident that justice will soon be done.'

It seemed logical that perhaps it was worthy of checking in on whether the police had indeed reopened the case as requested by Sherriff. When I called Peter Faris QC, he was sick in bed. Too unwell to conduct the conversation over the phone, he agreed to correspond via text. I asked him if there were any new developments in the Sherriff case. 'Nothing that I am aware of,' he wrote. 'Nothing.'

But didn't she have new witnesses? Had the police not suggested they might reopen the case if there was new evidence? 'I know nothing more. I do not have her contact number. I will try and pass your number on to a friend but more I cannot do.' When asked who the 'mutual friend' was, Faris replied, 'I repeat. I will try and pass it on. I cannot do more.'

Shortly afterwards, as promised, I received a phone call from the friend. This latest contact turned out to be a wild ride. The woman explained what a brave woman Sherriff was and how she simply wanted justice. She might be able to help me get in touch with her, she explained.

As she started to discuss other 'goings on' at Parliament House, it dawned on me that the woman must have worked there at some stage. 'Yes,' she confirmed. The woman was employed by a Liberal cabinet minister for several years. After she left Canberra, 'sick of the travel', she had returned to work for a senior Liberal Party MP at a state level.

She was reminiscent of Linda Tripp. During the Monica Lewinsky scandal, when the US President Bill Clinton had an affair with the young intern, the Pentagon staffer had befriended Lewinsky. Her secret wiretap recordings led to Clinton's impeachment trial. But Kathy Sherriff wasn't interested in partisan politics at all, her friend added. 'No, because for Kathy this is never about politics. It's about justice. In the hours and hours that we have talked, we have never discussed politics,' she said.

Later, I confirmed that Sherriff's Liberal Party 'friend' had set up the interview with Ben Fordham. She was effectively operating as de facto press secretary during the campaign. The former Liberal staffer claimed to have met Shorten at Parliament House and found him 'creepy', telling me a strange story about him once looking at her in a manner she regarded as lascivious. 'If a bloke wants to have a look, whatever. This was different. He actually made my skin crawl.'

However, she remained evasive about how she had met Kathy Sherriff and befriended her. The woman lived thousands of kilometres away. Nothing seemed to make sense. 'Oh, just through different contacts. You know, sometimes you just click with someone? You know how it is – there's always six degrees of separation.'

It wasn't clear if she had ever met Sherriff at all. The conversation also left unanswered the question of what role, if any, this woman had played in keeping the Liberal Party up to date with Sherriff's quest for justice. It seemed unlikely that this former Liberal staffer would not pass on information to other political contacts, given she was freely sharing her views with a stranger. But the day after our discussion, she sent a WhatsApp message demanding I never reveal her identity. 'It is my expectation that all communication with me is kept between us and my name is not mentioned in any context,' she wrote.

While she had not asked for anonymity in our first conversation, having an ugly debate about it after the fact seemed unproductive. I then attempted to make contact with Sherriff independently through a Facebook account. At first, she indicated she did not want to discuss the matter while the police might still reopen the case. I told her I accepted this and would respect it.

Sherriff's 'friend' contacted me promptly the next morning to complain that 'you have made contact directly with Kathy'. The tone suggested I had gone outside the rules by not going through her as a gatekeeper. 'She does not wish to speak about this matter for your book,' she said.

A few months later, I accidentally called Sherriff's Liberal Party 'friend'. In response, I got a message on Twitter from a Kathy Sherriff account, asking, 'What do you want?' It was enough to prompt me to ask if the account was not genuine and was actually being run by her Liberal Party friend. She never replied.

But the contacts around the Sherriff matter kept getting weirder. A self-styled 'vigilante', who said he had been banned from Parliament House for championing her rape claims, sent me hundreds of emails from Sherriff to him and to reporters. Sherriff later mentioned him in her emails to me.

'I also have a young vigilante who fought a very brave crusade for me. He even got himself "Barred for Life" from Parliament House, ACT,' Sherriff said. 'He was accused of rape but proven innocent. He knew from his experience what it was like to be accused of rape.'

Finally, after several months, Sherriff rang me. I explained that my interest was in terms of examining the election and whether she had been contacted by Liberal Party operatives. Did I know that an unnamed television journalist had 'employed a private investigator from North Sydney to hunt me down in 2013? I've got those emails too, even from the PI,' she said.

She also complained about her dealings with other journalists. 'Even Larry Pickering wrote a heap of bullshit,' she added. 'He had everything, word for word, that happened, from why and when I joined the ALP, until I left. And yet he misquoted me and turned a rape into a Mills & Boon book. Why?'

After our first conversation we had an entirely normal email exchange about some quotes I might use. But after we spoke I soon started receiving strange messages. The 'vigilante' contacted me to tell me Sherriff had told him he was 'in danger' after speaking to me. A documentary producer called me, clearly after a call from Sherriff about what I might have discussed about a project they were working on, and I assured her I wasn't writing about that. Finally, another friend of Sherriff's, also active in the Victorian Liberal Party, contacted me, urging me to chase Sherriff's story but demanding that the identity of Sherriff's friend and her Liberal Party links not be revealed. He then sent WhatsApp messages, insisting I never contact her again and that he was speaking for 'the girls'. It all seemed tied up with her friend in the Liberal Party.

It was all quite unusual, the cast of individuals clustering around Kathy Sherriff. It was like lifting up a rock to find a complex ecosystem of characters. Finally, Sherriff contacted my publisher, making a range of claims about me, despite the fact that our contact had been entirely friendly and civil. This was a pattern that had been repeated with many of the journalists she had contacted.

However, Sherriff had clearly picked up some skills in covert recording from *Sunday Night*. After we spoke, she emailed me one last time with the big reveal. 'I recorded all of our telephone conversations, legally!' Sherriff wrote. 'Obviously, you have not recorded our conversation because you never asked my permission, and you don't live in a state where the laws on secretly recording a private conversation are different to anywhere else in Australia. Recording a conversation without the other person knowing is illegal across every other state in Australia, and you are on record picking your kids up from swimming after school. Sorry to be a hard arse but I've had to tolerate the media in my face since I was ten years old and quickly learned that a majority of journalists are nothing more than a pack of poorly educated, alcoholic misogynists. No offence,' she concluded. 'Just facts.'

8

NEGATIVE GEAR

The famous metaphor to explain chaos theory, the science of how small changes can have large effects elsewhere, is known as the butterfly effect. The term was devised by Edward Lorenz, an American mathematician and meteorologist. In 1961, he was entering data into a weather-prediction program and discovered the big impact seemingly modest changes could have on weather patterns. Originally, he imagined a scenario where one movement of a seagull's wings changed the course of a storm, an idea that later gave birth to the more poetic notion that 'the flap of a butterfly's wings in Brazil could set off a tornado in Texas'.

Politics is no exception. The demise of Bronwyn Bishop set off a leadership crisis that accelerated the removal of Tony Abbott as prime minister. Malcolm Turnbull's ascension then triggered a ripple effect of further consequences. As prime minister, he enjoyed an early surge of popularity and promised to explore tax reform, including negative gearing. The discussion over whether Labor should tackle tax breaks for housing investors, long regarded as political kryptonite, crystallised. The negative-gearing experiment then emboldened the ALP to go further.

Sussan Ley's own entanglement with the Gold Coast property market, which delivered an abrupt ending to her ministerial career, was all about reaping the benefits of negative gearing. It was an investment strategy as dinky-di as Vegemite. The great Australian dream of home ownership is a tradition fuelled by one of the most generous tax regimes for housing investors in the world.

The basic idea is this: if you borrow to buy an investment property and the mortgage and costs associated are greater than the rental income of the property, it is negatively geared. The net loss on the investment property can then be used to reduce taxable income from your ordinary wages. Investors bank on offsetting their losses with a capital gain in the future when the value of the property rises. The higher your income, the greater the tax-minimisation benefits of negative gearing. For Ley, whose wage was slashed by more than $100,000 when she lost her job as a result of her investment purchase, it was perhaps not such a great investment. But for thousands of other Australians, an investment property is an important nest egg for retirement.

Labor's Treasury spokesman Chris Bowen had started examining negative gearing as a reform option immediately after the 2013 election. 'I took the view that negative gearing was one of those reforms where you could build a coalition of support,' he said. 'It sort of had everything in it. Fairness, generational fairness for young people, better access, budget savings and financial stability. Negative gearing accelerates the urban centre. We had the second-largest household debt in the world. I had the view it was a reform that could be ripe.'

Paul Keating, a political mentor who Bowen spoke to 'most days', egged him on. Labor powerbroker Graham Richardson, never a Bowen fan, would later complain that 'Keating's advice was a big part of the problem'.

But from the beginning, there were serious concerns raised about Bowen's reform plans. At the time, the ALP secretary was George Wright, who ran Labor's election campaigns, polling and political research. As Labor's review would find, the traditional links between the ALP's research program of focus groups being linked to policy-making would later break down, but Wright was highly engaged in the debates over negative gearing. He explicitly warned Labor's leadership group that it didn't want to get into the space of John Hewson and 1993, when the 650-page 'Fightback!' policy was described as the longest suicide note in Australian political history.

A political campaign veteran, he had served Labor leaders Julia Gillard and Kevin Rudd during the impossible years of the leadership wars. He had also worked on the Australian Council of Trade Unions' 'Your Rights at Work' campaign against WorkChoices during the Howard years. The reforms stripped workers of unfair-dismissal protections if they worked at companies with less than 100 employees.

The campaign remains revered in Labor circles as one of the most effective political operations in years. It was regarded as having a significant impact on Rudd's 2007 victory. Later, Wright would go on to create the 'Medi-scare' campaign – or, as Labor preferred to call it, the 'Save Medicare' campaign – that a furious Malcolm Turnbull would blame for nearly losing the 2016 election.

As a political campaigner, Wright could see immediately how the negative-gearing policy could be weaponised into a scare campaign. He was asked to do some research on it. Wright took the general view that it wasn't his job to offer a view on policy, just the politics. When asked his opinion, he told anyone who would listen that it was a bad idea. Or at least, it was a bad idea to pursue from opposition.

Labor's veteran frontbencher Jenny Macklin was also cautious. This caused some consternation in the budget's razor gang because Macklin had responsibility for one of the biggest spending portfolios. In theory, that gave her an even greater reason to find savings.

Bowen had publicly flagged his interest in negative-gearing reform months before the Liberal Party leadership challenge in September 2015. In April of that year, he had outlined his reform principles: do not disadvantage people who have made investments in good faith under current rules and do not risk reducing the supply of new housing.

In the lead-up to the 2016 election, Bowen said publicly it would be 'irresponsible to rule out going to the next election with changes to, for example, negative gearing'. His office considered a range of policy options, including caps on the number of houses you could negatively gear or the value of deductions you could claim.

Shorten was open to the idea. 'I wasn't getting push-back from him,' said Bowen. 'I was getting push-back from some, but not him. George Wright, Jenny Macklin were nervous, but ended up supporting it. Just general, "Oh shit, negative gearing, that's the third rail."'

The game changed when Malcolm Turnbull replaced Tony Abbott. Concerns quickly emerged over whether Shorten could beat him at an election. Generally speaking it would be unusual for an opposition to return to government after just one term, but Abbott had lost 30 consecutive Newspolls, a reason that was cited for dumping him as prime minister.

'Turnbull was obviously an enormously popular political leader,' said Bowen. 'The general consensus was he would beat Bill. I also took the view, and this could be construed as an attack on Bill and it's not, if there was going to be a personality contest between Bill and Malcolm, there needed to be a policy contest.' Had the rise of Turnbull fast-tracked the negative-gearing debate? 'I think that's true. But all the work had already been done while Tony Abbott was prime minister. Basically, I was on board for it and I think, in fairness, Bill was too. I would never say he was forced into it. That's not the sort of relationship we had. If he had said, "I don't want to do it," [negative gearing] would not have happened.

'We came out with this Big Bang policy. They had nothing, no agenda. We surged in Newspoll. The first Newspoll after we announced negative gearing was the first time it was 50–50. So, not ahead of Turnbull, but 50–50. I remember journalists texting me, saying, "Wow, there is a case for policy reform." There was a general comment made to me and my colleagues, "You saved [Shorten's] leadership."'

That's not the recollection of everyone around the shadow cabinet. Tony Burke, who served as shadow finance minister, disagrees that the negative-gearing timeline was driven by Turnbull's ascension.

'It certainly doesn't accord with my memories at the time,' he said. 'Chris had been working on the policy on that for ages. My whole experience is not that. It doesn't mean it's wrong. But I was shadow finance minister, so I was in all the discussions. I got there slowly on it. I had a wariness about it, because there was a reason people hadn't gone to it. But the boom in Sydney and Melbourne just became so big. It was parents saying, "I don't see how my kids are going to be able to live anywhere near me."'

Labor's shadow cabinet was also heavily influenced by the impact of broken promises on the standing of the Abbott Government. Abbott had spent the 2013 election pledging 'no cuts to schools, no cuts to hospitals, no cuts to the ABC'. After he proceeded to cut schools, hospitals and the ABC, his political reputation was in tatters.

The pressing reason to pursue negative gearing was also to pay for Labor's hopes to restore schools funding. Coupled with changes to capital gains tax, the changes were forecast to reap $32 billion in extra revenue over the following decade. As the ALP review into the election result noted: 'Beginning with $14 billion extra for schools, Labor had decided well before the election to commit large amounts of taxpayers' money to new spending initiatives. The total additional spending over 10 years was more than $100 billion. Having decided to spend this much more than the Coalition, Labor faced two choices: increase the budget deficit and public debt by the same amount or announce new revenue-raising measures to cover the cost. Going into an election campaign with unfunded expenditure of more than $100 billion would have exposed Labor to a highly effective attack of massively increasing budget deficits and debt.'

The Labor leadership group faced difficult options. By reinstating the deficit levy, Bowen was already proposing an increase in the top personal tax rate to 49 per cent. The ALP review added, '. . . the only alternative revenue source would be from lower and middle-income earners'.

While many of the voters most affected by the franking-credits policy would actually swing to Labor, it was the sheer volume of spending announcements released during the campaign that 'created a sense of risk in the minds of the main beneficiaries of Labor's policies – economically insecure, low-income voters – about Labor's economic management credentials'.

The policy the Labor Party ultimately settled on was retaining negative gearing for new house builds to stimulate new construction, but abolishing it for existing properties. 'It went to the Expenditure Review Committee something like 19 times,' Bowen said. 'Starting with a general threshold discussion. Should we do something about negative gearing? Starting with presenting about seven options. This would have been 2014. It only went to shadow cabinet once. You don't take things to shadow cabinet multiple times.' By the time it went to shadow cabinet most of them had heard about it and discussed it in private talks with Bowen or Shorten.

Labor's Brendan O'Connor recalls the debate over negative gearing was 'highly participatory' and there was intense discussion over the detail of the policy. Many options were considered, including alternative proposals for the cap on the number of houses you could claim negative gearing for, although these options raised less money.

Shorten announced his plan to tackle negative gearing during the Valentine's Day weekend ALP conference in 2016. The Turnbull Government responded by attacking Labor's policy as 'ill-considered', but flagging plans to target rich investors by either capping the number of properties that could be geared or limiting the annual tax deductions. Treasurer Scott Morrison said the 'excesses' of negative gearing would be tackled.

'The Liberals know that something needs to change, but they've chosen instead to run a cheap, shrill scare campaign,' Bowen responded. But soon a backbench revolt over the issue had the Turnbull Government running away from even tinkering with negative gearing.

After the 2016 election, the view emerged that the doomsayers were wrong. Malcolm Turnbull had tried a scare campaign on negative gearing, but in the words of one Labor strategist, 'It wasn't very scary.' There was a real sense Labor had won the debate and was dominant in parliament.

Over the years that followed, the housing market shifted. Tighter guidelines for lending slammed the brakes on prices at auctions and clearance rates. Some owners were concerned about falling prices, and worried that Labor's policy would help drive them down. Over the summer of 2019, Treasurer Josh Frydenberg spent the holidays defying his wife's plea to turn his phone off, instead penning opinion pieces on Labor's negative-gearing policy and generally stirring up voters' concerns.

The turning point was house prices coming down in Sydney and Melbourne. 'I don't concede it was a problem,' said Bowen. 'But it was much more contested than it was in 2016. Basically because property prices moved. The argument it [tackling negative gearing] would have made it worse, I don't accept. I did start it a bit later, in January 2020. I considered 2019 but I thought 2020 was pretty right.'

The summer before the 2019 election, the Labor Party conducted a series of focus groups, including one in Rooty Hill, Western Sydney. These groups, in which 'soft' or swinging voters are gathered in a room, fed snacks and questioned deeply about their views on various issues and various political leaders, are a vital part of political polling. 'Quantitative polling' – known by shorthand as 'quant' – is where a consistent question is asked of a large group of people. Quant is where a pollster rings you while you're cooking dinner and asks who you'd be voting for if an election were to be held this Saturday. As we know, the quant was spectacularly wrong in 2019.

But qualitative polling is altogether a different field. Here, a much smaller group of people is interviewed. The pollster recruits participants who are undecided, and explores their reactions to people and ideas, looking for their values. Their fears. What might drive their decision-making. Politicians are far from the only users of qualitative research. Advertising agencies use it all the time, to test which of their messages work best.

Labor's pollster John Utting conducted the research. And in early 2019, when he examined the feelings a random collection of Western Sydney residents had about the forthcoming election, alarm bells were ringing. Unprompted, focus group participants were raising concerns about Labor's housing policy. 'Sensitivity among those with an investment property is heightened now as the market is dropping,' Utting warned, 'and they don't want anything to exacerbate this. They fear ending negative gearing may do that.'

This was a policy the ALP had run with at the 2016 election against Turnbull, seemingly without problems. Though negative gearing had for decades been a political 'untouchable', it hadn't proved ballot-box poison; after all, Labor had nearly won. Soaring housing prices had inflamed ill-feeling about investors who owned multiple houses and claimed tax deductions, effectively for keeping first home-buyers out of the market.

However, just in the focus group alone, about 'one-third have at least one investment property and most aspire to get one in the future'. The focus group report noted the voters 'worry that it will lower the value of property investments because there will be fewer buyers when they want to sell'.

Another thing that had changed since 2016 for Labor was the opponent they faced. Malcolm Turnbull – a multi-millionaire who disliked negative campaigning – was an easy target for Labor's 'top end of town' campaign and would, moreover, not hit back with vicious attack ads. Scott Morrison, however, was another story entirely. Morrison's strategy was built very heavily around Labor's tax reform to negative gearing and franking credits that could be explained in intricate detail by its author Bowen. But Morrison didn't need detail. He called the negative-gearing policy a 'housing tax' – devastating shorthand. And as Labor's pollsters ran a temperature check on whose message was being heard among swinging voters, the news was not good.

Liberal ads that framed negative gearing and dividend imputation as tax increases had left a mark on the focus-group participants. 'We're taxed too much as it is,' one participant complained.

'It is an issue that is gaining in intensity, and critically in this set of groups we've picked up the first evidence, albeit at a low level, of vote switching away from Labor because of the issue,' the report stated. 'These voters have identified a weakness in Labor's arguments, that despite grandfathering, the changes will depress the resale value of their properties because presumably there will be less buyers in the market.' Investors complained, 'It will be harder to make money when I sell.'

There was 'less awareness' of cutting capital-gains-tax concessions but, when understood, it amplified voter concerns. 'Voters don't regard an investment property as the domain of the rich,' the Labor research warned. The report also warned that rebuttal or 'harm reduction' was difficult because it didn't address the central concern of many of these property investors. It suggested Labor stress the exemptions, grandfathering of existing investments and that the retention of negative gearing for newly constructed homes would boost construction and create jobs. The research suggested Labor stress the inequality of wealthy investors with many properties who reap the bulk of the benefits.

This was the advice that Shorten followed religiously in the campaign. 'Our changes won't apply to anyone who is currently negatively geared,' he said. 'In other words, you can still keep claiming a loss and claiming credits for the loss you make on your property investment, if that's what you currently do.' He insisted it was not a housing tax. 'You use the word "tax". If I'm not giving you a subsidy for you making a loss on an investment property, that ain't a new tax. That just means you're not getting a subsidy.'

Labor also considered other measures to address home affordability, but ultimately abandoned them. 'I considered other things like a first home buyer's grant to cushion the blow,' said Bowen. 'But I concluded it was pretty bad policy.' The idea never made its way to Labor's shadow cabinet. 'Just sort of my musings. And in the end, we didn't.'

As the election campaign was fought, the prime minister ramped up the warnings on Labor's plan to limit negative gearing to newly built homes and halve the 50 per cent capital gains tax discount. He warned Labor's policies would 'torpedo' the property market.

'If you now take the sledgehammer of negative gearing and capital gains tax changes – if you abolish negative gearing, as we know it – then you're inviting a housing market crash,' he said. 'We've seen house prices come back to a soft landing, and that's not me saying that, that's ratings agencies, it's the Reserve Bank.

'Everyone has recognised that one of the biggest economic risks that the country faced was a housing market crash. That's what the ratings agencies were concerned about, that's what the banks were concerned about, that's what economists all around the country were concerned about. That's what, as treasurer, I was very concerned about. So we needed to bring the housing market in to a soft landing.'

The prime minister liked to tell the story of his own journey on the property ladder. It was the sort of folksy narrative that worked beautifully with the social media posts being cranked out by the Liberal Party's digital team, featuring Morrison cooking his favourite curry and spending time with his two daughters.

'I remember the first place I bought with [wife] Jenny, it was 53 square metres, it was not very big,' he said. 'But that was what we could afford, and that's how we made our start. And it's always a big challenge for anyone to buy their first home. I'm for Australians setting their own expectations. I'm all for aspiration. I'm all for them having a big view of their future, and for us to be able to help them try to achieve that wherever they can. I'm not one who likes to lecture people about what their aspirations should be. I'm all for an aspirational Australia.'

But it wasn't just homeowners who would be 'torpedoed' – Morrison was adamant it was renters too. The prime minister claimed rents could rocket by as much as 15 per cent nationwide and more than 20 per cent in Queensland. This was a figure that included rent rises that would occur regardless of negative gearing, but he insisted they would increase more if Labor was elected.

During the campaign, Labor discovered that real estate agents across Australia were direct-mailing tenants, warning that if Labor's negative-gearing policy was introduced rents would soar and the unemployment rate would rise. The material claimed, 'Because you're currently renting, it might be tempting to dismiss the latest political battle over whether negative gearing should be abolished . . . but rents will rise.'

In one letter, a Raine & Horne agent wrote, 'Dear tenant, the Real Estate Institute of Australia has never been involved in politics but feel the changes that will occur if we have a change of politics will be devastating.'

It was completely untrue. The REIA had in fact run an identical campaign against Labor's proposed changes during the 2016 election. 'These are wild claims, not backed by any evidence whatsoever,' said the Australian Council Of Social Service Chief Executive Cassandra Goldie. 'Labor's negative gearing changes would not affect existing investors as their property is grandfathered; any impact on new investors will be gradual, and investment in new housing is exempt.

There's no evidence to back the wild claim that unemployment will rise.'

In an election campaign, you can always tell when an issue is working for a political party when it's all they want to talk about. On the Sunday heading into the final week of the campaign, Scott Morrison announced a $500 million scheme to help people buy their first home. The centrepiece of the Coalition campaign launch was a First Home Loan Deposit Scheme, to allow 10,000 homeowners to buy a property with a deposit of just 5 per cent.

'The election, friends, is about a choice,' he said. 'The choice of who you can trust to keep the promise of Australia, to all Australians, as prime minister: myself or Bill Shorten. The choice between a government that knows how to manage money, has returned the budget to surplus and will now pay down debt. Or Bill Shorten and Labor, whose reckless spending and higher taxes will put all of that at risk at the worst possible time.'

The scheme would be capped at 10,000 loans a year and be subject to an income test and limits on the value of the properties. Treasurer Josh Frydenberg confirmed that there was no modelling on the policy, which was based on similar schemes overseas. 'What we have seen is this program rolled out in New Zealand to great effect,' he said.

The prime minister said it was 'difficult to say' if the plan would push up prices. 'But I do know this: Labor's housing tax will force the value of your home down.'

In the environment of falling house prices, the Liberals could now argue that only they had a policy to assist first home buyers directly. The Labor Party, in trying to insist that the negative-gearing policy would have only a marginal effect on prices, was losing the argument that it could help affordability.

Chris Bowen thought the First Home Loan Deposit Scheme was poor policy. Shorten spoke to him on the phone that afternoon and told him bluntly that Labor was going to back it. Shorten said there was no way he was going to spend the final week of the campaign getting mowed down by the Liberals on negative gearing. He was making a 'captain's call'. 'We're matching it,' he said. And just like that, he spent another $500 million.

There was no time for a shadow cabinet debate. The election was so close, Labor couldn't afford a final mistake. Bowen was duly wheeled out to agree with the Liberals low-deposit home scheme. 'What Australians are sick of are political parties who say, "Just because somebody else thought of the idea, we say no,"' Bowen said.

The prime minister spent the final days of the campaign appearing magically at construction sites. It seemed clear the Liberals had based the final week around the hope that it would wedge Labor on the first home deposit scheme. To Shorten's supporters, the decision to match the policy was an example of his good political instincts when he was allowed to lead. The low deposit scheme was unlikely to have an inflationary effect on house prices if it was capped at 10,000 entrants. Neutralising the issue was the right thing to do.

Bowen wasn't thrilled by the policy but it was such a small program, it appeared to be more about trying to pick a fight with Labor. In the aftermath, negative gearing didn't feature as strongly in the post-mortems as the changes to franking credits, although some MPs said they believed on the ground it was a vote-switcher.

It was a big change from the mantra after the 2016 election when Labor was confident it had gambled and won on tax reform. 'Everyone said this policy is amazing,' said Bowen. 'You're taking on the Holy Grail! You've got young people on board! There was nobody suggesting to me we should dump the policy. In fact, some people were saying, "Can you go further?" And my answer was: "No, I think we've got that policy setting about right."'

What is not in dispute is that when Labor gambled on negative gearing and survived, it triggered the next big experiment: franking-credit reform.

9

RETIREES, KARMA AND THE DEATH TAX

Even before Scott Morrison talked of miracles on election night, the Labor Party was left wondering if the prime minister should be thanking the 'retiree tax', not Jesus. Labor's plan to reform franking credits was a policy that hardly anyone could explain, given a catchy nickname by opponents that nobody could forget.

Calling it a retiree tax was devastatingly effective. It terrified a good proportion of the 92 per cent of Australians completely unaffected by the policy. Across the country, Labor MPs reported being buttonholed by frightened pensioners, who had never owned a share in their life. As Bill Shorten would concede after the election, it was also the seed from which the death tax lie was born.

Two years earlier, when Chris Bowen had gone to see Shorten about the idea, it seemed like a pretty good one. The savings that the reform of franking credits could deliver were massive: $60 billion over a decade – twice the revenue raised from negative-gearing reforms.

Soon, Australia's budget would be handing out more cash on franking-credit refunds than it spent on public schools. But it was risky.

'Big call, digger,' Shorten said when Bowen first approached him. 'What does Keating think?' Paul Keating remained in almost daily contact with Bowen, who assured the Labor leader that the former prime minister thought it was a ripper. Keating was consulted on all of the big calls, including negative gearing and franking-credit reforms. 'Right on both counts, son, right on both counts,' was Keating's enthusiastic response.

But Labor frontbencher Jenny Macklin was concerned about the impact on pensioners. Bowen's submission to cabinet glossed over the risk. When it emerged that far more pensioners than expected were affected, Keating complained it needed to be fixed. It's not clear he raised that concern when he was first consulted. 'You've got to protect the bloody pensioners,' he said. Shorten felt he had been misled and let down by Bowen and had to wear the consequences of the climb-down when he announced pensioners would be exempt from the policy.

In the marginal electorate of Boothby, Labor's candidate Nadia Clancy told Penny Wong in April it was 'killing' her campaign, while ALP frontbencher Amanda

RETIREES, KARMA AND THE DEATH TAX

Rishworth was bailed up at a swimming lesson shortly after the election by a family friend who admitted he had voted for the Liberals. 'You what?' she said. He explained he was worried about his superannuation. 'But what sort of super do you have?' she asked. 'Industry super,' he replied. Labor wasn't doing anything to industry super, she told him. 'We love industry super,' she explained. 'Really?' he replied. Her friend was pretty sure his mum had told him Labor was doing something to franking credits that were bad for super. Rishworth towelled off her son, shaking her head, and drove home.

Then, there were the voters who really knew what they were talking about: the retirees who actually got franking credits and knew exactly how the system worked. In Perth, Labor MP Patrick Possum Gorman hit a pack of them one day while he was phoning voters in his electorate and it was a doozy. The former WA Labor Party state secretary was well versed in modern campaigning methods and had the organisation skills that you would expect from a former staffer to Rudd. But the day he called a retiree with franking credits who was enjoying a morning with his mates was not a great one. 'Yeah, actually, you've called at my coffee group – I will just put you on speaker,' the retiree explained. Gorman manfully accepted the challenge and recounts his comical attempts to listen respectfully as half a dozen seniors ripped into him on speakerphone over the noise of a Perth coffee shop.

'That was the worst call I did and I don't know how many retirees told me their views,' Gorman remembered with a rueful laugh. 'I knew I was on a losing streak with that call. They were not people who were persuadable.'

It was a complicated policy. The news coverage often included dramatic images of angry baby boomers shaking their fists at town-hall-style meetings at having their retirement plans stolen – but what the hell were franking credits? Even when journalists tried to explain the policy, it was confusing. The basic problem was that many did not really understand it. Journalists stopped trying and simply filed stories with words including 'retiree tax', 'franking credits' or 'dividend imputation', without a paragraph explaining what that actually meant.

Labor spent too much time explaining before they could talk about what they could do with the money. People who did receive franking credits understood the system in intricate detail and were disgusted that Labor and some sections of the media couldn't understand how cross they felt. It might not be much money they were securing through franking credits, but it was enough to pay for a holiday or Christmas presents for the grandchildren.

Australia's largest youth news website, Pedestrian.TV, gave explaining franking credits a red-hot go. In an article titled, 'What the F**k Are Franking Credits? What is Going On?', Deputy Editor James Hennessy wrote, 'Let me paint you a picture. Imagine for a moment that you're not eating Mi Goreng out of a dirty bowl in a share house, balancing your cracked smartphone on your knee reading this article. Imagine for just a moment that you are a person of means. Here's the basic idea: companies get taxed at the Australian corporate tax rate, which is presently 30%. If you're a shareholder of a company, and you receive dividends on the company profit, you sit down in front of your accountant at the end of the year and report those dividends as taxable income. The issue is that the tax office is, theoretically, getting two bites of the apple. People call this double-dipping, which invokes images of some maniac befouling your peri-peri dip with a chewed Dorito. Franking credits (also known as 'imputation credits') are intended to resolve this. The long and short of it is that Labor is trying to reform a system which, at present, gives retired members of self-managed super funds with no taxable income some extra cash thanks to a bit of investment trickery and reforms passed in 2001. Those people are pissed, and they're protesting.'

It wasn't a bad explanation at all, really, apart from the article noting Labor was 'headed to a landslide victory'.

Then, in the summer, Chris Bowen did something diabolical. He breezily urged those who didn't like the policy not to vote for it. 'If they feel very strongly about this, if they feel that this is something which should impact on their vote, they are of course perfectly entitled to vote against us.'

Labor powerbroker Graham Richardson later described it as 'madness'. Bowen ploughed on. 'What we're doing is reforming unsustainable, unfair concessions and loopholes in the system. It's necessary to invest more in schools and hospitals, to deliver bigger personal income tax cuts. We make all those commitments and we provide bigger budget surpluses.'

But Labor knew it would be risky to tackle franking credits and Bowen warned as much in his shadow cabinet submissions. The original submission is a 10-page document that describes the franking credit reforms as an 'Imputation and growth package'. It is an instructive document because it tells the story of an economic team under siege from big spenders in shadow cabinet. It notes Labor's success in pulling off the daring negative-gearing reforms and surviving the 2016 election.

'Labor has pursued several reforms that broaden the tax base and make the tax system fairer, such as reforms to negative gearing and capital gains tax, and reforms to family trusts,' the confidential submission began. 'The ability for individuals and superannuation funds to claim cash refunds for excess imputation credits was another Howard Government decision which is costing the budget dearly. Australia is the only OECD country with a fully refundable dividend imputation credit system.'

Bowen's original cabinet submission recommended that Labor reverse what Howard/Costello had introduced in 2001. Secondly, it noted that Bowen would bring forward a fully funded growth package that supported investment and jobs, which would include finalising Labor's position on the government's already legislated business tax cuts. Labor would consider a new 'investment boost' tax allowance, and a revamped national rental affordability scheme that would, over 10 years, underpin the construction of 100,000 new homes for public housing. Thirdly, it sought support for Bowen's goal of a 'superior budget position over the forward estimates than the Government on the basis of the additional revenue from the imputation measure'. In polite terms, that was Bowen saying to the shadow cabinet, 'Don't spend this money, you bastards!'

The submission sought agreement to 'return to the original dividend imputation system introduced by Paul Keating in 1987, whereby imputation credits could continue to be used to offset tax liabilities, but excess credits could not be claimed as cash refunds from the ATO.

The dividend imputation system had been introduced by Keating in order to avoid tax being paid twice on company profits. Under this system, cash refunds for excess credits were not allowed. But after the Ralph Review tax reforms, the Howard Government had changed the laws so that resident individuals and complying superannuation funds could claim cash refunds for any excess imputation credits. This meant people could use imputation credits to reduce their tax liabilities and, if credits exceeded tax liabilities, claim a cash refund from the ATO.

As Bowen's cabinet submission noted, when this decision was made, the budget was in surplus to the tune of nearly 1 per cent of GDP, and it was estimated to cost the budget around $550 million a year. 'It is now costing the budget more than $5 billion a year, with the cost expected to grow to around $8 billion a year by the end of the decade.'

The word 'pensioner' is not used in the main submission. It notes that 'Distributional data shows that two thirds of cash refunds accrue to superannuation funds (primarily self-managed super funds), with one third accruing to individual taxpayers. The largest beneficiaries of the current arrangements are typically wealthier retirees with large superannuation balances.'

Shadow cabinet was told that 92 per cent of all individual taxpayers did not receive a cash refund for excess imputation credits. The submission also stated that wealth data confirmed that 'share ownership is skewed towards high wealth households while low wealth households receive virtually all of their income from government payments and allowances.

'It's important to remember that this policy will not directly take money off retirees. Affected retirees will have the flexibility to adjust their investments in whatever way they wish to limit any adverse impact arising from the policy.'

Finally, the submission stated that with the finalisation of the growth package, the remaining revenue from the imputation credit decision should be quarantined to retain maximum flexibility in setting Labor's election policy agenda, achieving a stronger fiscal position, and for providing options to assist primarily low-income earners with cost of living pressures. That is code for tax cuts.

The timing and details of the announcement/s would be agreed between the leader, shadow treasurer, shadow assistant treasurer and shadow minister for finance. In other words, once shadow cabinet agreed to the architecture of the franking credit changes, the rest of the details would be handled by the boys – Shorten, Bowen, Andrew Leigh and Jim Chalmers.

Bowen notes that claiming cash refunds for excess imputation credits 'comes at an increasingly unaffordable cost to the budget'. 'It also worsens intergenerational inequity as it disproportionately benefits older, typically wealthier retirees at a time when younger working Australians are being burdened with higher taxes supporting the costs associated with an ageing population. The most recent data from Tax Statistics shows that despite the superannuation pool standing at well over $2 trillion in assets, superannuation earnings taxes are now a net drain on the budget.'

But the most important paragraph in the submission is the last. 'This policy does not come without its risks. There is broad support for the current dividend imputation system. And the Government will likely mount a scare campaign that our policy will adversely affect the share market and that it will damage investment and jobs. It will also argue we are hitting low income retirees. These risks will need to be managed.'

The risks were managed badly. Labor announced the policy on 13 March 2018, and it was immediately clear it had underestimated how many pensioners were affected. Shorten confirms he felt let down by the failure of the original submission to indicate how many pensioners would be affected.

The second cabinet submission to clean up the mess agreed to calibrate the decision by exempting all pension and allowance recipients, as well as self-managed super funds which had at least one pension or pension allowance recipient. The changes were not expensive, which made you wonder why they were not included in the original proposal.

The policy still saved $55.7 billion over the medium-term. In the second version, Jenny Macklin was more central in the decision-making process.

'The Government has run a deliberate scare campaign to inflate and mislead the impacts of our policy, centred on age pensioners,' the submission noted. 'The priority is to maintain the maximum policy integrity and revenue, while having the strongest policy response possible for pensioners. Pensioners are less able to change their situation to respond to policy changes. The submission confirms the new policy would not affect 93.5 per cent of individual taxpayers.'

To understand the psychology behind Labor's attraction to the idea of franking credits, you need to remember two things. Firstly, despite all the doomsayers warning that negative gearing was a hugely dangerous policy to pursue, Labor brought Malcolm Turnbull to the brink of defeat at the 2016 election. Nobody really expected that outcome and it emboldened Labor to not only retain negative gearing as a policy, but explore further reforms. Frequently, an election loss involves a policy clear-out. But Labor's success in 2016 meant it hung onto all the old policy and started adding more on top. Secondly, and this is critical, Chris Bowen had emerged from that election convinced that if their budget bottom line had been stronger, Labor may have actually won the election.

In the last week of the 2016 campaign Shorten's economic team was obliged to announce that, while Labor had a superior budget bottom line to the Coalition's over a 10-year period, its new spending commitments gave it a weaker bottom line over the four-year forward estimates.

'This was in the context of a very large budget deficit of almost $40 billion. Despite gaining 14 seats nationally, only two of these were in Queensland, both on the back of unsolicited One Nation preferences. The experience of the 2016 election led Bowen and the Labor leadership to conclude Labor must not go into the next election with a weaker budget bottom line than the Coalition.'

As one Labor frontbencher explains it, 'The problem with every political campaign is that the generals always fight the last war. And the problem with the last campaign was that there was a $16 billion difference between our bottom line and theirs. So we approached this term of opposition thinking we can't be behind them in the pre-election outlook numbers. We need to match them. And we needed to have enough money to spend on our priority policies. We did negative gearing before the 2016 election and that seemed to go fine. Actually in retrospect, the reason why people weren't that worried about it was they didn't think we were going to win the 2016 election.'

Labor campaigners observe ruefully that this is what politicians do. They have a bad week in the media and retrofit why they lost an election. But there's no evidence that a fiscal gap is the reason Labor didn't win the 2016 election, a campaign nobody expected them to win. For three years Bowen and the front bench have all believed this, but where's the evidence?

'This is a nice little thing that demonstrates the broader problem with all of these politicians,' a Labor staffer said. 'They have a shitty week in the media and they feel their credibility under attack with stakeholders and peers, then there's a poll and they connect the two. They make these big declarative statements and it's just not true.'

There's not a great deal of hard data to confirm Bowen's theory, which seemed to be accepted unquestioningly by the ALP review authors, Jay Weatherill and Craig Emerson. It seemed to be based purely on Bowen's perception that he got smashed around in the media during the final week of the 2016 campaign over the costings.

However, Labor's vote had actually gone up, not down, in the final week – as a result of the 'Medi-scare' campaign. Labor had falsely claimed the Liberals wanted to privatise Medicare, a campaign that became the prototype for the death-tax campaign in 2019. It was a campaign in which the Labor Party pulled out an old newspaper story confirming that the Liberals planned to privatise some of the back-office operations and tried to spin it into a plan to end Medicare.

There was zero evidence that the Liberals planned to do that. The report got no follow-up at the time and sunk without a trace. Labor campaigners will privately admit its own scare campaign was largely baseless. But it worked, because voters naturally don't trust the Liberal Party to protect Medicare, just as there is natural distrust of Labor on taxes and the economy, which was exploited to run a fear campaign on the 'retiree tax' and the death tax that didn't exist.

In the movie *Vice*, starring Christian Bale as Dick Cheney, there's a scene where the US vice-president attends an Americans for Tax Reform 'Wednesday meeting' with a conservative activist, Grover Norquist. In the Hollywood version, Norquist concedes that estate taxes are hard to eliminate, because they only affect those estates worth over $2 million. He then introduces a marketing guru Frank Luntz, who tells them simply by using the magic words 'death tax' instead of 'estate tax' they can weaponise a problem for the rich into a vote switcher for the poor.

It's not a historically accurate account but it does underline the emotive power of the words 'death tax' and the capacity to get people unaffected by the change riled up. But a campaign lie must always be based on a grain of truth, or amplify existing concerns about a political party.

After the election, in an interview for this book, Shorten accepted that it was the franking-credit reforms that opened the door to the death-tax scare campaign. Using the shorthand of calling the policy the 'retiree tax' amplified the death-tax message.

'I think this is a government that is prepared to lie about anything. But having said that, there's no doubt that not capping franking credits – or not sufficiently recognising the anxiety that older people felt. It provided the seedbed that allowed the government to grow a death-tax campaign.'

Even Labor staffers saw the connection between the franking-credit changes and a death tax when the policy was first announced. One press secretary turned to a colleague on the day the franking-credit policy was announced and said 'death tax'. 'We've just lost the election.'

Within 10 days of the election campaign starting, the Labor Party was tracking thousands of Facebook shares of 'fake news' on the death tax. It was an internet link to a legitimate three-month-old press release from Treasurer Josh Frydenberg but it was combined with fake news that 'Labor, the Greens and unions have signed an agreement to introduce a 40 per cent inheritance tax'.

'Everything you own cannot go to your kids or next of kin at death,' the post reads. 'Forty per cent will go to the government. If you die before your spouse she will have to pay 40 per cent of what you're worth to the government. When she dies your kids will have to pay 40 per cent of what she had left to the government and this includes the family home.'

During the campaign Bowen had been growing more concerned over the impact of the 'death tax'.

'We can argue about what went wrong, but clearly we got things wrong. We didn't do enough about it. I think the death tax was huge. We were talking about it on those 6.15 am hook-ups. I first raised it. Someone texted me about it and I raised it. At first I thought it was fairly isolated. Then I realised it wasn't. The impact of the death tax on Facebook was a huge concern.

'We complained to Facebook about the fake-news elements of it. We were assured that everything that could be done was being done. If you searched for death tax, you were taken to our page, as opposed to, you know, a page with lies about Labor's policies. But I had many, many more people raising the death tax with me on election day than any actual Labor policy. The difficulty was if they raised franking credit or negative gearing, you could convince them. So it was almost impossible to win.'

After the election, the ALP outlined its extensive contact with Facebook to stop the spread of lies. The new Labor National Secretary, Paul Erickson, wrote to parliament calling for an examination of fake news, the death tax and asking what could be done to stop it. It warned of threats to Australian democracy that had been amplified by the economic and social transformation that digital platforms have enabled.

Guardian Australia ran a data project during the election to track hidden social-media campaigning. The death-tax scare campaign started with three key events: a *Daily Telegraph* article on 21 July 2018 reporting that the Australian Council of Trade Unions supported an inheritance tax, an uncritical follow-up discussion on the *Sunrise* program the following day, and a media release by Josh Frydenberg on 24 January 2019, warning of Labor's supposed plans.

But the Liberal Party insists there was no big strategy. As both Andrew Hirst and his deputy, Isaac Levido, observes, 'If we wanted to run a death-tax campaign, you would have known about it.' They insist it was largely organic. It wasn't something they needed to feed, although they clipped up the denials and made a video as soon as Labor rose to the bait and responded.

On the night of the 2016 election, Malcolm Turnbull was so stroppy over Labor's Medicare campaign that he famously called for the cops to investigate. 'The Labor Party ran some of the most systematic, well-funded lies ever peddled in Australia,' he said. 'And the SMS message came from Medicare. It said it came from Medicare. An extraordinary act of dishonesty. No doubt the police will investigate. But this is the scale of the challenge we faced. And regrettably more than a few people were misled.'

It was, he said, a pretty shameful episode in Australian political history. The words could have been cut and pasted into Bill Shorten's own speech on election night. But this simple truth is hard to deny: if Labor had done a better job of selling and framing its own policies, it wouldn't have ended up at the mercy of baby boomers on Facebook, sending dumb memes about a death tax that never existed.

After the defeat, Anthony Albanese confirmed that he was among the scores of Labor MPs who realised on the ground that retirees genuinely believed they were going to be taxed, even if they didn't even own shares.

'During the election campaign one day, I had a woman come up to me and she said, "I'm very worried about this franking stuff." And I said, "Oh yeah. What are your circumstances?" She said, "Well, I'm a pensioner. I can't afford to pay any more." I said, "Well, pensioners are exempt from the policy. How many shares do you have?" "I've never had a share, love."

'That was the problem. When you've got to explain dividend imputation and franking credits from opposition, tough ask. And it was a tough ask.' He conceded some of those affected weren't very wealthy people. 'They were people for whom a small cheque was what they paid their rates with or their car rego, or other essentials in life when it came in, so that clearly had an impact for us.'

Hindsight was a wonderful thing. But when Kevin Rudd criticised Labor's campaign, Shorten let rip to colleagues. 'Mate, I've got all the texts from all of the revisionists,' he complained. 'Hagiography texts. Fuck, it's awesome.'

Keating, for example, was explaining to Bowen how to sell franking-credit reforms, not telling Labor not to do it. But in his characteristic style, Shorten did not confront Keating directly. After the election, he got Kelty to send a message to the former prime minister, who responded by diplomatically refusing to conduct any further post-mortems on the election.

10

BLAME GAME

Labor's Campaign Director, Noah Carroll, slept on a mate's couch on election night. He was so busy fighting the campaign and spending a lazy $30 million trying to get Bill Shorten elected, he had flown down to Melbourne and forgotten to organise himself a hotel suite. By Sunday morning, the blame game for the defeat was underway. Its prime suspect was identified: a 40-year-old, male, measuring 180 centimetres, asleep on a sofa. Newspaper reports variously described him as 'extinct', 'dead meat' and as 'dead as a dodo'.

Carroll was a highly experienced Victorian ALP campaign director, but he had never run a federal campaign – or even worked in the national office – before he was appointed to the job in 2016. The Liberal Party's new Federal Director

Andrew Hirst was in the same boat, although he had never run an election campaign at all. He had worked for every Liberal prime minister since John Howard but was in some ways a surprise appointment. His record in the lead-up to the 2019 election was failing to pick up a new seat in the Super Saturday by-elections in July 2018. When Scott Morrison won the unwinnable election, he emerged as a Liberal hero. Carroll was going to be remembered for something different.

As a younger man, Carroll had worked alongside Labor Right powerbrokers Stephen Conroy and Robert Ray, before rising to the job of Victorian ALP secretary. After the 2016 election he was hand-picked by Shorten to run the next federal campaign.

Some in Shorten's office were quick to point the finger at him. Labor frontbenchers complained he was too secretive about the research, too vague about the campaign messages. Carroll, they complained, was not going to survive a victory, let alone a defeat.

It would be wrong to suggest Carroll was in awe of Shorten, but it was true to say he admired him and was respectful. They didn't have the sort of relationship that involved him reading the riot act to the boss. Certainly not in public, anyway. Carroll prided himself on not humiliating people and dispensing any tough advice privately. He had watched Shorten 'take the bullets' for others' mistakes, most notably when the party underestimated the impact of the franking credits on pensioners and he had to backflip. He admired him for it. Not all leaders had been able to survive that sort of decision, but Shorten had taken the blame for the team.

When Carroll came face to face with Shorten backstage at Essendon Fields on election night, he was grateful that the Labor leader didn't seek to blame him for the result. 'Bill was exceptionally composed, dignified and very professional. He was also thinking of those around him and their welfare, so it was very impressive and showed great leadership. And Chloe was exactly the same.'

Carroll believed that Shorten's instinctive understanding of how to conduct himself in defeat was an example of his leadership qualities. Whatever the polls said about his popularity, which was sub-optimal, the fact was that most of his staff were incredibly loyal and believed he would make a good prime minister. Those who didn't disappeared. Chloe Shorten also spent the entire evening thanking staff and reassuring those in tears that they could not have worked any harder. She understood how devastating the result was for all those who had put their lives on hold for a different outcome, all the nights and months they had spent away from their families because they had believed Bill Shorten would make a good prime minister.

The actual result was so traumatic and unexpected, Carroll was left thinking that a more fragile person than himself might have been psychologically destroyed by it. In the days immediately after the defeat, he sounded in shock. 'It is physically and psychologically gruelling and exhausting. It's brutal.'

The simple fact was that politicians 'judge a campaign director by one key performance indicator and it's winning', Carroll admitted. He understood that reality when he accepted the job. And now he had lost, there were calls for him to resign. With a young family, he had planned to leave after the 2019 election, but not on these terms. For the entire election period he'd been away from home, deployed to a high-rise office block at Labor's Parramatta campaign headquarters.

He had been around politics long enough to remember the story of Victorian Labor MP Greg Wilton, who had committed suicide after media reports that police had found the 44-year-old distressed in his car with his two young children in the You Yangs, near Geelong. There was never any evidence he planned to harm his children, but newspapers reported the incident as an attempted 'murder-suicide'.

Victorian Premier Jeff Kennett attacked the media coverage that 'subjected this young man to national humiliation' without considering his acute depression. He spent some weeks in a psychiatric hospital. In June 2000, Wilton did take his own life in a national park near the town of Labertouche, Gippsland, an incident that shocked parliament.

The story of Wilton and his lonely death was something that was never forgotten by Carroll, who had joined the Labor Party around the time the MP died. He had reflected on it over the years and it was one of the reasons he took care to ensure that Labor staff were looked after during the campaign. Halfway through, Carroll had thought how lucky he was to be working with the people in campaign headquarters. How he believed they didn't have an issue with bullying or getting into trouble in bars in drinking-related mishaps, a not uncommon occurrence.

He had heard all the stories of leaders who turned on their staff after an election. 'Some of the horror stories I have heard from other Labor campaigns . . . where the campaign director received text messages or was demon-dialled by an unsuccessful candidate telling them that the loss is all their fault, that there is no future for them or that they should blame only themselves for the loss.

'The presumption is that every person is made of steel. But what happens when someone in that role with a scenario like that isn't able to cope? I have worked alongside a number of people in very senior roles that I would be concerned about under that kind of pressure. This presumption that everyone's made of steel and there's no harm in what you say. That's wrong.'

Perhaps the only people who truly understand what it's like to run a federal campaign – the high stakes, the disasters, the management of political egos – are the opposing team. After the election, as Labor colleagues anonymously ripped into Carroll's performance with gusto, former Liberal Party Director Brian Loughnane, Liberal Campaign Director Andrew Hirst and his deputy, Isaac Levido, paid tribute to him as 'a good operator'. They had plenty of observations about Labor's campaign and its failings, but did not seek to kick the man they had fought, who they respected.

However, Levido did think Labor was cocky. 'The commentariat and the media class, their shock at the result, was a demonstration of how not just the media but the Canberra bubble generally are completely out of touch with mainstream Australia,' he said. 'Labor was very complacent.

They had a two-year run-up thinking they were a sure thing for government – then they campaigned in a way that was quite intellectually lazy.'

Labor's failure to readjust to the change in leadership to Scott Morrison was a significant problem. But as the Liberal Party's own review into the result found, it was hardly a thumping victory. 'The successful election result was achieved through sheer grit and determination from the top of the Party,' it stated, 'laid over a clear political strategy, with the help of a Labor opposition that made many missteps. It is important not to overlook that the margin of victory was very small. There is no room for any complacency in the Liberal Party following the 2019 election campaign. Candidate selection processes need to be improved. Ten Liberal candidates had to be disendorsed.'

After the federal election, Levido returned to London to run newly appointed Prime Minister Boris Johnson's campaign machine as director of politics and campaigning in the lead-up to the 2019 British election. He would secure another historic victory and the highest of Australian praise from his old friend Liberal Senator Andrew Bragg who declared him 'not a wanker'. 'If I were federal director, he'd be the one I'd want running the campaign,' Bragg said. 'He understands politics, polling and . . . modern campaign infrastructure. He's an earthy machine man.'

Carroll was impressed that Liberal Party Director Andrew Hirst had actually got the Liberals to shut up and stop talking about themselves. 'Suddenly, he manages to put Barnaby Joyce in witness protection,' he said after the election. 'Angus Taylor is the invisible man. They ripped Ian Goodenough's phone off him for three weeks. Even Turnbull went quiet, mostly. They did something that had eluded them for the whole cycle and that is impose discipline and/or tell people to zip it and just go away, so they could try to actually get a message out there.'

The success of the mild-mannered Hirst in gently facilitating the confiscation of Goodenough's mobile phone still managed to make Carroll laugh in the grim days after the loss. Goodenough had briefly derailed the Liberal campaign by telling a reporter he may have met with a far-right extremist who was 'dressed like a rapper'. After the campaign, the activist, Neil Erikson, admitted he made the whole story up. Goodenough confessed to a meeting that never occurred. His phone remained clutched tightly in the hands of a staffer after that and he had to ask for permission to use it.

Before the election, Labor's deputy leader Tanya Plibersek did raise concerns with Shorten directly over whether there was a problem with Carroll that would require a restructure in the office or whether he was even the right person to run the campaign. Shorten rejected this idea.

The reality was that Carroll was his pick. When George Wright resigned after the 2016 election, Labor's Victorian factional powerbroker Stephen Conroy pushed for Carroll to get the job. His credentials were sold on the basis of his successful campaign to elect Dan Andrews as Premier of Victoria in 2014 after just one term in opposition.

As a political strategist, Carroll's strength was data and polling. But it was his communication of this data to the leadership group that came under sustained criticism. Labor's leadership group consisted of Bill Shorten, Tanya Plibersek, Labor's Senate leader Penny Wong and deputy Don Farrell, but other senior members of the shadow cabinet were brought in, including Chris Bowen, Jenny Macklin and Tony Burke.

Even this group were not given hard copies of Labor's polling. Instead, there were verbal briefings by Carroll. Some participants complained that these briefings made no sense. The leadership group kept asking what it all meant. Could they win? Carroll would never give a straight answer. Or, not an answer that some could decipher. When the election result was not what they expected, some of them came after him in a big way.

Carroll maintains that presentations were made to shadow cabinet on polling. 'There's always a judgement to be made and every campaign has different challenges and tensions,' he said. 'There is no doubt it must be shared and it was. Multiple presentations were made to the shadow cabinet, the leadership group, staff and the caucus. The state secretaries had unprecedented access to research in their state, both before and during the campaign.

'It's very common in campaigns that some remain unhappy about not having full access to the research. Shadow ministers would often approach us to undertake dedicated work for their portfolios in terms of communications and we would often oblige, but it's understandable that there is always someone aggrieved about their level of access.'

The truth is that politicians can be a demanding, egotistical bunch. There is a natural tendency to assume that any victory is the leader's win and any loss is the campaign director's fault.

Another problem was the fact that most of the politicians around the table in the leadership group – Shorten, Plibersek, Wong and Farrell, along with Bowen, Macklin and later Brendan O'Connor – didn't have any background in interpreting polling at all. Naturally, they wanted to be assured the research could guarantee a victory. Clearly, many remained at a loss to determine whether they could actually win on the basis of Labor's political research.

In contrast, Scott Morrison's own office and his campaign team was rich with experience in understanding and analysing polling. The prime minister himself had worked as a Liberal Party state director in NSW, commissioning polling and working on campaigns that implement the findings. His principal private secretary, essentially his political chief of staff, was Yaron Finkelstein, one of a large number of alumni of the Liberal Party's preferred pollster, the Crosby Textor Group.

Carroll's engagement of more than one political researcher to run a national tracking poll and focus groups was regarded as unorthodox. It was against this backdrop that the idea propagated by Shorten's office in the final week of the campaign that victory was assured with an expected 82 seats seems bizarre.

Carroll concedes he never suggested a seat haul of 82 in that final week. 'I did think we were going to win. But

I would never be stupid enough to say we were going to win by 82 seats.' The ALP campaign director was never hopeful of more than 78, a razor-thin margin to win an election by, considering a majority was 76 seats, or 77 seats if Labor wanted to provide a speaker.

It was also the view of Andrew Hirst, and deputies Isaac Levido and Simon Berger, that the election was close and you don't run around predicting the final seat count like you're popping down to Sportsbet to put some money on a win. As Levido explained, you campaign to influence the outcome, not to predict the outcome, and once you start doing that, 'You've lost the discipline.'

On the Sunday after the election, Shorten spoke briefly to the media as he left his hotel. In exquisite timing, his unplanned press conference as he was door-stopped by reporters clashed with Anthony Albanese announcing his candidacy. The result was 'devastating', said Albanese, who called for an overhaul of policy.

Had Shorten been a factor in Labor's loss and could Albanese have won the election? 'Can I say this about Bill Shorten?' said Albanese. 'No-one could have worked harder for the cause of Labor and the election of a Labor government than Bill Shorten. He has fought a tough campaign – he has led our great party for six years. He has been an inclusive leader and is someone who has campaigned on a policy agenda in the interests of working people – and is someone who has my respect. We respect our former leaders and I have the utmost respect for Bill Shorten, and you will see no criticism of him from me.'

There were 'lots of lessons for Labor to learn from yesterday's results', Shorten said. 'I know that my party will. I am now looking forward to spending some overdue time with my amazing wife. After all, I am Chloe Shorten's husband. And to see the kids.'

He only took one question: what went wrong?

'We didn't get enough votes,' he replied.

11

AN UNEXPECTED WEEK AT PORTSEA

Bill Shorten drove down to a beach house in the Victorian seaside town of Portsea with his family after the election loss. The house belonged to millionaire liquidator Mark Mentha, an old friend. Friends from the neighbourhood came and went. It was good to get away from the television cameras that would be otherwise camped outside his home. Shorten was more focused on the kids and long walks on the beach than politics. The leadership contest to replace him was underway and Anthony Albanese was quick to declare. Former NSW Premier Kristina Keneally promptly stripped her social media of photographs of Shorten and replaced them with smiling pictures of her with 'Albo', who she had voted for in the original 2013 ballot. Her colleagues reflected on the brutality of her Shorten erasure with a mixture of awe and nervous laughter.

Down at the beach, Shorten did make some calls, urging colleagues to support Tanya Plibersek if she ran. This did not pass unnoticed by his critics. 'Shorten loses again, trying to undermine Albanese leadership' was the headline in *The Saturday Paper*. 'Defeated Labor leader Bill Shorten has stunned colleagues by actively involving himself in the selection of his successor and attempting to hinder the run of left-wing powerbroker Anthony Albanese,' was the story in *The Sydney Morning Herald*. Labor MPs accused Shorten of 'actively lobbying people, making sure someone runs against Albo'.

As his deputy for six years, Plibersek built a close relationship of trust with Shorten. She regards as absurd the suggestion that he should have remained mute on his replacement. 'Why shouldn't he have a view? Everyone else had a view,' she said. 'It's the Labor Party. He wasn't the only person making phone calls – everyone was making phone calls.'

Former Prime Minister Julia Gillard and former ACTU Secretary Greg Combet were urging Plibersek to make a run, as was former Labor frontbencher Jenny Macklin. 'There were many people urging me to run. He wasn't the only person who wanted me to run.'

Plibersek explains Shorten's conduct as a simple expression of loyalty to her for serving as his deputy, not an attack on Albanese. 'He and I were never close before we became leader and deputy leader. We worked very well together. He was always honest and honourable with me and I was honest and honourable with him. I think you see something in someone's character over time. The fact that he supported me after six years of working closely with me – I take that as a compliment. I think that's him being grateful for the unity and stability I had provided as his deputy.'

Plibersek had made a sombre appearance on the ABC's *Insiders* program on the Sunday, congratulating Scott Morrison on his victory. 'As to what went wrong, I think there's two main features,' she said. 'We faced a very cashed-up scare campaign from the United Australia Party. Eighty million dollars is the estimate of how much Clive Palmer spent, not to – it seems – win himself a spot, but to trash Labor. And secondly, our policy agenda was big. It was bold. And I think perhaps we didn't have enough time to explain all of the benefits of it to the people who would benefit.' Asked if she was considering running for the leadership, she said, 'Well, of course I am considering it.' She planned to announce her candidacy within 24 hours. Unions were calling in with support too.

However, on the Monday morning after the election, she was at home in Sydney, a rare event during the recent campaign, with her eight-year-old son. 'I was lying in bed at 5 am and Louis climbed into bed with me and he was so happy that I was there at 5 am on a Monday morning.'

After six years of working six or seven days a week, she thought about what taking on the job of opposition leader would mean. She had been away from home on and off for years, but particularly so during the final weeks of the campaign, when she and Penny Wong seemed to be surrounding Shorten like a kind of female human shield. 'When you step up to that leadership role, whether it's prime minister or leader of the opposition, the time away from home is just so much greater. I had seen it up close.'

She was starting to think that perhaps running wasn't such a good idea. She knew it would be a decision that would invite criticism and suggestions she was bowing out because she couldn't win.

'Of course, the people who are cynical about that are generally people who wouldn't ever make a decision that prioritises their family – that's their choice, good luck to them. I actually don't want to be lying on my death bed, divorced and with my children not turning up because they hate my guts. I had a family for a reason.'

Plibersek has three children – Anna, Joseph and Louis. She had made a conscious decision to step back to help balance her family responsibilities previously in her career, and it did not hinder her subsequent ascension to the role of deputy leader. It was a responsibility she shared with her husband Michael Coutts-Trotter, a senior NSW public servant. In a remarkable story of redemption, he now leads the NSW Department of Justice, despite previously being a prisoner himself, for heroin importation. In the 1980s, when he was a drug addict, he was convicted and sentenced to nine years' jail. He spent time in NSW's most dangerous prisons, before being released on parole after serving three years.

Overcoming his past was not a simple matter. In 1995, he secured a job in the office of Brian Howe, Labor's then deputy PM, only to have ASIO veto his security clearance, which was vital to do the job. Soon after, he was denied an interview for another job in the Carr government as a press secretary. Eventually, he got the job as press secretary to the NSW treasurer but was warned his past would become political fodder. It didn't take long before the Sunday papers exposed the story. When his criminal past blew up again in 2007 after he was appointed to run the NSW education department, he tackled it head on.

'To a degree we all make mistakes in life,' said Coutts-Trotter. 'Mine was far more significant than a mistake anyone here will ever make. But you can't carry it around like a ball and chain forever. And that's true of me. Redemption is possible, a second chance is possible. Twenty-three years ago I was convicted of a very serious drug offence. I was a drug user and a drug seller, and luckily and remarkably in life I've been given a second chance. For every job I've applied for, I've indicated the facts of my life. I've told people about who I am, what I've done. And I've gone for those jobs on merit.'

When the Indonesian Government announced it would execute Bali Nine drug smugglers Andrew Chan and Myuran Sukumaran in 2015, Plibersek delivered an emotional speech in parliament.

'In 1988, my husband left prison after being charged and convicted of a similar crime to these young men,' she said. If he had been arrested overseas, she accepted he could have suffered a similar fate. 'I imagine what would have happened if he had been caught in Thailand, instead of in Australia. I think about – I didn't know him at the time, this is 30 years ago – what would the world have missed out on? They would have missed out on the three beautiful children we have had together. They would have missed out on a man who spent the rest of his life making amends for the crime that he committed.'

If Plibersek had stood for the ALP leadership, the story would have inevitably been reheated, but that had nothing to do with her decision. She has been an open book on her husband's past. Instead, it was simply a matter of doing the right thing for her family. 'I just thought, "I can't do this to the people that I love,"' she said. 'Both my husband and I have, at different times, had to make decisions about combining our work and caring responsibilities – families all over Australia do this all the time. But that extra demand to be away is just something I thought wasn't right for us at this time.'

Although she had already decided she wouldn't run, Plibersek appears to have allowed herself one indulgence. The former Prime Minister Julia Gillard's endorsement of her as a leadership candidate was still released by her office. The statement said that she was 'honoured to have the support of such a distinguished former prime minister and Labor hero'. Plibersek must have known, at the time she did that, she wasn't going to run.

Shortly afterwards, she confirmed she would not be a candidate. She insisted that she could not 'reconcile' responsibilities to her family with taking on the job as Labor leader. 'I am overwhelmed by the confidence my colleagues, the union movement and Labor party members have placed in me. I thank them from the bottom of my heart for their support. I know some people will be disappointed with this decision. But now is not my time.'

The observation that 'now is not my time' carefully left open the possibility that it might be her time one day, in the future.

With Plibersek out of the race, the remaining contenders who could stand against Albanese included Labor's Finance spokesman, Jim Chalmers. He was less experienced than the other candidates but had always been regarded as a future leadership option. He also had something money can't buy: his mother, Carol, had given birth to her son in Queensland.

Chalmers was born on 2 March 1978 at the Mater Hospital in Brisbane. It's a birthday he shares with Anthony Albanese. The date is also the anniversary of the defeat of the Keating Government and the election of John Howard as prime minister in 1996. 'I turned 18 the very day that the Keating Government lost office,' he said. 'I will not claim to remember much about the late evening of 2 March 1996 – but I do recall that election being a formative experience. He convinced me of Labor's greatest strength: that we are the only ones capable of combining market economics with an active social contract and global engagement.' That year, Chalmers joined the ALP.

In his maiden speech to parliament, he addressed the attempts by Labor to distance itself from the Keating Government under Kim Beazley's leadership. 'After 1996, I came to agree with those who argue Labor's great mistake was its failure to defend the towering achievements of the Hawke and Keating governments. For a time this denied us a rich inheritance – the marriage of sweeping economic reform with progressive social policy – leaving us without a solid foundation from which we could rebuild and renew. We will not make the same mistake this time around. The Rudd and Gillard Labor governments have a phenomenal legacy and we are proud of it.'

He described his family as unconventional. His mother worked nightshift as a nurse for much of his childhood. As the youngest child, he ended up living by himself with his mother after his older sisters left home. 'For a great portion of that, it was just the two of us. It was not easy for her and at times I made it harder, but what I know of selflessness and service I learnt from her, and I will always be grateful for that gift.'

Perhaps showing a greater commitment to the cause of Keating-ism than is strictly necessary, Chalmers penned a 90,000 word PhD on the former prime minister. Its title: *Brawler statesman: Paul Keating and prime ministerial leadership in Australia.* His thesis will no doubt provide a rich vein of scholarship if, as expected, he becomes leader in the future.

For example, there is the sobering news for his colleagues that sometimes you need to cut controversial ministers loose. 'The general observation about Prime Minister Keating's management of resignations and dismissals was that "you stick by people and defend them [and] you don't show weakness",' he wrote. He notes however that it 'could be argued that Keating's personal loyalty and political stubbornness was detrimental to his ability to manage ministerial scandals and resignations'.

Chalmers' PhD wasn't all clinical political analysis. When he interviewed Bob Hogg, the former ALP national secretary said that Keating was often late to cabinet and 'you'd find out

Paul was fucking around at the Lodge until 3 pm in the afternoon', while another former minister gripes to Chalmers that 'we're all busy people and he'd be out with his two singlets and an overcoat on listening to bloody Mahler'.

At just 41, Chalmers was on the younger side for a potential Labor leader. Shorten was 46 when he secured the top job and Albanese was 56. Kevin Rudd was 49, Julia Gillard, 48, Mark Latham, 43. Chalmers was an unusual specimen in the sense that he arrived in parliament with a widely held expectation that leading the party was a real prospect. He was well-liked by his colleagues, and often displayed a good deal of emotional intelligence when dealing with them, but apart from working for Treasurer Wayne Swan as chief of staff during the global financial crisis, there were not many big reforms or political victories you could assign to him. This was hardly surprising given he had only entered parliament six years earlier.

On the flipside, he had spent years working for the federal secretariat gaining an understanding of polling and, more importantly, years preparing cabinet submissions and working with ministers and understanding the mechanics of government. But he was vulnerable to attacks regarding his lack of experience as an MP. After the election, Scott Morrison used a Star Wars reference to attack him in parliament and highlight his links to Wayne Swan, calling him 'Obi Swan's Padawan'.

Chalmers had worked for Labor governments since 1999. At the age of 21, he started work as a research officer in the Queensland Department of Premier and Cabinet when

Peter Beattie was premier. Jobs in the Labor Party's headquarters in Canberra quickly followed. In 2002, he went to work as the ALP's national research manager, a job that basically involves polling and commissioning policy analysis with the Chifley Research Centre.

He stayed for the 2004 federal election, which may help explain his futile attempts to reconcile Mark Latham with the Labor Party. In the lead-up to the 2013 election, Latham wrote a *Quarterly Essay*, titled 'Not Dead Yet: Labor's Post-Left Future'. It was a thoughtful piece, which called for a clear-out of the apparatchiks and dead wood and examined the question of how to reconcile the party with Keating's economic legacy. Chalmers and Latham started talking to each other. By this time the Queenslander was working for the Chifley Research Centre.

In December 2017, Latham repaid the favour in his signature style by penning a column for *The Daily Telegraph*. 'The shadow finance minister, Jim Chalmers, has released some of the worst policies in the history of the Commonwealth – yet few people seem to have noticed. This is the twilight zone which Australian politics has now entered. Chalmers' policy agenda has more black marks against it than Harvey Weinstein's reputation.'

Chalmers was first elected to parliament at the 2013 election, replacing Craig Emerson in the Queensland federal electorate of Rankin. Between securing his preselection and getting elected, there was the small matter of Kevin Rudd's resurrection as prime minister. Rudd regarded Chalmers as a spear carrier for Swan.

In his book *The PM Years*, Rudd conducts an extended character assassination based on the idea that Chalmers came to his office, begging and pleading for his career. In Rudd's version, Chalmers is dragged before Labor's new king, *Game of Thrones* style, in mortal fear he would kill his preselection. 'The thought had crossed my mind,' Rudd wrote. 'He broke down in tears in front of me. I simply said to him, "Jim, why don't you learn from this experience that sinking a knife into someone's shoulder blades is not the way to go in the future?"' Rudd then asks Chalmers what he would do in similar circumstances. 'He paused. He cried again. He said, "I probably wouldn't have me in caucus." I told him that was the first honest thing he had said all day.'

Chalmers disputes this version of events and has suggested that Albanese was present at the meeting. Albanese declined to comment on the differing recollections for this book.

Rudd goes on to claim Chalmers never thanked him for winning his seat, which he would have lost under Gillard, and never heard from him again. This is untrue. In fact, Chalmers rang him two days after the election and thanked him. They also had a long chat in his office the day after Rudd resigned from politics.

But Chalmers proved a reluctant starter to run for the leadership himself. He made it clear to all those urging him that he wouldn't stand if Chris Bowen was. This perplexed some observers, including Shorten. 'I never asked for permission from anyone before I ran for the leadership,' Shorten told a colleague.

It was obvious enough that Bowen was not a serious contender, because of his proximity to the franking credit reform fiasco. Chalmers' supporters regard Bowen's decision to throw his hat in the ring as a 'dog act' designed to stop him from making his own run. By the time Bowen withdrew from the race, it was too late for Chalmers to make a serious run. This is an interesting observation given that Chalmers and Bowen appear to get along well and have a good relationship.

Within the Right faction, there were various attempts to encourage Chalmers to find a suitable left-wing woman for a ticket, and Victorian MP Ged Kearney was raised. However, it was never a serious prospect. On the Monday night after the election, he appeared on the ABC's *Q&A* program. 'I'm considering it,' Chalmers said. 'I don't think it's unreasonable that a few of us take some time to work out what we want to do – remember, we were hoping to be forming a cabinet this week. I want to play a substantial role in rebuilding our electoral fortunes, a rebuilding of our policies up to the next election.' Some MPs believe if he had run for deputy, he could have beaten Albanese's deputy Richard Marles.

Chalmers' reasons for subsequently declining to throw his leadership hat in the ring included his young family. During the election campaign, his daughter, Annabel, had been unwell with a bone infection. He had spent 20 nights camped out in the Queensland Children's Hospital with Annabel hooked up to an IV drip.

On 23 May, Chalmers announced he would not contest the leadership. 'A few people said you should run and lose and get in the queue. I am not into that. I am not into running and losing. There were good reasons to run but I thought I was a one-in-three chance of winning. But genuinely I did not want to be away from home six nights a week, rather than three or four. I had a five-month-old kid. I spoke to Albo about being the deputy, but what I discovered was the more I thought about it, the less I actually wanted to do it. I thought I could provide more value to the team just focusing on being shadow treasurer.'

Chalmers' friend and colleague Chris Bowen knew he didn't stand a chance in the leadership ballot. However, he decided to put his hand up, largely to have the opportunity to explain himself after the election defeat.

On the Sunday after the election, the Right faction held a national phone hook-up at 8.30 am. Included on the call was the NSW ALP Secretary, Kaila Murnain, who was at war with Bowen. Joel Fitzgibbon and Tony Burke were backing the NSW Left's candidate, Albanese. When Bowen indicated during the conversation that he was considering running, there was no suggestion from Murnain that the NSW Right would swing in behind him.

He announced his candidacy on the Tuesday, standing out the front of his fibro childhood home, in the suburb of Smithfield in Western Sydney. 'I think the party does deserve a contest – I think the party deserves a choice. I think it would be wrong of me not to provide that choice to the party.'

Bowen was quick to dump on the 'class war' rhetoric that came to define Shorten's leadership. 'I haven't gone down the road of talking about so much top end of town. I do think, as I said before, there is a two-class tax system in Australia.' He also raised the need for Labor to reconnect with people of faith. 'I have noticed as I have been around during the election campaign and even in the days since . . . how often it has been raised with me that people of faith no longer feel that progressive politics cares about them.'

Bowen defended the franking-credit reforms as necessary to fund Labor's agenda on hospitals and schools. 'Franking credits was a controversial policy, a controversial policy for which, no doubt, we lost some votes. But I don't accept it's why we lost the election in entirety. We also lost the election because of policies we don't have, like a death tax. I had more people raising the death tax on polling booths with me than ever raised franking credits. And the death tax, of course, was an invention of the Liberal Party.'

Bowen knew his leadership tilt was a completely doomed mission. 'I'm happy to concede Albo probably goes in as the favourite. The Labor Party winning on Saturday was the favourite too. I'm a bit over favourites. It doesn't always work out so well.'

He planned to announce he was withdrawing from the leadership contest later that week, but after it leaked that he was expected to withdraw, leaving the way clear for Albanese to be elected without a ballot, he brought that timetable forward. He confirmed at a media conference that he did not think he would have won. 'I've been on the phone to colleagues. I've been very pleased with the response – it's clear to me that I would have majority support in the actual caucus ballot. But it's also clear to me – I'm a realist – that

Albo would win the rank and file, for good reason – he's a popular character . . . Hence I have reached the view that it would be unlikely for me to win the ballot.'

The big-target strategy was a decision he did not resile from. 'We paid a price for some of our policies. I will never be part of an opposition which lies about its plans and hides its plans. Whether I'm leader or in any other capacity, I will argue against that.'

But there was still drama brewing over Victorian MP Richard Marles' attempts to secure the deputy's job unopposed. Marles had enraged Queensland colleagues when he declared before the election that the potential collapse of global coal markets was 'a good thing'.

Marles had issued a public mea culpa just days after the election in an attempt to defuse the issue ahead of a potential leadership ballot. 'Well, the comments I made earlier this year were tone deaf and I regret them and I was apologising for them within a couple of days of making them,' he said.

Meanwhile, a Labor frontbencher from Victoria, Clare O'Neil, had ruffled feathers by putting put her hand up for consideration, an awkward state of affairs that meant Marles' own Victorian Right faction was among the last to endorse him for the job. O'Neil's candidacy was regarded as precocious by some colleagues. In fact, she had been in parliament exactly as long as Shorten when he was elected leader, but the same rules don't always apply to everyone.

She was being urged to run against Marles by Victorian frontbencher Mark Dreyfus, which proved a lightbulb moment for some on how much Dreyfus must dislike

Marles. There was much tut-tutting about it being Albanese and Marles' 'turn' and O'Neil, who didn't stand much of a chance, agreed to withdraw, perhaps wiser on the etiquette of Labor's game of queues and 'turns'.

But the prospect of an all-male leadership team in the House of Representatives, the Albanese-Marles deal, would have flow-on effects in the Senate under the ALP's quest for gender equality. If Albanese was elected leader – and there seemed no logical alternative – and his deputy was Marles, that would mean three of the four leadership positions were held by men. It seemed fairly obvious who would be pushed out of the pram: Labor's deputy Senate leader, Don Farrell. During that phone hook-up on the Sunday, the issue was raised, but NSW ALP Secretary Murnain insisted it wouldn't be a problem.

Nobody seemed to be keen to discuss this looming execution on the conference call. Or raise the obvious, which was that waiting in the wings was Kristina Keneally, a NSW Right faction member who could be parachuted in to deliver an all-woman Senate team to balance out the blokes in the House of Representatives. Only after the phone hook-up did Labor frontbencher Joel Fitzgibbon admit the truth. 'I'm not sure I can protect Don,' he said.

Senator Farrell had always struck some of his colleagues as having the demeanour of a chivalrous Southern gentleman from the United States, whose 'culture of honour' might also involve some Old Testament retribution for those who crossed him. His staff were fond of him and his old saying, 'If we don't look after our friends, who will?'

But Farrell's tensions with Labor's Senate leader Penny Wong were long-standing. Some years earlier, Albanese had intervened when Farrell was preselected at the top of the SA Senate ticket, describing putting Wong second as 'gross, self-indulgent rubbish'. After a great deal of pressure, Farrell agreed to be dumped to the second spot. He was booted out of parliament at the next election before, eventually, returning.

Farrell had a wicked sense of humour about the fiasco, discussing with colleagues that Wong might actually be closer to Lucifer than Mother Teresa. 'What you do need to understand is that she's evil, as in, like in the Bible evil,' he once told colleagues.

Despite the halo that hovered somewhere above her head, Senator Wong was well known for being a tough taskmaster on staff and sometimes having to curb her temper. She admits as much herself. During one outburst, a former chief of staff walked into her office, closed the door and gave her a good talking to, before she emerged, chastened, and apologised. Staff did find her intimidating. In fairness, this is a complaint rarely made about men who exhibit the same behaviours or abilities. But her old sparring partner, Senator Farrell, was well aware that she was not always as close to sainthood as her legion of fans believed.

Farrell still had good relationships with unions around the country and several said they would back him if he wished to stay on as deputy leader. The South Australian fought the fight for a desolate few days before bowing to the inevitable. Albanese had made it quite clear he wanted

Farrell out and Keneally in. The emergence of Marles as his preferred deputy had sealed Farrell's fate.

History seemed to be repeating itself. After Wong organised for Farrell to be dumped from the top spot on the Senate ticket in 2012, her factional supporters and friends had also moved to block him entering state parliament. During university, Wong had been in a long-term relationship with Jay Weatherill, who later became the South Australian premier. He remained a close friend. When Farrell announced his intention to run for state politics in January 2014, Weatherill went berserk, arguing it would cripple him as premier.

A few weeks earlier, Farrell had gone to see Weatherill about the parachute plan. The talks were witnessed by Peter Malinauskas – the former state secretary of the powerful Shop, Distributive and Allied Employees Association – who would later become the SA Labor leader. 'This is crazy,' Weatherill told the pair. 'You can't do this to me eight weeks out from an election. I am just not going to cop it. For better or for worse, you are seen as one of the architects of the Rudd-Gillard-Rudd mess. That will be visited on us as a destabilising influence.' If Farrell wanted a seat in SA Parliament, he wasn't opposed to finding him one, but not like this.

The meeting ended with Weatherill confident it had been resolved. Two weeks later, he picked up *The Australian* and there it was in living colour. Farrell was going to run for Napier. 'That's it,' said Weatherill. 'He's just declaring war.' He called in to ABC Radio and announced, 'If he comes in, I will go.'

Former SA Treasurer Tom Koutsantonis still remembers hearing the premier's interview and, like other Labor MPs listening in, he 'just about drove into a stobie pole'. The hairy-chested display by Weatherill, who was regarded as a nice guy but not as formidable as his predecessor Mike Rann, was great PR. It made him look like he had a spine and Labor won the state election. Once again, Farrell agreed to stand aside.

Farrell turned his attentions to resurrecting his Senate career. Wong tried to block him again, but he returned to parliament after the 2016 election. Later, he was elevated to the role of deputy Senate leader after Stephen Conroy quit. Now he was out once more, to make way for Keneally.

'How many times do these people have to fuck me over?' Farrell asked. The answer was apparent. He resigned as deputy leader but was assured he could remain part of the leadership team meetings.

Wong and Keneally never had a single conversation with the man they dumped from the role of deputy Senate leader about what happened. No thank you for your service, no handover between the incumbent and the successor. Keneally just took over the job and that was it. Farrell's latest knifing was a forbidden topic of discussion.

But the tensions lurked beneath the surface. After the 2019 election, during a Senate tactics meeting, Labor senators discussed how to respond to the climate change strike by school students. The Greens were proposing a motion of support, but Victorian Senator Kimberley Kitching declared that supporting the motion was an exercise in 'virtue signalling'. It would be better to amend the Greens' motion to support 'peaceful assembly'. Penny Wong responded sharply that it was an issue parents did care about. 'Well, if you had children, you might understand,' she said.

To claim that a woman didn't understand something because she wasn't a parent is the sort of observation that, if a man made it, would spark outrage. Don Farrell's eyebrows shot up when Wong said it, according to witnesses. There was a large group of senators and staffers in the room and it did not take long for gossip about the exchange to circulate. News of it leaked to the ABC, but for reasons that were unclear, the report chose not to identify Wong as the person who made the remarks. Considering how the issue could have blown up, she'd got off lightly. Privately, Wong insisted she would never suggest what was being implied, that a woman could not have a view because she was not a mother.

12

SILENCE OF THE LAMBS

Four days after the 2019 election, the man who Anthony Albanese would appoint as his economics adviser penned a brutal assessment of where Bill Shorten went wrong. Of all the places he could choose to publish this, he decided to put it up on his LinkedIn account. Perhaps it was something of a job application. Alex Sanchez argued that the election 'ripped a big scab off Labor'. He accused the party of prosecuting a world view thoroughly inconsistent with its successful tradition by flirting with the anti-business policies of UK Labour leader Jeremy Corbyn and US presidential hopeful Bernie Sanders.

'Australian Labor, once the beacon for how moderate, Centre Left parties govern, allowed itself to uncharacteristically stroll into the world of Sanders, Corbyn and the climate-change zealots.'

The party may spruik Paul Keating, he said, but its spiritual character is Jim Cairns.

Cairns, a left-winger and Whitlam minister, was treasurer for seven months before being removed from the job over his role in the Loans Affair. He's also famous for his controversial relationship with Junie Morosi, his principal private secretary.

Sanchez argued that Rudd's victory in 2007 had simply 'kicked Labor's post '96 existential crisis along'. 'How else can one explain a Labor agenda that managed to swirl from anti-WorkChoices to explicit economic conservatism to Rudd declaring before the 2007 election that "this reckless spending must stop" to declaring climate change the greatest moral challenge of all time.

'At first I thought it was me, believing that I had missed the new zeitgeist and that the modern Labor project was being developed by Rudd,' he said. 'But unfortunately the Rudd (and Gillard) Labor project ended as it started – confused, inconsistent and with nothing but the unbearable lightness of being. Labor now encounters the big challenge it has hitherto avoided.'

His diagnosis was that Labor also needed to grapple with a membership base that believes there is no problem that cannot be solved by more government and more spending.

'How to pay for it doesn't really matter,' he said. 'Take schools for example. In the ALP, the problem with our schools is not good money being spent badly, but good money not being spent.'

This analysis touched on a great unspoken dilemma for the Labor Party. Given that the party's membership base is more left-wing than the electorate, is there a danger that extending the right to choose leaders to the membership will deliver increasingly left-wing leaders and policies that render the party unelectable?

Sanchez argued there was a 'monoculture' that defines modern Labor, consisting entirely of lawyers, ALP officials and unionists, with little experience of private enterprise. 'There is just no way that Hawke's first cabinet – complete with shearers, farmers, lawyers, academics – could be elected today,' he said. 'These days, most Labor figures have come from within the ranks of unions, party officials or paid staff, and in several cases, are partnered up. When you develop your own Labor royalty, then it is patently easy to be out of touch – because by nature, you are.'

There was also a culture within the progressive political groups of ridiculing the ordinary voter. He pointed to the tension between reporters and frontbenchers on the road over the economic impact of Labor's climate-change policies. 'When Bill Shorten said that asking about the cost of climate change was a "dumb" question, he basically was telling the Australian people they were dumb for asking it. Of course, nothing could be further from the truth – these are decent, hardworking Australians looking after their own.'

Once upon a time, Sanchez had worked for Mark Latham. This was enough to prompt critics of Albanese's new leadership to complain he had assembled a 'freak show' in his office, including, they would mutter indignantly, an ex-Latham staffer. A conga line of suck-holes may have been more apt, if one wanted to pay direct homage to his former employer's vernacular. But Sanchez, who left Deloitte Economics to join the leader's office, hardly fits either bill.

The question he asked lies at the heart of how Labor responds to the electoral loss. 'As Labor goes about its post-mortem of the 2019 election, the one question that must be honestly answered is how did Labor land here?' Sanchez asked. 'How on earth could the party of Hawke/Keating adopt a big taxing, big government, big climate agenda? Is it really possible that modern Labor could be that out of touch? How on earth could the ALP breezily claim it believed in the Hawke/Keating model and then just sidestep its philosophy? How is it possible that absolutely no-one, not in the party, caucus, or unions, pipe up and say this path is just madness? Where were all the strong women and men, the dissenting voices in the great Australian Labor Party?'

It's an important question. Once you start searching for the answer, a babushka doll of excuses emerges, with everyone handing responsibility to a higher power. The Labor caucus blames the shadow cabinet. The shadow cabinet blame the leadership group and the budget razor gang. The leadership group blame the bilateral deals the leader made with his big-spending ministers. You end up with one babuksha doll left: Bill Shorten. But surely every Labor MP must have some shared responsibility that they did not speak up?

Did Albanese oppose the franking-credit reforms in shadow cabinet? No. Did anyone in the leadership group tell

Bowen when he raised the idea of taking franking credits from pensioners, 'Mate, that's a terrible plan?'

Surely, you imagine, there must have been some absolute fights about that in shadow cabinet? A modest backbench revolt in the ALP caucus, perhaps? A delegation to the leader's office? With the benefit of hindsight, it seemed obvious this was a big, risky reform to argue for from opposition. But here's the curious thing – there was little or no dissent in the parliamentary party. There don't seem to have been any great battles about the big reforms at all.

Open warfare in Shorten's shadow cabinet was rare. In fact, it seems to have been borderline non-existent. Tanya Plibersek, the deputy leader throughout the period, confirms that fights within these decision-making bodies were unusual.

'I don't really recall anyone raising concerns internally about negative gearing or capital-gains tax or the dividend-imputation policy,' she said. 'There was never a big fight about it, but I think we absolutely underestimated the capacity for scare campaigns to be run off it.

'After we did the pensioner and the part pensioner exclusion, the people who were going to be affected by it were really people with substantial assets. Heaps of people on a pension or a part-pension thought they were going to be affected. But what's worse, a whole lot of people believed the lie – they just heard retiree tax and thought we were going to tax their super or their pension.'

There are those who point out that the spend came before the tax. Bowen and Tony Burke, and later Jim Chalmers, argue they had to go looking for savings and revenue measures to pay for huge expenditure on schools, which was Plibersek's own portfolio.

Former Labor frontbencher Kim Carr is blunt. 'Not one of those senior people argued against the policies at the time,' he said. 'Not one of them. Not one of them in the shadow cabinet spoke or voted against them. No-one opposed the spending on schools, on hospitals, on child-care workers, on the environment, on the defence policies, or any of the other commitments that we made. And it would have been a horrendous situation to go into an election having an argument about where the money was going to come from for any of the social programs. You can argue that we've got to spend less, that's a reasonable proposition, but you've got to say where we should spend less, and how that would then end up defining the Labor Party.'

If you ask backbenchers and Labor MPs, they'll tell you that by the time risky policies made their way to the ALP caucus for debate, the deals were done. And raising questions could get you marked down as a troublemaker.

'There's a bit of a "go along to get along" culture,' a Labor MP said. So much so that he didn't want his name used in this book. If you speak out, even on policy issues, you get punished and overlooked for promotion. 'It doesn't encourage people to fight policy issues. Because none of these fights are had, when it does happen, it's a big deal. If you were having fights all the time, like in the Hawke/Keating era, then the dogs bark and the caravan moves on. In Paul Keating's day, they would have a fight a week. It was just part of the culture.

'Now what happens, if there's the slightest hiccup you get half a dozen calls straight after caucus from journalists. I am not blaming the media. And if I say, "Nah, not much in it," they move onto the next person and you read about it the next day. So you don't have any fights and, if you do have fights, frankly, it costs you down the track. Then, if the way to get promoted is not to have the fights and to be agreeable, well, those people are not going to have a fight in shadow cabinet, are they?'

The issue is also at play with Labor's election strategy, as the ALP review into the loss noted. 'Labor's campaign lacked a culture and structure that encouraged dialogue and challenge, which led to the dismissal of warnings from within the party about the campaign's direction. High expectations of a Labor victory led to little consideration being given to querying Labor's strategy and policy agenda.'

Under Shorten's leadership, unity was preserved at all costs. According to the – large – number of MPs on the front bench, dissent was managed out of the process. The entire party was managed to minimise conflict, centralise decision-making and stop leaks to the media.

After the 2016 election, there were 69 Labor MPs in parliament and more than half of them were on the frontbench in some capacity, even if it was junior. That is, there were more frontbenchers than backbenchers. There were 21 people in shadow cabinet. There were 25 people serving in the outer ministry and junior ministries. The collective responsibility for adopting a tax-and-spend agenda lay with shadow cabinet. But did the original decision?

According to Labor frontbenchers, the answer was no. How can this possibly be so? They argue that the real engine room was the leadership group. The decision-making was outsourced to that smaller decision-making body that consisted of just seven Labor frontbenchers. Albanese was excluded from this group. The Gang of Seven consisted of Bill Shorten, Tanya Plibersek, Penny Wong, Labor's Senate Deputy Leader Don Farrell, Treasury spokesman Chris Bowen, Tony Burke as manager of opposition business in the House of Representatives, and Jenny Macklin. Later, she was replaced by Victoria's Brendan O'Connor.

It was a bloodless coup that usurped the power of shadow cabinet and sidelined dissent. The Gang of Seven made the big calls. Sometimes the expenditure review committee or budget razor gang was more central, a separate group which essentially was the leadership group but with the addition of Jim Chalmers as finance spokesman and Andrew Leigh as assistant treasurer.

However, members of the leadership group assert that the situation might have been even more problematic than it first appears. They accuse Shorten of being renowned for what they describe as 'bilateral', making side deals with big-spending ministers, including Education spokeswoman Plibersek and Health spokeswoman Catherine King.

As one MP described it, the long-suffering Chris Bowen would raise concerns in the expenditure review committee over new spending, only to be shot down by the Labor leader. Or, Jim Chalmers would come 'flying out of the trench', arguing that a policy was a good idea but too expensive. Suddenly it would become clear that Shorten had already cut a deal with his ministers to get their pet projects through. Labor's economic team of Bowen and Chalmers would be confronted with a stitch-up. They could knock the edges off a policy and make it cheaper, but did not have the power to veto it.

There were endless discussions with Shorten about this. At various points, Penny Wong had even canvassed those concerns. The argument then follows that Bowen and Chalmers were driven to revenue measures because Shorten and Plibersek were not prepared to rein in expenditure.

Other members of the group argue that the arrangements often worked quite well. As a clearing house for strategy decisions, including parliamentary tactics on contentious legislation, it was efficient. These were decisions that needed to be made quickly and without rancour. The upside was less dissent. The downside, less contestability.

This was a reflection of Shorten's desire to preserve unity at all costs after the Rudd/Gillard years and to reduce leaks to the press. But in doing so, Labor repeated the pattern of centralised decision making that sidelined the ALP caucus. During the Rudd years, Australia was governed by a Gang of Four. The strategic priorities and budget committee of cabinet, known as the SPBC, consisted of Rudd, Deputy Prime Minister Gillard, Treasurer Wayne Swan and Finance Minister Lindsay Tanner. The big downside of these centralised decision-making processes is well established. At the time, Lenore Taylor wrote in *The Australian* that the dominance of the SPBC seems to have evolved from a habit developed in opposition — where the four members were called 'the planning group' and formed a kind of kitchen cabinet before the 2007 election campaign.

As former Labor Treasurer Wayne Swan notes in his book, *The Good Fight*, Rudd centralised a great deal of decision-making in his office because of a pathological fear of leaks.

'This was at the heart of the malaise that fell upon the government through this period,' he wrote. 'Kevin was an extremely poor chair of cabinet meetings. They would drag on for hours as he sought to use them as his own personal briefing session because he had not carried out the necessary preparation by reading his papers in advance. And finally, there was a culture of fear and blame that had its origins in Kevin's temperament. He was often quick to anger and his outbursts were regularly disproportionate to the matter at hand. This was invariably followed by retributive action of some sort.'

Those sorts of temperamental issues were not ones that Shorten suffered from. He was a good chair of meetings. But the centralised decision-making was an issue.

Labor frontbencher Tony Burke, who was regarded as an Albanese supporter internally after the 2016 election, believes it would be wrong to put the blame for the defeat entirely on Shorten. According to Burke there were high levels of consultation about every decision.

'In defence of Bill, you would be hard pressed to find a more consultative leader,' he said. 'Anyone who tries to retrofit it to claim that Bill was making all these calls on his own, that's not how it was done.'

That's not to suggest there were not substantial discussions at shadow cabinet about the design of certain policies or how they would operate or be rolled out. But it's strange that nobody in shadow cabinet opposed the decision to limit negative gearing, or abolish refunds for franking credits.

Why was this so? Clearly, the aftermath of the turmoil and personal animosity of the Rudd/Gillard years was a huge factor. Many of the frontbenchers who worked with Shorten were scarred, and desperate to prove that the ALP could conduct itself with collegiality and dignity. Labor frontbenchers concede there were consequences that flowed from that. Shorten placed a great priority on unity and avoided big fights on shadow ministers' spending. It was left to Bowen and Chalmers to nip and tuck, rather than conduct major surgery.

As the ALP review into the 2019 election notes, Shorten himself was damaged by these events, because 'the unexplained termination of Rudd's leadership and the role played by Bill Shorten in that process and in the subsequent demise of Julia Gillard had a negative effect on Shorten's standing'. But Labor did benefit from presenting a unified front afterwards, particularly as divisions were on display under Tony Abbott's leadership and later during Malcolm Turnbull's tenure. This is confirmed in the results of ALP focus groups where voters raised Labor's leadership stability and unity as a positive.

The review of the election result noted that the entire Federal Parliamentary Labor Party learned a bitter lesson from the internal instability that had marred Labor's time in government and made the party unelectable in 2013. 'Caucus placed a premium on stability from the time of the election of Bill Shorten as leader. Moreover, the second Kevin Rudd-led Caucus changed the rules to assure the leader's position. Labor's period in opposition from 2013 to 2019 was characterised by stability, as a result of the collective decision of the federal caucus to prioritise unity.'

The time to have those arguments is surely in the first year after an election loss, as Labor tries to reconcile its past with the future. As Sanchez wrote in his LinkedIn manifesto, the 2019 election certainly picked a big scab off Labor. 'Who knows, maybe the 2021 election will sort it out for them – winning an election usually does that. But with a deceased estate in NSW and federally, it's hard not to think that Labor is going to be in the wilderness for a while. Nothing short of a complete renovation is needed. Labor should not waste its crisis, even one that has been hanging around since 1996.'

13

THE QUIET AUSTRALIANS

When Scott Morrison thanked 'the quiet Australians' for his win on election night, the search to identify this mysterious and exotic group of voters, who had somehow hidden in plain sight despite the powerful gaze of pollsters and pundits, began in earnest. Much of the instant analysis was ill informed. The term itself annoyed many. As Anthony Albanese observed, most Australians 'aren't that quiet'. It implied that voters who were passionate about issues were somehow unAustralian. But if you accept that a group of voters did help secure Morrison victory, it's a reasonable question to ask who these voters were and where they live.

The expectation that Labor would win was so pronounced, it must have felt like a political earthquake to many viewers watching the election coverage at home. Would it surprise you to learn that the Coalition's first preference vote actually went backwards? In fact, it went backwards in a majority of states and territories. Not by much, as it was essentially an election that delivered the status quo. Morrison's miracle was that he held on. He did not lose seats where he was expected to, and where he did lose ground, he made up for it elsewhere. He campaigned strongly and stuck to his message.

It was surgical, but it was hardly a landslide. Only nine seats changed hands in a 151-seat parliament. The Liberals won five seats – Bass and Braddon in Tasmania, Longman and Herbert in Queensland and Lindsay in NSW. However, they also lost Warringah, held by Tony Abbott. The Labor Party gained three new seats. Two were in Victoria – Corangamite and Dunkley, which, although held by the Liberals, had been designated notionally as marginal Labor seats after a boundary redistribution. The Liberals, the Labor Party and Clive Palmer collectively spent around $120 million on the campaign. The upshot was that the Morrison Government secured a net gain of a single seat.

None of this should be used to excuse or underestimate the magnitude of the Labor Party's defeat. Particularly after the leadership madness of three prime ministers in three years, Labor should have performed strongly. Instead, the party recorded its lowest primary vote since the Great Depression in the 1930s. Given the Liberals' fortunes when he took over the leadership on 24 August 2018, Morrison's victory was remarkable. But it did not involve some sort of landslide.

Just one in three voters – 33.3 per cent – gave Labor their first preference vote. That means 67 per cent of Australians did not vote for the ALP. But it's been that way for a long time – over a decade. The last time the Labor Party secured a primary vote of more than 40 per cent was when Kevin Rudd led Labor to victory in 2007. Julia Gillard secured 38 per cent in 2010 and it's been downhill ever since.

The Australian National University's research into the election result, a survey of over 2000 voters, also noted significant differences between the way men and women voted. The Australian Electoral Study found 45 per cent of men gave their first preferences to the Liberal Party, but only 35 per cent of women did so. A gender gap was also in play with the minor parties, with 15 per cent of women giving their first preference to the Greens, compared to only 9 per cent of men.

So, how did the Liberal Party win, despite the fact that its primary vote was slightly down? Critical to the victory were preference flows from Clive Palmer's United Australia Party and One Nation. The Morrison Government secured slightly fewer first-preference votes in 2019 than it did under Malcolm Turnbull. In New South Wales, Morrison's home state, the Liberals lost ground but the swing was less than half a per cent. The Liberals also went backwards in Victoria. The only states in which they got more first-preference voters compared with the last election were South Australia, up 5.48 per cent; the Northern Territory, up 4 per cent, and in Queensland, the supposed dragon slayer for the Coalition, where the first-preference vote increased by a piddling 0.41 per cent.

It's only when you look at the two-party-preferred vote that you can see how strongly the voters' preferences flowed to the Coalition. Off the back of One Nation and Palmer preferences, the two-party-preferred swing in Queensland rose to 4 per cent. UAP and One Nation secured a combined swing of 6.7 per cent and the majority flowed back to the Liberal-National Party.

The real question Labor has to confront is this: which voters turned on them and why? How does the ALP attract more voters in the future? Easy question to ask, but a harder question to answer. If you read the newspapers in the days after the election, you may have been told the culprits were, in no particular order: wealthy retirees who feared the 'retiree tax' on franking credits, property investors who loved negative gearing, Queenslanders, middle-class families, Christians, and climate-change sceptics. Even the mythical tribe of 'Shy Tories' – who supposedly tell pollsters they will vote for Labor and then do the exact opposite in the privacy of the polling booth – was raised as a possible culprit.

Former Prime Minister Paul Keating said the lesson of Labor's surprise defeat lay in the failure to understand voters. 'If you're talking about the Labor Party and why it lost the election, it failed to understand the middle-class economy that Bob Hawke and I created for Australia,' he said.

The headline in *The Sydney Morning Herald* was 'Bill Shorten failed to understand the middle class', which was not exactly what he said, but the idea was off and racing. The only problem, as Labor Senator Kim Carr points out, is that the data does not support the conclusion. 'I really admire Paul Keating enormously. But I think statistically the evidence is against him. The Labor Party's problem was that we were not able to connect to blue-collar communities in sufficient numbers, in Queensland and Western Australia. The Labor Party had committed to important changes in education, health and housing. Our messaging was wrong, not the policy. On climate change, I think we failed to understand just how deep the anxieties about the future were for working-class communities.'

Not all of his colleagues agree with Senator Carr's claim that the problem was simply the sales pitch. But he's correct to argue that the data does not support the idea it was the middle class that abandoned Labor. In fact, it was the working class, the ALP's own base, that turned on them in states like Queensland. Blue-collar workers, who might benefit from some of Labor's policies, baulked at voting for Shorten.

After the election, the Labor Party conducted a comprehensive demographic analysis of who didn't vote for them. The analysis found that Labor went backwards with blue-collar workers in outer suburban and regional areas. However, these voters did not switch directly to the Liberal Party. Instead, they parked their vote with One Nation or Clive Palmer.

The states where the ALP lost vote share were Queensland, New South Wales and Tasmania. Then there were areas Labor failed to gain vote share – a status-quo result. These included South Australia and Western Australia and Victoria's outer metro seats, as well as areas with lots of families with children under 15 and culturally diverse communities.

Where did Labor gain vote share? White-collar and highly-educated areas, safe Coalition areas where Labor had performed poorly in 2016, seats contested with the Greens, inner-metro seats in Victoria. Effectively, inner-city seats packed with university educated, middle-class voters. The lesson of the 2019 election is that a good deal of university-educated voters, enjoying good incomes, were relaxed and comfortable, as John Howard used to say, with paying more tax.

That's why Tanya Plibersek argues that the idea voters were casting their ballot against Labor's tax policies does not completely stack up. 'People were voting on both sides against their economic interests,' she said. 'There were a lot of wealthy people who might not have done well out of our tax policies, but they voted for us because they wanted action on climate change – they liked the progressive agenda. There were a lot of people who would have been economically better off with our policies who voted against us, because of the scare campaign. We didn't rebut the scare campaign well enough. There's never one answer and the answer is different in different parts of the country. I don't think that "we lost the middle-class" argument really works, because solidly middle-class seats in Sydney and Melbourne had significant swings towards Labor.'

However, the ANU's election study, released in December 2019, which surveyed voters after the election, found Labor's tax policies polarised the electorate. The proposal to limit negative gearing was supported by 57 per cent of voters, while 53 per cent supported the franking-credit reforms. Voters were divided, providing opportunities for the Liberal Party.

'No other major tax change proposed in an election has produced such division among voters since the Coalition's proposal to introduce a goods and services tax (GST) in 1998,' the ANU study found. 'In that election, 42% saw the GST as the most important issue, and 42% supported Labor on the issue (who opposed the tax) while 44% supported the Coalition.'

Low-income workers in jobs that lack security are, of course, on the frontline of an economic downturn. It makes sense that they would detect changes in the economy faster than those cushioned from the impact. Don Farrell poses the theory that blue-collar workers were more sensitive and attuned to the weakness in the economy.

'One theory is the economy was in much more trouble than people thought or anticipated and in those circumstances people stick with the devil that you know,' he said. 'Since the election, there have been three interest rate cuts. The Reserve Bank doesn't cut interest rates when the economy is going well. I think the people who get affected in any downturn are on lower incomes. They deserted us in significant numbers. I think they realised, before anyone else did, that the economy was tracking badly. If you go back to 1993, which I think was the last time an opposition lost the election and a government won an unwinnable election, the economy was also in strife. They are just worried about making a change when economic times are tough.'

Kos Samaras, a former assistant secretary of the Victorian ALP, tells the story of sitting down with a family friend who works in the construction industry. 'He went into a lot of detail about how precarious his work is. Periods of intense work followed by periods of no work. His experience is shared by most he works with. They are largely placed into jobs by agencies. If they get work, like a job for six months, they work as much as possible, racking up as many hours as possible to earn as much as possible.

'He told us about how many work 20 days straight on non-union sites, as they desperately try to gulp up the work before the boss taps them on the shoulder and gives them their marching orders. No notice, on the spot – no more work. What struck me about his story is he is highly skilled, has skilled up for multiple jobs in the industry, but the work is so unstable and irregular that he fears starting a family and planning ahead. It explains in some part why people like him have become a political problem for established parties.'

Workers in low-income and low-security jobs might not like their boss, but like any rational worker would like unemployment less. The rhetoric of taking on 'the top end of town' must have sounded good in focus groups when Malcolm Turnbull was leader, but it clearly did not work in the 2019 election.

After the election, some Labor supporters criticised Albanese's support for the Liberals' tax cuts. 'Naturally, the criticism is based on a well-founded principle that those better off should not be given more money, but instead those funds should be distributed to those further down the economic ladder,' Samaras said. 'This position is ideologically correct but politically wrong. Here is why. Lower-income earners do not bemoan higher-income earners getting a tax cut. Ignore all the usual surveys you read in this space. If they get a tax cut, then they are agnostic as to what happens further up the income ladder.'

According to Samaras, the lesson is that these voters, when feeling frustrated about their personal economic health, do not punch up to attack employers or big business. 'They punch down. They have a strong sense that income is a product of hard work. They have no issue seeing someone on $180,000 get a tax cut, but they do object to someone not working being given more money. Like many, I always find this mindset personally confronting, but I have lost count how many times I have seen this expressed in focus groups. You will only ever see this expression if the focus group is run by someone capable of triggering the cognitive dissonance in people.'

Another critical factor was the concern of working-class voters when the Labor Party was promising radical changes and action on a 'climate change emergency'. 'Climate emergency as a term sends shockwaves through these communities,' Samaras said. 'The word emergency insinuates rapid, sudden and unprecedented action. Action which they will immediately interpret as more of the same but only faster. More of the same being the last 40 years of upheaval. Communities in the Hunter Valley, regional Queensland and northern Tasmania have endured nearly four decades of economic decline. The upheaval has been so great that you could say people living within these communities are traumatised by change.'

Another persistent myth was that retirees turned on Labor. Three days after the election, ABC journalist and professor of global affairs at Griffith University Stan Grant wrote, 'Retirees, middle-class parents and those dependent on the mining industry for their livelihoods all felt they were in the firing line.'

It is a reasonable analysis that sounds completely logical. There was a generational gap in how Australians voted. Older Australians were more likely to vote Liberal. It's true that retirees were told they faced a 'retiree tax' under the franking-credit reforms. It's logical to assume they felt in the firing line, but how did they actually vote? Did seniors abandon the Labor Party? The answer, according to the hard data, appears to be 'No'. That's not to say the policies did not suppress the vote, but it's not clear it caused voters to abandon Labor.

'So, one of the surprising results is that we didn't find a very strong correlation between the swing and the age of voters,' the Australian National University's Associate Professor Ben Phillips said. 'I was reasonably sure there would be quite a big impact for older Australians. I know there was a lot of concerns around the franking credits, and a lot of older Australians have got franking credits, particularly in their self-managed super funds.

'We didn't find that. In fact, we found quite the opposite, in that we found that people who were most likely to be impacted by Labor's tax increases – so that's the negative gearing, the franking credits – who were largely higher-income people, were more likely to vote towards Labor, or swing towards Labor. Of course, this data does not mean that Labor's franking-credit policy did not do the party damage, particularly in terms of suppressing the vote where

Labor might otherwise expect to pick up seats. But it does not suggest older voters abandoned Labor in droves.'

He found that age was not a major factor in the election. The sweet spot for Morrison was voters with low education. They were on low incomes or, in some cases, good incomes but experiencing financial pressures with credit-card debts and big mortgages.

The picture of the typical voter who delivered victory for the Liberal Party looks something like this: a family man with children, who did not attend university, who might earn good money of $100,000 or more a year. Whether or not they regularly sang hymns at church on Sunday, they regard themselves as Christian.

The idea that voters will happily cast a vote against their economic interests seems, at first blush, surprising. As Nick Dryenfurth recounts in his book on the Labor Party, *Getting the Blues*, former NSW Premier Neville Wran lectured Bob Hawke in 1983 over his election slogan, 'Recovery, Reconciliation and Reconstruction'. Wran complained it sounded 'like a meeting of the fucking Hare Krishnas. Give them something to vote for. These greedy bastards want a quid in their pockets.'

But at the 2019 election, workers decided they didn't trust Labor's promises of bigger taxes and a quid in the pockets of schools and hospitals, particularly if an economic downturn meant they didn't have a job.

Some Labor strategists believe there are also emerging issues with migrant voters. 'The fastest-growing migrant communities in this country are from mainland China and subcontinent India,' said Samaras. 'They are entrepreneurial, socially conservative and seldom vote for political parties based on economics, although health and education are factors in their thinking. On top of Labor's growing problem with voters of faith is an equal and much more worrying decay of its tenuous hold on tradies. In these same electorates, where some people of faith opted for minor parties, Labor lost ground within the tradie cohort.'

'We defied the iron law of Australian politics,' Senator Farrell said. 'The iron law is that governments lose elections, oppositions don't win them. And we lost that election. It was our policies that the electorate rejected. They rejected them pretty comprehensively in the heartland. The paradox was that the swings that we got in that were in the wealthier parts of the electorate. They were people most likely to be affected by our tax changes. So, I am not sure you can draw the conclusion that our tax policies was the reason. There was something deeper going on.'

What Labor is left with as rusted-on supporters are inner-city, university-educated, middle-class voters. People that look a lot like most Labor MPs and the staffers that work for them. In the workplace, feminists have long complained of unconscious bias, the tendency of male bosses to promote workers who think and look like them. It turns out that the highly educated, middle-class men and women on Labor's frontbench designed policies that appealed to people like them and sold the policy with language that appeals to people just like them. Little wonder that Labor believed the election was in the bag.

14

AN ACT OF BASTARDRY

Labor's Campaign Director Noah Carroll had devised one of the most complicated polling operations in the ALP's modern history and he sat astride a dancing octopus of different pollsters and techniques as a self-appointed pollster-in-chief. He had engaged YouGov to conduct that quantitative research, the nightly tracking poll of 20 key marginal seats, and he had Labor's veteran pollster John Utting – the co-founder of Utting Mills Research – conducting the focus groups in every state except Queensland. In the sunshine state, another UMR alumnus, Stephen Mills, was running the focus groups. Then there was a robopolling operation run by a New Zealander, which acted as a second tracking poll in a different group of seats.

These complicated arrangements reflected Carroll's belief

in new strategies and technology. They were also a reflection of ancient Labor feuds. ALP President Wayne Swan had insisted on having a different focus group pollster in his home state of Queensland. The decision seemed to have been prompted in part by his scepticism about the abilities of Carroll and Utting. But the potpourri of pollsters didn't end there.

Eric Goddard, a former business partner of Carroll's, was running the robopolls. His company was registered to a boat at a marina in Wellington, NZ. Robopolls were not always the most respected device, although they ultimately did quite well in the 2019 election, largely because they can skew conservative. Essentially, the inherent bias of the robopolls neatly matched the underestimation of the Liberal Party primary vote.

This byzantine arrangement made sense to Carroll. He had a strong view that you shouldn't have the same people doing your focus group who were doing your quantitative tracking polls. The idea was to provide cross-examination and rigour. He believed it helped to have a focus-group moderator who would test assumptions in your tracking poll and vice-versa, to double check you were on the right track. In theory, that sounds sensible. To sceptics, it was a hot mess.

The ALP's official pollster, YouGov's Dr Campbell White, was a mystery man to Bill Shorten. In fact, the Labor leader hadn't spoken a word to him in nearly five years. It's not clear that he had his own pollster's mobile phone number. A New Zealander, White had worked on Labor's campaigns in Australia for nearly 20 years under the tutelage of John Utting. He had also worked for Newspoll, the political oracle that MPs consult with most, when deciding whether or not to neck a prime minister.

This election, he was taking over responsibility for running Labor's marginal seats polling operation from his old boss Utting for the first time. It was a big responsibility. But he would soon discover it did not come with a great deal of access. His frequent offers to brief the Labor leadership group on his research were rebuffed. It was a point of contention raised in his confidential submission to the ALP's post-mortem into the election result.

When he did brief the Labor Party on his findings, White didn't even get to speak to the campaign director. Instead, he mainly emailed his results to Bruce Cohen, a Victorian consultant brought in to work closely with Carroll.

It is fair to say that Utting did not appreciate being usurped by his protégé. But the older man shared the younger man's experience of having little or no contact with the Labor leader or campaign director. Both men had to talk to Cohen and he briefed Carroll, who, in turn, briefed the Labor leadership group, who complained they couldn't understand what Carroll was talking about. To put it mildly, it was less than ideal.

White was invited to visit the Parramatta HQ only a handful of times during the election. His requests to include questions in the tracking poll to test how the campaign was travelling were brushed off. Even more bizarrely, the contract for YouGov to conduct the party tracking poll was delayed for months and finalised just weeks before the election was called. By comparison, the Liberal Party started ramping up a sophisticated polling operation soon after Morrison was elected leader.

The $500,000 deal to conduct the ALP's quantitative polling was signed in April, just days before the prime minister called the election. By comparison, the Liberal Party's pollsters, Crosby Textor, had been conducting nightly tracking polls for months, building up the intensity since summer, in the lead-up to the 2 April budget.

There are some suggestions that the Labor Party toyed with the idea of not using a traditional tracking poll and relying on robopolls instead, and that this was one of the reasons for the late decision to sign White. It's true that his relationship with the ALP was already established because he had also conducted the polling for the by-elections. But regardless of whether it was widely expected he would be signed to conduct the tracking poll, polling companies don't start working for free before a contract is signed. As a result, the formal tracking poll for the ALP only commenced shortly before the election was called.

Was this a strange set-up? It certainly was if you compared it to the Liberal Party campaign. London-based pollster Michael Brooks, of Crosby Textor, who flew into Australia before the campaign, spent most mornings on a phone hook-up with Scott Morrison. He would brief the prime minister on his findings and if there were any questions, he was there on the call to answer them.

Crosby Textor, founded by former Liberal Party Director Lynton Crosby and pollster Mark Textor, was an institution in conservative circles that had guided successive Liberal prime ministers to historic victories since the Howard years. It acted as a Swiss finishing school for generations of Liberal strategists. Or, to use a Harry Potter analogy, a Hogwarts School of Witchcraft and Wizardry for conservative hacks.

Its alumni was scattered across the party's headquarters and parliament. Everyone from Morrison's chief political adviser, Yaron Finklestein, to the Liberal Party Director Andrew Hirst and his deputy Isaac Levido had worked there. For the last decade, it had also forged a relationship with British Prime Minister Boris Johnson, culminating in Levido helping to devise the strategy for his stunning December 2019 election victory against Labour's Jeremy Corbyn.

Pollsters are critical to election campaigns, driving announcements, determining which states the leader should campaign in, which seats to target, which to abandon, and where millions of dollars in the campaign will be spent. Sometimes, political leaders live and die by them.

But in what should have been his moment of triumph, White did not join the intended celebrations with Shorten's campaign team on election night. What does that tell you about how confident he was of a Labor victory? His own polling suggested a much tighter race than the media and voters expected from the published polls. In fact, White hoped for the best, but, based on his own work, feared Labor would lose. That's why he remained at home on election night, grimly watching the television coverage.

The ABC's analyst Antony Green captured the mood early. 'At the moment, on these figures, it's a bit of a spectacular failure of opinion polling,' he said. The result defied the betting markets, stunned the Labor Party and tarnished the reputation of Newspoll, the nation's most trusted election oracle.

For over 50 consecutive surveys, Newspoll had declared that Labor would win an election. Even the exit polls, which asked people how they voted after they left the polling booth, got the result wrong. In the aftermath, *The Sydney Morning Herald* announced it was pressing pause on the IPSOS poll, which had correctly called the Labor Party's low primary vote but still managed to tip a Labor victory. Some claimed it was one of the worst polling failures since Brexit. The Brexit and Trump debacles had been warning signs, but easily dismissed given the different voting systems in the UK and US. But there had been signs in the gap between the polls and the results in recent state elections in Victoria and NSW – both predicted very close results, even hung parliaments. Both were badly wrong, but in opposite directions.

Examining the carnage, the nation's pollsters blamed all of the usual modern problems that make it harder to get accurate results, including the dwindling number of home landlines. As more Australians rely on mobile phones, it's tougher to get representative samples in marginal seats. It's one reason pollsters have increasingly turned to online panels of voters. These results are then weighted to better reflect the community. These are the 'secret herbs and spices' that pollsters use to manipulate results to ensure they are more representative and thus more accurate. During this election, the 'recipe' clearly went wrong.

After the election, Shorten reflected that he had encountered 'the most corrupted polling in Australian history'. But that's not why he believes Labor lost the unlosable election. Mostly, he blamed Clive Palmer's campaign. 'I don't think the polls were all that wrong for most of the time. I think they changed in the last two weeks and missed the undecideds.'

However, Australian Electoral Commission data confirms Labor won a majority of votes on election day – 50.4 per cent on a two-party-preferred basis – but trailed badly on millions of pre-poll votes cast earlier in the campaign. That doesn't entirely support Shorten's theory that pollsters missed the undecided voters, even if there were a lot of them. The exit polls may have been close to accurate in terms of votes cast on the day. The Liberals, with 54.6 per cent, trounced Labor on pre-polls and postals of just 45.4 per cent.

But for Campbell White, it was an election defined by another trauma, a betrayal that he describes as 'an act of bastardry' – the leaking of the ALP tracking poll. Less than 48 hours after the election result, his confidential research was published on The New Daily website. The $500,000 research project was far more sophisticated and expensive than the polling published by newspapers.

But what stunned Carroll and White was that the leak of the ALP tracking poll included the graphs and analysis. According to party officials, that had 'never happened', or not in their memory. This was material that had not even been provided during the campaign to ALP state secretaries.

In an interview for this book, White said the betrayal left him gutted. 'What disgusted me is that act of bastardry – it was an act of betrayal. I mean to Bill Shorten, to Noah [Carroll], to the Labor Party as a whole.' Internal party polling often has a 'mythical' status, because it's secret, but leaking the entire ALP track certainly provided a disturbing image of how the sausage was made. 'That mythical image has persisted because, before now, people involved in the campaign have respected the sanctity of the campaign,' said White.

It was a kick in the guts as Labor was still taking in the shock of the election result. The pollster feared the leak was an attempt to blame the loss on the polling. But what came as a surprise to many, including in the Labor Party, was that it revealed that YouGov was conducting Newspoll for *The Australian* newspaper, the Galaxy polls for the News Corp tabloids, Channel Nine's election-night exit polls and now the ALP's own internal polling.

Utting dropped another bomb on the same day the tracking poll leaked. He revealed that he had repeatedly raised concerns about the potential conflict of interest of having the Newspoll pollsters also running Labor's research operation.

'I raised concerns with Noah Carroll and no-one acted on them,' he said. It 'beggars belief' that conflict was not declared to the public. 'YouGov/Galaxy Research presented itself to the Australian people via the media as an honest broker and dispassionate observer of the political scene, while being intimately involved in Labor's political campaign.'

YouGov managing director David Briggs confirmed his company did prepare the tracking poll for the Labor Party in the national campaign, and had also done the ALP polling for the NSW election. 'We don't boast about it,' he said. 'We don't deny it.' He insisted there was no conflict of interest in the business arrangement. 'How can it be a conflict of interest? The two things can happen very independently. Everything is very siloed.'

Briggs said the polling for the ALP and Newspoll was kept completely separate and did not cross over or use the same research. 'When you look at the polling record here, we were the most trusted brand. We did the exit poll for Channel Nine. But also we've been doing work for Seven-West Media.'

While the company explained that these were separate polling operations, the revelation shocked many, including the Liberal Party's legendary pollster Mark Textor, who was 'stunned'. Firstly, Galaxy and YouGov are not traditional political campaign pollsters – a specialised field that is different to public polls published in newspapers. Also, they hadn't previously declared publicly that they were doing the work on *The Australian*'s Newspoll, the News Corp tabloids' Galaxy polls, Nine's exit polls and the ALP's own tracking poll.

The leak of the ALP's tracking poll highlighted the fact that even the internal polling had overestimated the Labor primary vote. The poll was a basket of 20 marginal seats they needed to retain or win. The seats tracked were divided into inner-metropolitan (Griffith, Reid, Chisholm, Stirling,

Swan), outer-metro (Petrie, Lindsay, Boothby, Dunkley, La Trobe, Hasluck), provincial (Herbert, Longman, Robertson, Corangamite) and rural (Flynn, Leichhardt, Eden-Monaro, Page, Braddon).

The methodology used by the poll was different to Newspoll, which provides a national snapshot of the two-party-preferred vote. Newspoll was using a combination of robopolls – automated messages to phone lines – and online panels of voters selected by YouGov. By comparison, the tracking poll was a nightly poll of 20 voters in the 20 key marginals. That is, 400 voters being asked how they intended to vote.

Any cursory glance of the tracking poll published provided little evidence that Labor was a sure bet. The support for the party was patchy and bouncing around. Those within Labor who were convinced they were going to win the election either didn't have access to the poll or didn't know how to read it.

The ALP's review of the election result commissioned former Queensland State Secretary Evan Moorhead to examine the research strategy. His report is packed with coded criticisms.

The Newspoll survey was considered more reliable than the other published polls, but Moorhead had identified a big problem. 'First, the publicly available Newspoll figures had a persistent technical error that overstated Labor's primary vote,' he wrote, 'understated the Coalition's primary vote and consistently suggested Labor was in an election-winning position. While the YouGov campaign track had a similar but smaller error, the fact the campaign track reported a Labor two-party preferred vote that was less optimistic than published polling every night of the campaign, provided warnings about key problems for the campaign.

'Seat polling conducted during the campaign also provided early warning Labor's campaign was struggling, particularly in regional Queensland. However, the persistent Labor lead in Newspoll (and other published polls) created a mindset dominated by high expectations of a Labor victory, and this affected the Party's ability to process research findings that ran counter to this.'

In short, Labor disregarded its own $500,000 polling operation because of the Newspoll results, which some MPs seemed to be unaware was being conducted by the same company.

'Second, there was a lack of integration between the various research elements. Research methods and providers were not exposed to robust interrogation where there were inconsistencies or differences in their findings. Instead, when inconsistencies arose, the campaign's response tended to be to interrogate and analyse the accuracy of individual research findings. This was particularly the case where the research findings were inconsistent with published polling.'

But the diabolical problem was that the relationship between polling and policy development appeared to have broken down. In the past, Labor might have brought ideas to former ALP Secretary George Wright – for example, negative gearing – to test them before further policy-design work was done. This didn't happen as much after the 2016 election.

Intriguingly, several Labor sources insist that Wright tested the idea of franking credits before the 2016 election and found it was risky, because people didn't know what it was and it was dangerously vulnerable to a scare campaign. Both Shorten and Bowen insist there was no polling done on this idea until after the 2016 election, or that if it was conducted they were not aware of it. This is disputed by former ALP campaign secretariat staff, who insist that Wright did commission focus-group work on franking credits, which might make sense because it had been raised from time to time in recent years, including in the review of tax policy by then Treasury Secretary Ken Henry in 2009.

During the 2019 campaign, Labor's shadow cabinet lobbed new policies on ALP campaign staff without warning and then wondered why there was no polling explaining how to sell it.

'The research program was not embedded in the strategic decision-making of the campaign,' said Moorhead. 'Decisions in favour of policy continuity after the 2016 election, and a view that turbulence within the Parliament and the Government could lead to an early general election, meant strategic options were continually being framed by tactical pressures. This left the research program focused more on the tactical implementation of decisions already taken, rather than building a strategy that could inform campaign planning and tactical decisions.'

Some ALP campaign workers complain that the polling was mainly used to devise television ads.

But despite the headlines that the Liberal Party had known they were going to win based on the Crosby Textor polling, victory was never locked in from the Liberals' perspective. Liberal Party Director Andrew Hirst confirms that nobody knew what the precise outcome would be. The party's polling identified a range of outcomes anywhere between securing seats in the low 70s and high 70s.

In the 151-seat parliament the Liberals needed 76 to win a majority. They were optimistic about Herbert and Longman in Queensland and Lindsay in NSW. They were also optimistic about seats like Bass and Braddon in Tasmania and Wentworth in Sydney. They expected to lose Tony Abbott's seat and Gilmore in NSW. That already had the Liberal Party going forwards and Labor going backwards.

The Liberal Party's last tracking poll ran on the Thursday night before the election. So, that was 48 hours where they were not polling – and something like 12 per cent of voters make their mind up on the day.

'Of course, nobody knew what the precise outcome was going to be,' said Hirst, 'because you can't poll every seat all the time, right up until the moment that people vote. But we could consistently see a pathway – albeit a very narrow pathway – to victory. The key point is our polling was accurate. It showed us the pathway and you try and utilise that research as best you possibly can to get the best possible outcome.

'It wasn't like the public polling. But, again, the public polling was measuring something else, the national two-party-preferred vote. It got that wrong, but that isn't what we look at.'

The man who had previously conducted the ALP polling – in some form or another since 1996 – was John Utting. He had founded Utting Mills Research with Stephen Mills. The back story to the links between the various pollsters working on the ALP campaign was as complicated as the polling operation they were working on.

Utting had first hired the ALP pollster Dr Campbell White nearly 20 years earlier. White rose to become the CEO of UMR, with the three men going their separate ways in 2016 after a merger with Essential Media. Subsequently, Utting left his old company to start a new business. White joined the Newspoll pollster David Briggs and his Galaxy-owned YouGov polling arm. Stephen Mills also departed, taking the UMR name and basing himself in New Zealand. Utting formed his own company, Utting Research. By engaging all three – Utting, Mills and White – the ALP believed it was putting the band back together. But the trio were not encouraged to work as a team, and Utting remained annoyed by the decision to appoint White to run the tracking poll.

Utting revealed that he had repeatedly raised concerns about the potential conflict of interest of having the Newspoll pollsters, YouGov, also running Labor's research operation.

'I raised concerns with Noah Carroll and no-one acted on them,' he said. It 'beggars belief' that conflict was not declared to the public. 'YouGov/Galaxy Research presented itself to the Australian people via the media as an honest broker and dispassionate observer of the political scene, while being intimately involved in Labor's political campaign.'

More importantly, the poll underestimated the Liberal Party's primary vote. 'No wonder Bill looked shattered on the night,' said Utting. Labor's NSW Campaign Director Kaila Murnain had also used YouGov in the state election in March. Utting's assessment of those results was dripping in sarcasm. 'They also did a fantastic job for Kaila Murnain in NSW. Look at the smoking crater that was. What it tells you is Bill Shorten went in expecting to win. A Hillary Clinton moment.'

But despite Utting's brutal dissection of the ALP tracking poll, it hadn't offered much comfort that Labor was going to win. There was nothing consistent over the election period about the results, which had dipped up and down like a seesaw.

Victoria's Assistant Secretary Kos Samaras said the first time he saw the tracking poll was after it leaked. 'It indicated a close race,' he said. 'Once you factored in the margin of error, Labor was always within striking distance of losing. Victorian Labor's 2018 tracking poll produced a similar discrepancy, but on this occasion no-one paid much attention to its inaccuracy because the victory was so great.'

In other words, plenty of internal tracking polls get it wrong – it's only a massive problem when you think you're going to win and you lose. As traumatic as the leak was, it was a blessing in disguise for YouGov, because it undermined the claim that Shorten was lulled into believing he would win based on the ALP's internal polling.

The fallout from the drama continued to simmer. After the leak, Labor's Assistant National Secretary Sebastian Zwalf phoned YouGov. One of Zwalf's responsibilities was co-ordinating the polling and research. People were starting to ask him what had gone wrong and he needed an answer. But White had been told by Noah Carroll not to speak to anyone other than the two men conducting the ALP review into the election campaign – Jay Weatherill and Craig Emerson. With the leaks already flowing out of the ALP HQ about what had gone wrong, Carroll was trying to keep the lid on things.

Acting on this advice, the pollster told Zwalf he would give his answers to the review. White's refusal to discuss the matter with the Labor official – who didn't realise he was following the instructions of the party secretary – became the subject of gossip within Labor circles and was subsequently leaked to the media. For his troubles, White ended up in a *Sydney Morning Herald* gossip column in a story claiming he was refusing to tell the ALP what went wrong – an entirely false accusation given that he was following the instruction of his client.

After his first blast, Utting penned a column for *The Australian Financial Review*, outlining his thoughts on the polling debacle and how to fix it. 'Discredited, distrusted, even despised, after last Saturday's election the polling industry in Australia has reached its nadir,' he wrote. 'It would be hard to imagine how things could get worse. The reason I write is to ensure this doesn't happen again and suggest a series of initiatives to clean up and rehabilitate our industry and the health of our democracy.'

He noted that the largest-ever exit poll undertaken, the Channel 9 YouGov-Galaxy Research poll, based over 3300 interviews, showed a 52–48 per cent ALP lead, when the reverse was the case. He posed an alarming question: what if Labor's vote had been overstated for years and polls had created a parallel universe?

'The last 50 or 60 Newspolls showed Labor comfortably ahead. What if, in reality, Labor was at best level pegging or even behind? How has this affected our political commentary and political behaviour? Did polling create a parallel universe where all the activity of the past few years, especially the leadership coups and prime ministerial changes, were based on illusions, phantoms of public opinion that did not exist?'

Watching this all unfold from the United States, polling guru Nate Silver took the view that some of the claims of the Australian polling catastrophe were overblown. A best-selling author and statistician, he rose to fame after successfully predicting the outcome in 49 of the 50 states in the 2008 US Presidential election. Then, in 2012, he picked 50 out of 50, before he got the rise of Trump spectacularly wrong.

On his FiveThirtyEight blog, Silver wondered if the collective unhinging in Australia didn't say more about the numeracy of journalists. 'Polls showed the conservative-led coalition trailing the Australian Labor Party approximately 51–49 in the two-party-preferred vote. Instead, the conservatives won 51–49. That's a relatively small miss. The miss was right in line with the average error from past Australian elections.

'Given that track record, the conservatives had somewhere around a one in three chance of winning. So the Australian media took this in its stride, right? Of course not. Instead, the election was characterised as a "massive polling failure" and a "shock result". When journalists say stuff like that in an election after polls were so close, they're telling on themselves. They're revealing, like their American counterparts after 2016, that they aren't particularly numerate and didn't really understand what the polls said in the first place. They may also be signalling, as in the case of Brexit in 2016, their cosmopolitan bias; the Australian election, which emphasised climate change, had a strong urban-rural split.'

Silver did believe the polling results suggested signs of 'herding', in which pollsters fiddle with their own methodology to ensure the findings are in line with those of their competitors. 'Still, some of the headlines in the Australian media are idiotic and embarrassing. When polls show a race within a couple of percentage points, nobody – least of all journalists, who are paid to be informed about this stuff – should be shocked when the trailing side wins.'

Nobel Laureate Professor Brian Schmidt, the vice-chancellor of the Australian National University, penned a column titled 'Mathematics does not lie: why polling got the Australian election wrong'. His conclusion echoed Silver's that there was evidence of herding. The collective similarity of the Australian opinion polls 'violates the fundamentals of mathematics', he said.

'Since the election was called, there were 16 polls that published two-party-preferred results ahead of Saturday's vote. Every single one of them predicted the LNP winning 48% or 49% of the two-party-preferred vote, with Labor winning 51% or 52%. You can think of the uncertainties in the polls much like what happens when you flip a coin 10 times. You can expect to get the "right" answer of five heads quite frequently, but not every time. If you do a similar calculation for the 16 polls conducted during the election, based on the number of people interviewed, the odds of those 16 polls coming in with the same, small spread of answers is greater than 100,000 to 1. In other words, the polls have been manipulated, probably unintentionally, to give the same answers as each other.'

But Australia's pollsters had an enviable reputation of getting it right and the fact they collectively got it wrong was horrifying. Newspoll's David Briggs declared himself to be feeling 'shithouse'.

'It is of note that in my 33 years of administering opinion polls in Australia, we have not had one Trump, Brexit, Scottish referendum or UK election-style miss until now,' he said. 'The result on Saturday has many similarities to the election of Donald Trump in 2016. Trump had been written off by political commentators, and most of the published polls had Clinton with an election-winning lead.'

Briggs had been warning for months that it was always possible for prime ministers to surprise. 'In 1993, Paul Keating started the election behind with a two-party-preferred vote of 52.5 to 47.5, which is pretty similar to where we are now,' Briggs had said in April. In the 1998 election, when John Howard was attempting to introduce the GST, he was also trailing Labor when the election was called. 'Mr Howard also started the 1998 election with Labor in front on 51.5 per cent.'

In 2004 as he faced Labor's Mark Latham, voters were evenly split at the beginning of the election. 'They started the campaign neck and neck, with Labor in the lead midway through the 2004 campaign with 52–48,' said Briggs. Despite that lead, Howard defeated Latham on election day. 'It comes down to the risk. If people think there's a risk, they will stick to what they know.'

But Labor had been in front for years. Scott Morrison had trailed the Labor Party 56–44 on a two-party-preferred basis in his first Newspoll. Even a month before the election, the gap was still 54–46.

Now Head of YouGov's Public Affairs and Polling Asia-Pacific, White argued that, in previous elections, skilled practitioners were able to get great results despite the technical difficulties. 'The reason we have not seen the failures that have occurred elsewhere is that Australia has very skilled people like David Briggs, who have been able to adjust for deficiencies in the samples. And in an odd sort of way, Australian pollsters are actually the victim of their own past successes, because this set up expectations that polling was completely infallible and it isn't. It's sort of insane to look at 51–49 and think that's a complete fait accompli.

'This is not saying the polling industry didn't get it wrong. It absolutely did. We have to take actions to do things differently and do things better. One of the things we are doing is shifting our state and national polling to 100 per cent online. We have a lot more information, such as demographics and broader political attitudes.

'Another factor that made this election different was the massively different trends in certain marginal electorates, compared to others. There were seats where there was indeed a swing to Labor. That's why seat polling was generally rather accurate in terms of picking winners. Seat polling is generally regarded as less accurate than other forms of polling, so perhaps it wasn't given sufficient weight by commentators.

'We shouldn't lose sight of the fact there were unusual characteristics of this election, which were evident in hindsight, which may have affected how pollsters interpreted the data we had. What made the election different was the dynamic of the election. The election basically became a referendum on Labor. Almost every election you can point to in this country's history, it's usually a referendum on the government. There's one exception, apart from this one, and it is 1993. There are obvious parallels.'

15

CLIVE PALMER AND ADANI

Clive Palmer signed the deal to rebirth his political party over a seafood dinner at Scratchleys in Newcastle in June 2018. The billionaire property developer turned mining magnate, who learned the art of politics working with Queensland Premier Joh Bjelke-Petersen in the 1980s, flew into town on his private jet. It was an evening that would have profound consequences for Bill Shorten.

On the menu at the harbour restaurant was a $230 hot and cold seafood platter, featuring prawns, blue swimmer crabs, Balmain bugs and 'A' grade oysters and fries. But all Palmer needed from his dining companion, the One Nation Senator Brian Burston, was a signature.

After he'd quit politics before the 2016 election, with regulators circling over the collapse of his Townsville nickel refinery, the Australian Electoral Commission had deregistered his party. When Burston agreed to defect and sit in parliament for Palmer's United Australia Party, Palmer automatically secured party status for his non-existent political organisation. 'That's accurate,' Burston said in an interview for this book. 'That was my dinner with Clive at Scratchleys.'

The dinner, on 15 June, satisfied the Australian Electoral Commission rules that would otherwise have required Palmer to prove that he had 500 grassroots members. Three days later, Burston announced his defection in Canberra.

Why was party status so important? Without it, there would be no box above the line on the Senate ballot paper at the 2019 election for voters to mark '1' for the 'United Australia Party'. His candidates, buried beneath a mountain of other names below the line on the ballot, wouldn't stand a chance. Burston, who was known to have fallen out with Hanson, was the perfect vehicle for the billionaire to get back in the game.

'I'm 65 years old,' said Palmer. 'The options are either croquet, bowls, going for a sail every Sunday or dribbling in a nursing home. I've got a good revenue or income – $400 million a year – so I thought I would put it to use.'

Palmer and Burston had met the day before in Townsville. With Burston's vital signature hanging in the balance, Palmer agreed to fly his private jet, which was registered to the Cayman Islands, down to Newcastle for the dinner.

'I met Clive up at Queensland Nickel,' said Burston, 'and had a chat with him for about an hour and liked what he had to say, didn't make any commitment. That was the day before the Newcastle dinner. He said, "Do you want to catch up for dinner tomorrow night?" I said, "No, I'll be back in Newcastle." The flight was already booked. But Palmer said, "Oh I'll be in Sydney. I'll fly up from Sydney and we'll catch up." I said, "Yeah, okay." So he flew to Newcastle.'

Shortly after the meeting with Burston that helped secure his political comeback, Palmer announced he planned to reopen the refinery in Townsville, in the federal electorate of Herbert. It was widely speculated he would run for the seat, the most marginal in the country, although he later abandoned that idea and ran for the Senate.

Palmer and Burston had met the day before in Townsville. Just two years earlier, Queensland Nickel had collapsed with debts of about $300 million, leaving close to 800 people out of work. But things were looking up for Palmer, after Chinese company Citic was ordered to pay more than $200 million in royalties to his company Mineralogy. Soon, he would re-enter the Forbes rich list with a $1.8 billion fortune. All of a sudden, his lease deals in Citic had started making real money, at a rate some speculated was as high as $7 million a day.

So, that's why they met up in Townsville and how the pair ended up at Scratchleys for dinner the next day. But what did Burston get for his troubles? It was not publicised, but the two men had a secret handshake agreement.

'Clive did say to me at the time that he would indemnify me against any legal action that One Nation may take, with me leaving the party and hooking up with him,' Burston confirmed. 'I said, "I am happy to come across and let's register the United Australia Party." So, it was on my Senate position that it was registered without requirement for members. So when I expedited that, he gave me a commitment that if there's any attacks on myself, he will indemnify me against any legal expenses. He volunteered that. I was not concerned about anything. He may have had something in the back of his mind where Hanson or others may attack me. Which they did ultimately. But we couldn't foresee that. He just said, out of the blue, "I will indemnify you against any legal costs."'

That promise would come in handy for Burston, because the break-up with Pauline Hanson was certainly rocky.

In the lead-up to Valentine's Day 2019, Burston was involved in a scuffle at Parliament House with Hanson's Chief of Staff, James Ashby. It resulted in Ashby being briefly banned from parliament. Blood was then smeared on Hanson's door, which Burston at first denied and then later admitted to his involvement in.

'Whilst I do not recall the incident of blood on the door, I now have come to the conclusion that it was myself and I sincerely apologise for that action,' he said. Asked if he should resign, Burston said, 'Why would I? I barely even remember it. I was traumatised.'

Ashby agreed to be sin-binned by Senate President Scott Ryan. 'As a member of staff to a senator, I respect the jurisdiction of the president of the Senate,' he said. 'To that effect, I have surrendered my pass. However, there must be a full investigation of this matter, the allegations that preceded the altercation and a range of other issues regarding the alleged treatment of female staff that may be relevant to this matter.'

The row had erupted over sexual-harassment allegations. After Burston left One Nation, Hanson gave a speech under parliamentary privilege saying an unnamed MP was facing unfair-dismissal claims and sexual-harassment complaints. 'This gutless wonder we call senator should hang his head in shame,' she said.

The next morning, I ran into Burston in a lift on the Senate side of Parliament House. Who could she be talking about? It seemed highly likely she was having a crack at her recently departed colleague. 'It's me,' he confirmed. As the lift doors opened, we got out and he complained it was a pack of lies being peddled by his former colleagues. In fact, he argued it was actually him who had been sexually harassed. Twenty years earlier, for example, Burston said Hanson had touched his back. 'Right back when we had our first One Nation AGM at the Rooty Hill RSL, that was the first time she hit on me,' he said. Shortly afterwards, Burston went public with his claims in the media.

Hanson laughed off his sexual-harassment claims in a series of television interviews. 'I might be 64 but I'm not that desperate,' she said. 'These are allegations that have been made up, there is no truth to them whatsoever and I feel sorry for his wife, I really feel sorry for his wife.'

Just to communicate the message loud and clear, shortly afterwards Hanson sent a text message to Burston's wife, Ros, on Valentine's Day. 'You are being taken for a fool by Brian,' she wrote, according to court documents. 'He is the last man I would ever hit on. I am definitely not attracted to him now or ever. He is vindictive as you well know. He is being investigated for sexual harassment by more than one of his former female staffers. They can't all be wrong.'

Claiming that the speech, text message and the two other incidents caused damage to his 'personal and professional reputation', Burston lodged defamation action seeking aggravated damages of $1 million.

His defamation legal team was led by Sam Iskander, Clive Palmer's lawyer. Asked if Palmer was paying for the legal action against Hanson under their deal to cover his legal expenses, Burston was coy. He didn't wish to comment publicly and suggested you should 'read between the lines'.

Iskander is a busy lawyer running a busy practice. He was also representing Palmer in seeking an apology from comedian Jordan Shanks, also known as Friendly Jordy, who had referred to the UAP leader on YouTube as a 'nutty turd', 'Fatty McFuckface' and a 'crackpot'. A legal letter sent by Iskander to the comedian said he had suffered 'actual damage as a result of defamatory comments published, including but not limited to extreme embarrassment and humiliation and damage to professional, personal or political reputation'.

But a defiant Shanks insisted he wasn't worried. 'He made one tiny miscalculation and that is – I'm a millennial. Going bankrupt doesn't scare me. I don't have a house. I have as many assets as you have seats in parliament: none.' His video reply has been watched over 700,000 times on YouTube.

Iskander's firm was also the legal team advising Palmer's fugitive nephew Clive Mensink Jr, the son of Clive Mensink Sr. For three years, Mensink Jr had remained on an overseas holiday after the collapse of Queensland Nickel when he was the sole director. There were two outstanding Federal Court arrest warrants for Mensink, who was wanted for questioning. The collapse put around 800 people out of work and left them chasing $70 million in unpaid entitlements.

Just weeks after Burston and Palmer dined at Scratchleys, Iskander told the Federal Court he had never actually spoken to his client, Mensink Jr. 'No,' he said. 'My understanding was Mr Palmer was the main conduit of instructions and he had the authority to act on [his nephew Mensink Jr's] behalf, and so therefore I would follow those instructions accordingly.'

Interpol had experienced some difficulty in locating Mensink, although he was tracked down by News Corp living in Bulgaria, having shed half his body weight and acquired a glamorous new girlfriend. As to those who questioned whether or not Palmer was sending money to his fugitive nephew, the billionaire urged them to get stuffed. 'It's my money, he's my nephew and if I want to pay him $1 million a week I will, because I've earned my money hard,' Palmer said.

A few months after his dinner with Burston, Palmer announced he was appointing his nephew to a new job as the European chief of his Titanic II project, including running a new London office. It was hard not to wonder if Palmer's wicked sense of humour was involved in the press release. 'Mr Mensink is the perfect candidate to deliver a world-class experience with Titanic II,' Palmer said. Sadly, however, he explained Mensink could not return to Australia in relation to matters brought against Queensland Nickel, due to a refusal by the special purpose liquidators to meet his travel expenses.

'He has always been available for any actions required by the liquidators. They have always known where he is. I caught up with Mr Mensink in Bulgaria recently and he is most excited about this opportunity. He shares Blue Star Line's passion for recreating the ship of dreams as a symbol of love and peace in the world, playing to the Jack and Rose in all of us.'

Having secured Burston's vital signature to create the United Australia Party in June 2018, Palmer had to wait for the Super Saturday by-elections to take place before he could officially register his new political operation. Under the electoral commission rules, the political party register was frozen until the writs were returned for the by-elections. But the ads for his new party were already starting to pop up all over the country.

On Facebook, Palmer had been pumping out the memes for months. Mostly, the jokes revolved around Tim Tams. 'Gee, that Tim Tam was good,' was a classic post. The sillier the jokes, the more shares. 'Satisfies a woman eleven times in one night,' was another Tim Tam favourite, a meme that featured a photograph of a packet of biscuits. Some involved a Trump-esque rubbishing of the media, including one featuring a police officer approaching a parked car and telling the driver, 'Mate! This spot is for garbage vehicles only!' The comic-strip-style meme then features an image of Buzzfeed reporter Mark Di Stefano's head superimposed into the car, responding, 'I work at Buzzfeed.' The police officer replies, 'Oh, my mistake, sorry for bothering you sir.'

Palmer already had 100,000-plus Facebook followers when he created the 'Palmy Army' to build an online force that could be deployed on social media to attack his enemies. 'Bring your pies, bring your sausage rolls, bring your Yowies, bring your memes,' it declared, 'but DO NOT bring the Greens.'

Members were encouraged to create their own memes about Palmer. After a few days of online meme crafts, the Palmy Army was deployed on 'Operation Turnbull Turnip', targeting Malcolm Turnbull's Facebook page. 'All PALMY ARMY members go to Turnbull page and call him a Turnip!' Palmer's account ordered. 'Yes Turnip. Turnip memes Turnip jokes turnips anything . . . we are going to make this a meme. We will get this all across Facebook and media. Let operation Turnbull Turnip begin!! The force is with us.'

As the media continued to dismiss him as an idiot, the billionaire was assembling an online army of disaffected voters turned off by traditional politics. It was the classic Trump-style tactic. Barnaby Joyce calls them 'I've got the screaming shits' voters. 'They are not Pauline Hanson voters, they are not Howard battlers, they just are angry,' he said. 'And they look for the best mechanism to kick the parties that should have been looking after them in the backside. Clive goes into that space on the same modus operandi as Trump does.'

When Palmer emerged back into public life in 2018, Turnbull didn't have much to say about the new developments. 'As far as Mr Palmer is concerned, I guess all I can say is we have seen that film before,' he said.

But Burston told journalists that Palmer planned to spend $50 million on the election campaign. Australia had not seen that film before at all. 'We have quite an extensive advertising campaign – the media are putting it at $31 million – I believe he's spent more than that,' Burston told the ABC's *7.30* program. 'I believe it will end up around $60 million, so it's going to ramp up from now. We've run about 60,000 TV advertisements across the country to date, and that number is going to increase to about another 90,000, so it's going to be very, very significant.' Once again, nobody believed him. Burston's entirely accurate warning about what Palmer planned to unleash was dismissed by the media as the ravings of a crackpot.

It was probably one of the greatest philanthropic investments in journalism in years: despite bagging the media on Facebook, Palmer's advertising was bankrolling it. He was shovelling money into News Corp, Fairfax and 2GB. However, journalists understandably had doubts about where this would all end up.

'Surely Clive Palmer is one soufflé unlikely to rise twice – although predictions are hazardous when we're talking about a man dedicated to buying votes,' press gallery veteran Michelle Grattan wrote. 'It beggars belief that Palmer, discredited in the political shambles and business disasters and disgraces of the last few years, can be starting out again, planning to run candidates in "all seats" in the House of Representatives and for the Senate.'

CLIVE PALMER AND ADANI

But Palmer was serious. What was hard for the media to decipher in the beginning, though, was how he measured success. Was it really a seat in parliament? Or something else?

Burston had appeared at a press conference in Canberra with his new backer just days after the Newcastle dinner. 'We will unite Australia and we will bring integrity back into the Senate,' Burston pledged.

Labor MP Cathy O'Toole heckled Palmer and Burston throughout the press conference, asking when he was going to pay the former Queensland Nickel workers who maintained they were owed money.

'I don't owe anyone anything in north Queensland,' Palmer replied. He blamed the liquidators and said he planned to reopen his Townsville nickel refinery. 'It was the administrators of Queensland Nickel who, despite the direction of joint venture partners, refused to transfer employees and assets to a new operator, which would have allowed workers to keep their jobs.'

Before too many questions could be answered, the sprinklers erupted in the Parliament House courtyard, and the media and Palmer had to flee his own press conference.

When Palmer had launched the first incarnation of his party in 2013, he had stood as a candidate himself, winning the seat of Fairfax in Queensland. He was catapulted into the House of Representatives, as three of his candidates – Jacquie Lambie in Tasmania, Glenn Lazarus in Queensland and Dio Wang in Western Australia – also secured spots.

He declared, 'If you can't twerk, you can't be prime minister,' before gyrating during FM radio interviews. But two of his senators would ultimately dance out the door and sit as independents. First, Lambie quit just a year after the election. Lazarus followed a few years later, complaining that at times Palmer could be a bully.

'If you're continually berated and, I guess, yelled at, that's got to be a form of bullying, and that was just something I couldn't tolerate for a long period of time,' Lazarus told *Four Corners*. Palmer was photographed falling asleep in Parliament and rarely turning up for votes and divisions.

But for a few years there, he was the kingmaker. Palmer even did a deal to abolish the mining tax that included a surprise element nobody saw coming in September 2014. In the compromise with the Palmer United Party, the Abbott Government agreed to delay the increase in the compulsory superannuation rate to 12 per cent by 2022 until 2025. It seemed to come out of nowhere too, because it wasn't on the original list of demands from Palmer.

Shorten noted that Abbott had promised Australians 'on at least 14 separate occasions not to make any adverse changes to superannuation'. Abolishing the mining tax was a core Coalition commitment, but the delay in the superannuation rise was another broken promise. Labor described the deal, struck by Palmer with Finance Minister Mathias Cormann, as a 'dirty, devious deal'.

It was during this period that Palmer and Cormann got to know each other. Five years later, Cormann was quarantined to barracks at the Liberal Party's campaign headquarters in Queensland during the 2019 federal election. The Western Australian senator copped some criticism from locals for his disappearing act for the duration of the campaign, but his role in the Liberals' war room was more important. As the 'minister-in-residence' at the Coalition HQ in Brisbane, he was embedded in the campaign policy unit. Of course, his location allowed him to catch up with old friends in Queensland, including the billionaire Clive Palmer.

Cormann and Palmer had been dining and dealing for years. Chopsticks at the ready to devour dumplings at their favourite restaurant, China Plate, during parliamentary sitting weeks, the two men loved to eat and talk politics. When Palmer was an MP, the pair sometimes attracted a crowd of photographers and journalists. Palmer was usually ready with a quip about 'doing a deal' over some contentious piece of legislation over fried rice. The billionaire would then return to parliament the next morning in his bright-red electric Tesla car, erupting out of the vehicle to insist nothing had changed.

But dining with Clive Palmer could be a dangerous business. It had previously plunged Malcolm Turnbull into hot water after the pair had enjoyed a meal at another Chinese restaurant, the Wild Duck. The evening fuelled leadership speculation because critics argued Turnbull should not be dining with Palmer. Another dining companion, Treasury Secretary Martin Parkinson, was forced to flee out the back entrance to avoid the television cameras. With Turnbull regarded as a leadership rival, Tony Abbott kept a watchful eye on him, and his supporters flew into a frenzy that the dinner was an act of dishonesty designed to showcase Turnbull's ability to do deals with the key crossbencher.

Palmer loved the attention. 'I had a wonderful banana split – it was fantastic,' he told journalists who'd gathered outside the restaurant. 'I recommend it to all of you, a caramelised banana with coconut ice cream. That was the highlight of the evening for me; that was my focus of the night.' Turnbull was left to fend off claims that what he was really hungry for was Tony Abbott's job as prime minister.

But there were no photographers or television cameras in Brisbane if Palmer and Cormann wanted to catch up during the 2019 election. The journalists were on the road, travelling Australia on the 'Bill Bus', crashing through supermarkets with microphones and cameras and pens and notepads. Cormann and Clive were free to plot and gossip, if they chose to do so, far from the prying eyes of the travelling media party.

Palmer has confirmed they ran into each other a few times, but insisted they did not talk about politics. 'Not politics,' he said. 'Just, you know, have a nice day. I can't recall. I only saw him once or twice.'

Cormann rejected suggestions the pair may have compared notes on advertising or strategy. He dismissed claims he went to Palmer's house for dinner as fanciful, but declined to say how frequently they caught up. 'I don't talk about my campaign diary,' he said. 'I can assure you that Clive did all his own work. We were able to persuade him to preference the Liberal National parties ahead of others – that's it.'

'I can tell you, it wasn't a conspiracy between us and Liberals,' Palmer said in an interview for this book. 'No, there was no direction from any Liberal people to me, in terms of what to do. I don't want to mislead you, I know all of them. But "Shifty Shorten" came out of our focus groups.

'We did some focus groups. We asked them about Bill Shorten. What they said [was] there was something they were not happy [with] about Shorten but they can't put a finger on it. So, I thought about it and I thought, "Well, he's a bit shifty,"' he laughed. 'That's what I came up with. So we conducted a massive advertising campaign on "Shifty Shorten".'

If the attack line did come out of the Palmer focus groups, there's probably one good reason. As any simple Google search reveals, 'Shifty Shorten' was a Liberal Party slogan for years and it was used in multiple advertising campaigns. It was also used by Scott Morrison in parliament, who called Shorten a 'rolled gold failure' and a 'rolled gold fake'. 'What we see in the leader of the opposition is a shifty character – he is shifty as,' Morrison said. Turnbull used the word as well, referring to his 'unaccountable shifty conduct'. That's a big clue that the word came up in Liberal focus groups too and the party was keen to repeat the word to reinforce voters' negative perceptions.

The idea that the Liberal Party entered into a Faustian pact with Palmer to win the election against the odds is a seductive idea for the Labor Party. Former Nationals leader Barnaby Joyce dismissed it. 'I am a cynic but I don't think for one second there was some sort of a clandestine plan between Palmer and the Liberals,' he said. 'Something as Machiavellian as that would have to come out. That is a secret just too big to keep.'

Interestingly, he argues it was not Scott Morrison who won the election but the Nationals Senator Matt Canavan. 'Matt Canavan won the last election, because against the edict that nobody should talk about coal, he went out and talked about coal in central Queensland. And the Labor Party couldn't extinguish that. The Liberals were having conniptions about it. We thought we were going to lose all those seats in central Queensland and we held the lot and won one. So, it is a Coalition agreement spelt C-O-A-L.'

After the election, the Labor Party commissioned an analysis of Palmer's ad spend for the ALP review into the election result. It found the impact of his expenditure was unprecedented in its size, duration and breadth. 'The United Australia Party's campaign spend was more than the advertising budgets for the same period of McDonald's, Foxtel, Telstra or any of the banks,' it stated. 'In fact, the only organisations in the country who outspent Palmer were Harvey Norman, Woolworths, Wesfarmers, Toyota, the Commonwealth Government, and the New South Wales and Victorian state governments. No other political party made it into the top 50 Australian organisations' spending on advertising over that period.'

The impact of the expenditure was to drown out the Labor Party's own advertisements. In advertising, the penetration of a campaign is measured in what is known as a 'share of voice'. Labor's analysis found that if the United Australia Party's advertising activity from January to March was included, the ALP's share of voice declined to about 14 per cent and in some regional markets, such as Townsville and Rockhampton, as low as 10 per cent.

'In the closing stages of the campaign the volume of Palmer's expenditure rapidly increased, and the themes of his advertisements shifted to a much harsher anti-Labor message. Palmer's closing argument was a cartoonishly exaggerated version of the Liberal Party's campaign messages,' it states. 'An industry analysis of Palmer's expenditure commissioned by the National Secretariat demonstrates in the final week of the campaign the United Australia Party's most prominent messages were anti-Labor advertisements which directly targeted Bill Shorten.'

Palmer confirms this was the case. It was a deliberate change in strategy. He said that two weeks before the election he received polling that showed Labor would win and that the UAP would secure several Senate spots but not control the balance of power.

'Let's go back to about maybe 16 days before the election. We got a very extensive poll done, right across the country. It showed we would get about 10 per cent primary at that stage.' The polling, which Palmer claims to have spent $300,000 on, was a robopoll that showed Shorten would have won 84 seats. 'We might have won four seats. The Greens and the ALP would control the government. Who knows if that was right, but we had that poll. We concluded it would be a bad thing for Australia for Bill Shorten to be prime minister. So about that time we directed that we had to attack Shorten to make sure he did not become prime minister. The most important thing, the message was "Don't vote for Labor". We had a deal with News Corp that we would have two pages in every newspaper for the last 14 days of the election.' This was worth millions of dollars alone.

When UAP did the polling again seven days later, Palmer claims the Coalition went up by 7 per cent. These claims are not supported in the polling of the major parties. 'That was a natural consequence of polarising the electorate,' he said. 'But that wasn't enough to get Morrison elected. He still needed our 3.5 per cent of the vote we got on election day. And there was a big flow of our preferences to the Liberal Party.' Does Palmer think he is responsible for getting Morrison elected? 'Yeah, I think so. I think it's generally recognised in Australia that's what happened.'

After the election, Labor President Wayne Swan backed calls for spending caps. 'A $60 million spend by a conservative-aligned billionaire in a preference recycling scheme for the Liberal and National parties cannot be allowed to stand,' he said. 'The characterisation of the Labor policy agenda as radical says more about the state of conservative politics in Australia than it does about Labor.'

But Palmer said his spending would likely be more than the $60 million speculated when he lodged his final expenditure statement with authorities. 'I would have thought $65 to $70 million if you take all the expenditure going back to the billboards. The final figures have got to be lodged with the Australian Electoral Commission, so we are doing a double-check. It will come out somewhere around there. We did pump a lot of money into it.'

Palmer, who previously boasted of 'polarising' the electorate with negative ads, said it was a joke the ALP was calling for caps on spending. 'Let's examine that objectively. First of all, Labor was happy for me to spend as much as I wanted to when they thought I might give them my preferences, right? They asked for my preferences.

'Politicians should focus on the message. Shorten was a flawed leader in the electorate's eyes and, combined with franking credits, that gave us credibility. It's not based on "Clive Palmer spent a lot of money, so we lost government". They need to look closer than that. Remember when Chris Bowen said, "If you don't like it, don't vote for us?" They didn't.'

Shorten would later describe Palmer as 'bombing us into the Stone Age' with his advertising. He believes that Palmer 'doesn't do a deal if there's nothing in it for him'. But Shorten was a shape-shifter himself on climate-change policy. After installing Julia Gillard as prime minister in 2010, he became alarmed that 'the carbon tax is killing us', just one of the reasons he agreed to return to Kevin Rudd as leader, a man who despised Shorten and demanded that he publicly endorse Rudd's return as prime minister as the blood price for him standing as a candidate. Inside the Gillard camp, Shorten was regarded as the weakest link.

However, during the election Shorten restyled himself as a climate-change warrior, albeit one who struggled with answering the question of how much his climate-change policies would cost Australia. It took him a while to settle on the right answer, which was that the cost of doing nothing was greater.

Australian voters repeatedly tell pollsters climate-change action is needed, but baulk at options which would apply price signals and penalties for polluters. The idea you can reduce emissions without any impact on the economy is a nonsense.

And into this debate, three weeks before the election, arrived Bob Brown's Adani convoy. It was a travelling roadshow of activists determined to stop the Adani mine who rumbled through mining towns, including Clermont, the closest to the Adani mine, pissing off locals and generally leaving a trail of furious voters wherever it travelled. Locals shouted abuse at the convoy as it arrived and as it departed.

Massive swings were recorded to the LNP in the Queensland electorates of Capricornia and Dawson, 12 per cent and 11 per cent respectively, despite the controversy surrounding George Christensen's frequent trips overseas. Or perhaps it was because of that, given that, once again, the attacks appeared to come from 'southerners' in the media. Labor recorded a primary vote in the state of 23.7 per cent.

After the election, Greens leader Richard Di Natale said Labor's real problem with issues like the Adani mine was that Shorten didn't pick a lane. He conceded that the Adani convoy hurt Labor for that reason. 'The reason it didn't help Labor was because the Labor Party refused to take a clear position.'

This much Di Natale and Kevin Rudd can agree on, with both accusing Shorten of making the mistake of being 'neither Arthur nor Martha' on the issue of coal and on the Adani mine.

'We should never find ourselves defined, in terms of the appropriateness or otherwise of our climate-change strategy, by what the Greens party says,' Rudd said. 'For them to define the Labor Party's climate-change credentials simply in terms of Adani, I think was a profound political error. To win nationally, you must win Queensland. It is hard. It is not just Brisbane. It is wider southeast Queensland and each of those provincial cities is different.'

Labor also needed to recognise Queensland had 'certain religious sensibilities'. 'You can't just ignore that,' said Rudd. 'You can't just disparage it. You have to work with it.'

As journalist Lech Blaine writes in his essay, 'How Good is Queensland?', the best post-mortem on the state written since the election, Rudd has barely spent longer than a fortnight in Queensland since 2014, but still understands the sensibility. 'Morrison is not dumb,' Rudd said. 'He didn't wave his hands in the air on the Sunday before the election because he was led to do so by the Holy Spirit. He was sending a clarion-clear message that these were his people.' There is one unifying element. 'One thing that unites all Queenslanders,' he said, 'is a general "fuck you" towards people from the south.'

Shorten accepts he read the mood wrongly. 'It pains me that I misread some of the mood in Queensland and Western Australia, where they saw some of our policies as Green-left and not for working-class people. It pains me to realise that people thought we weren't putting jobs first and foremost.'

Soon after the election, Annastacia Palaszczuk's government suddenly fast-tracked the Adani approvals. 'The community is sick of it, I'm sick of it, everyone is sick of the delays,' the Queensland premier said. 'Everyone has had more than enough time to resolve these issues and for some reason that has not occurred. That all ends now.'

Less than a month after the election, on 13 June, it got the tick of approval. Both the Australian Marine Conservation Society and the Australian Conservation Foundation warned the decision put the Great Barrier Reef at risk. 'If it goes ahead, Adani's mine and its coal will wreck our climate, steal our groundwater, trash Indigenous rights and irreversibly damage the Great Barrier Reef,' the ACF said. 'Adani's mine is a climate crime – a crime against humanity and our planet.'

Shorten admits that if the Queensland state government had made a decision earlier, it may have saved Labor a lot of grief. It also would have saved his office a lot of grief. They'd taken to referring to Labor's climate-change spokesman Mark Butler as the 'Grim Reaper', for his propensity to pop up somewhere giving a speech on why he didn't like Adani every time Shorten travelled to Queensland. 'I've personally said that I think that opening up a new coal basin in the Galilee Basin in Queensland is not in the national interest,' said Butler in February, 'because I think the business case that was presented for opening up this basin 10 years ago was dissolved – it has disappeared.' As he spoke, Shorten was in Townsville, in the marginal Labor seat of Herbert.

In his final address to the ALP caucus after the election, Shorten laid the blame on Palmer's ad spend. 'We were up against corporate leviathans, a financial behemoth, spending unprecedented hundreds of millions of dollars advertising, telling lies, spreading fear,' he said. 'Powerful vested interests campaigned against us through sections of the media itself, and they got what they wanted.'

But what was it that Palmer really wanted? The 85-year old Australian Workers' Union President Bill Ludwig offers a blunt assessment. 'He just wanted to fuck us over,' he said. 'He got what he paid for.'

However, Ludwig was not surprised Labor lost. 'No, I wasn't surprised at all. The mining industry in Queensland is paramount. You see you can't make policy in Melbourne and Sydney for Queensland.' Ludwig points to Deputy Labor Leader Richard Marles' claim during the election that it was a good thing the coal industry would soon be a thing of the past. 'That was stupid. I've known Richard for a long time. That's the very thing I am talking about – some guy in Melbourne criticising Queensland.

'They don't understand the impact. It's not just the coal miners but everything that goes with it. It's entrenched in their DNA. All the workers, the support staff and contractors. You can't just overnight say, "This is bad." If you raise concerns you are anti-mines, workers may decide, "Well, we can't take the risk." [Queensland Treasurer] Jackie Trad, in particular, she was on the wrong tram, being anti-coal mining. Queensland. You can't do it.'

After the election, *Guardian Australia* reported that a Clive Palmer controlled company, Waratah Coal, had applied for a mining lease to build a massive coal mine four times the size of Adani's in Queensland's Galilee Basin. A modest notice in the classified section of a weekly newspaper based in Emerald, Queensland was the only sign to the outside world of the latest developments. But Palmer's ambitious plans were hardly a secret – in the final 10 days of the election campaign he had promised to build the new coal-fired power station. He predicted the new venture would help bring down power prices for Australian families.

But what about politics? Would Palmer have another crack at parliament? It's not like he doesn't have the cash. This is Labor's fear. It would seem, however, that Australia's mining billionaire is content for now. His political foray, dismissed as a circus and a joke by the media, has helped secure the future of his mining interests and potentially millions of dollars in profits. He is a man with the contented air of someone who has just played Australia's political elite for mugs.

'I think my days in politics are over, don't you? I just want a quiet life.'

16

NOT CHANGING THE RULES

Sally McManus, the woman who would become the ACTU's first female secretary, and Bill Shorten were among the 58 new recruits to the ACTU's inaugural trainee program in 1994. The program was the brainchild of Bill Kelty and another union leader, Chris Walton. After surviving the 1993 'Fightback!' election against John Hewson, the union movement began sandbagging for a Labor defeat. It was a 12-month training course including some residential retreats. The chances of Labor winning another term were slim and the ACTU wanted to prepare for a more deregulated industrial-relations future under an incoming Liberal government. Walton travelled overseas to examine union organising in the United States. Kelty, an AFL fanatic, was a student of the regeneration of teams and was interested in what the Australian union movement could learn from the US, where workers were far less unionised and organising workers was more difficult.

Shorten was 27 and straight out of the law firm Maurice Blackburn. 'The union was only a stepping stone to his political career,' Walton said. 'He found a way in, which was this traineeship.' He had started work at the AWU the same year. 'I am pretty sure his first day on the job was with us – he became a trainee with the Australian Workers' Union. Obviously, it was an orchestrated entry into the union movement and on to a broader career with the AWU.' Shorten was a man on the rise – it was obvious that federal politics or state parliament was his destination and the union movement was the vehicle.

Shorten, who was bulkier and wore glasses at the time, was a notable character among his colleagues in the training course.

'He was always pointed out by others in the group to be there for his political career,' Walton confirmed. 'They would say, "Bill, you're going to be PM one day, are you?" Because he was so ambitious and he was such a player at the time. It oozed out of him. He was very funny about it, joking, "You better look up to me, because I *might* be PM one day."'

A *Four Corners* documentary later captured the former lawyer turning up at building sites having ditched his business suit for a denim jacket. He learned on the job. One union official had to tell him that his blow-ups and aggression in a meeting with an employer were 'embarrassing' and he moderated his conduct. The lesson was that getting a better deal for workers also involved good relationships with employers.

Sally McManus appeared to be more of your garden-variety Macquarie University student radical. She had also joined the first ACTU trainee intake after accepting an invitation from Kelty to join the Australian Services Union.

'He [Shorten] was in Victoria and Sally McManus was in Sydney,' said Walton, 'so they didn't have a lot to do with each other, except at the residential. But George Wright had a bit to do with him. He was at the LHMU [Liquor, Hospitality and Miscellaneous Workers' Union]. He got on pretty well with Bill but they were pretty different people. George is a pretty strapping, football player type. Bill was your classic, retail politician. But he was a prolific organiser – I think he signed up 400 people. And he was on the rise.'

Wright recalls that everyone knew Shorten was someone who was going to be a significant figure in the union movement.

Working for the AWU changed Shorten. 'Despite Bill really using it as a stepping stone, he did genuinely connect with people,' Walton said. 'He said to me later – that year or two really got him to connect with real people, rather than politics being a game. I remember him ringing me one night in tears because one of his key leaders in a workplace had been killed in a forklifting accident. It was very genuine how upset he was.'

Shorten rose to national prominence as a result of the Beaconsfield mine collapse in 2006. Three of the miners working underground were trapped and unaccounted for: Larry Knight, Brant Webb and Todd Russell. Knight was killed in the rock fall, but Webb and Russell survived. The miners kept alive for 14 days drinking groundwater collected in their helmets and sharing a muesli bar. When the owners of the mine showed little appetite for media updates, Shorten stepped in, emerging as a daily fixture on *Sunrise* and the *Today* show. Later, it provided more evidence of his friendships with the top end of town – he borrowed billionaire Richard Pratt's private jet to return to Beaconsfield when the men were found.

For years, Shorten had been spoken of as a potential Labor leader, as had Greg Combet. Some colleagues saw them as rivals. Some Labor officials claimed they hated each other.

Bob Hawke had anointed Combet as a potential Labor leader for years. But Kelty, who was close to Paul Keating, was pushing Shorten as the man most likely.

Some Labor officials familiar with the pair's relationship say Combet regarded Shorten as 'insubstantial' and 'a PR machine with no depth'. Some Victorian leaders called him 'Showbags Shorten'.

But Combet insists talk of a rivalry with Shorten is overblown. 'He's a talented guy – I didn't have any objection to that,' he said. 'But typically what it was about was – I was the Left person and he was the Right person. We were both cast into that role. And I was NSW and he was Victoria – like, every traditional faultline in the Labor Party, we fell on either side of it.'

Over the years, McManus had developed a reputation as an innovative campaigner at the ASU and helped run the 'Medi-scare' campaign at the 2016 election. This featured union members handing out fake Medicare cards, claiming the Turnbull Government planned to privatise Medicare. Her union was also involved with a landmark equal pay case that won pay rises of up to 50 per cent for 150,000 community workers. When the ACTU Secretary Dave Oliver resigned in 2017, she stepped up.

During McManus's first televised interview, she was asked by *7.30*'s Leigh Sales if she would distance herself from the militant Construction, Forestry, Mining and Energy Union, which had faced 118 separate legal proceedings in various courts around Australia.

'There's no way we'll be doing that,' McManus said. 'The CFMEU, when they've been fined, they've been fined for taking industrial action. It might be illegal industrial action according to our current laws, and our current laws are wrong. I believe in the rule of law when the law is fair and the law is right. But when it's unjust I don't think there's a problem with breaking it.'

The Liberal Party went berserk over the remarks. Liberal frontbencher Christopher Pyne described her comments as 'anarcho-Marxist claptrap'. Home Affairs Minister Peter Dutton announced that 'a maniac is leading the ACTU'. Shorten was forced to distance himself from the remarks. 'I just don't agree,' he said. 'If you don't like a law, if you think a law is unjust, use the democratic process to get it changed,' he said.

Business Council of Australia Chief Executive Jennifer Westacott said McManus's comments could have dangerous consequences by 'signalling to individuals around the country that it's okay to take the law into their own hands'.

'What kind of society will we have if everyone can simply choose to ignore any laws they don't like?' she said. 'How do you explain this to your children? You don't like the law so you just ignore it?'

But if the media expected McManus would issue an apology when she addressed the National Press Club just weeks later, they were mistaken. 'The very wealthy have too much power in our country, and ordinary Australians – working people – do not have enough,' she said. She spoke of defying 'unjust laws' and 'wage theft' and flagged that the ACTU would seek a $45 a week increase in the minimum wage.

In many ways she outlined the core issues that would form the basis for the ACTU's 'Change the Rules' campaign. She also claimed that 'the neoliberal experiment has run its course' as an effective economic framework. Dutton continued his attack, describing her as 'a modern-day communist'. But McManus was confident that the time for real change had arrived. 'We're going to change where the centre is,' she said. 'If we win public opinion, we expect Labor to deliver on that.'

It was with the same goal in mind that the ACTU launched 'Change the Rules'. 'To change the rules, we need to change the government,' said McManus. 'We will do this by talking to as many people as we can about which political parties have, and which have not, committed to a fair go for working people. We want to live in a country where people have jobs they can count on and fair pay rises. The Morrison

Government and big business are standing in the way of secure jobs and fair pay rises, and the union movement is ready to restore the fair go.'

Unions spent somewhere between $17 million and $25 million on 'Change the Rules'. The pendulum had swung too far toward big business,' McManus said. 'We need to change the rules at work so working people can't be held to ransom by bad employers who will use loopholes to cancel agreements, cut pay and slash conditions.'

The campaign evolved into a plan to target 16 seats at the 2019 election. These included Gilmore in NSW and Dunkley and Corangamite in Victoria. But Labor was defeated in Bass and Braddon in Tasmania, and so delivered a net gain of a single seat – before you consider the loss of Herbert in Queensland, which takes the equation down to zero. Every single Queensland seat targeted – Forde, Capricornia, Flynn, Petrie, Leichhardt and Herbert – was lost. Even more controversial was the targeting of blue-ribbon Liberal seats, including Kooyong, Higgins, Flinders, Menzies and Deakin. It was a big investment for little result.

But there were concerns about the cut-through of the campaign slogan months before the election.

'When you go in with a slogan that's "Change the Rules", you've got to wonder, what are people going to think that means?' said Greg Combet. 'When we did "Your Rights at Work", we tested everything. I am not sure the "Change the Rules" campaign was resonating.

'The temptation in the union movement, and I was guilty of it too often, is that you are so enmeshed in the system – the industrial relations system – that's where your mind is. You're thinking about the rights of unions. Whereas of course for the real issue, where you need to live, is people's rights. For example, arguing for right of entry for a union official, as distinct from the right of an employee to have someone to come and help them. I made that mistake too.'

Critics of the campaign, including ex-ACTU Assistant Secretary Tim Lyons, described it as a 'hubristic vanity project'. 'What does it actually mean? If you think back to "Your Rights at Work", there was a very confident proposition, which was the repealing of WorkChoices, which is something people could get their heads around. I am just not sure anybody could really answer the question about what "Change the Rules" actually meant. Now I think the idea was probably for people to read into it their pet issue, but I think the evidence is in now – it just didn't actually work.'

After the election, a review of the 'Change the Rules' campaign, led by former Queensland MP Evan Moorhead, found it wasn't well understood beyond officials and activists. 'Even for simpler messages like "Australia needs a pay rise", it was hard to explain the direct and immediate link between election outcome, policy reform and changed wage levels,' the report found. 'The focus on establishing a policy reform mandate for an incoming Labor government meant that the Change the Rules campaign became focused on policy prescriptions rather than problems facing voters.' This was the idea raised by the ALP's own election review about affiliates and supporters 'banking the win'.

The ACTU review describes Scott Morrison as 'a clever marketing executive' who worked to define himself as a humble suburban father in a baseball cap, making awkward attempts at sport, who separated himself from the toxic LNP brand by running a one-man campaign. Morrison also accepted the recommendations of the migrant workers' inquiry on wage theft in an attempt to remove workers' rights from the election agenda.

'The Change the Rules campaign had started with a Prime Minister who the public understood as a risk to their working conditions, but now faced a Prime Minister that sought to portray himself as someone on the side of working people … In fact, the LNP Government went to extraordinary lengths to avoid workplace rights being an issue at the Federal election, desperately trying to nullify issues like wage theft and casualisation.'

There was also a danger that talk of increasing the right to strike and industrial action could prove a turn-off for some voters. 'If a policy proposal is too radical, the LNP will undoubtedly use that proposal as an attack on the Union campaign or Labor. In previous election campaigns, State and Federal, LNP campaigns have attacked Labor and Union policies for working rights as radical or as an example of wrong priorities.'

During the election, Morrison did try to ramp up the idea that McManus would enjoy too much power under a Labor government. 'Sally McManus will now be a board member, figuratively, on every single one of your companies,' he said. 'The union movement will be in control of your businesses if the Labor Party are elected. So much for you running your business if Bill Shorten is elected. They want control of Australia's building industry again. They want control of every site. They want control over every decision you make.'

At the 2018 ALP national conference, the 'Change the Rules' policy agenda was embedded in the ALP policy platform. It was another sign the union movement was focused on locking Labor into what changes it would introduce after the victory — assuming the win, rather than campaigning for votes.

'The widely held view that Labor would win the election also meant that the campaign became incredibly dependent on policy announcements from Labor,' the ACTU review found. 'The Change the Rules campaign ended up being swamped by an LNP fear campaign on tax, and a Clive Palmer fear campaign on tax and a Labor campaign that did not make Change the Rules issues a key choice at the election.'

The election result was not entirely a surprise to McManus. Even though the union's polling had Labor in front, it was too close to be confident. Months earlier, its polling had started detecting that the Medevac laws that allowed sick asylum seekers to return to Australia were creating issues for the Labor Party in Queensland.

'I knew that something was not right, especially in the last two weeks,' McManus said. 'For most of the election campaign there was an uneasy anxiety but the polls kept saying something else.' And then there was the retiree tax, including fake claims that McManus supported a death tax. 'It just grew and grew and grew. What I saw happen was a subterranean social media campaign. It's an area that's unregulated and is almost impossible to stop.'

The election result left McManus's reputation as a formidable campaigner bruised. But worse was to come when the scandal she had been quietly grappling with for months, surrounding the arrest of CFMEU leader John Setka, exploded into the media. On Boxing Day 2018, it emerged Setka had been arrested after police were called to an argument at his home. He was later charged with sending a woman abusive text messages. It was an open secret in Melbourne that the woman was his wife, Emma Walters, but under Victorian family violence laws it could not be reported. The couple were well known in Melbourne in union and legal circles.

Setka and his wife, a lawyer, were in the grip of a marriage breakdown, and it would soon emerge that, after his arrest, Walters had fled Victoria with her two children en route to family in Adelaide. On the way, she was arrested for speeding and drink driving. Months later, she escaped a criminal conviction after pleading guilty to driving with a blood alcohol level more than five times the legal limit. Instead, the court imposed a 12-month community correction order focused on rehabilitation and suspended her licence in Victoria for two years.

Setka's arrest and the allegations against him sparked a bitter rift with his deputy Shaun Reardon, who, among other jobs, had earlier operated and controlled Setka's Twitter account. It was something of an in-joke in union circles that the technologically challenged Setka didn't even write his own tweets. The men had previously been close. They were arrested and charged with blackmail in December 2015 over a dispute with building products company Boral. The case took a heavy toll on both men, with Setka blaming the ordeal for some of his behaviour towards his wife. He was arrested in front of his children. Three years later, the charges were dropped.

McManus was on a train in Europe when she read a leaked dossier of the range of family-violence allegations against Setka. The leak was designed to put pressure on the union movement to force him out. But complicating matters for McManus was her friendship, not only with Setka but Walters. It was Walters who urged the union and McManus not to sack her husband, after the couple reconciled and attended counselling together. Walters saw the attempt to remove her husband from his job in the wake of their family-violence issues as an intrusion into their personal lives.

But McManus formed the view that the union movement could not possibly countenance the allegations contained in the dossier. 'If any of these allegations are correct, John Setka must resign,' she said. 'There is no place for perpetrators of domestic violence in leadership positions in our movement.'

Setka's response to the leak of the dossier was to try to explain the circumstances he found himself in to the next meeting of the CFMEU. It was during this meeting that he complained that while women had previously been badly treated by domestic violence laws, now the pendulum had swung so hard in the opposite direction that he couldn't speak to his own wife. He struggled to understand that the law was also there to protect both parties after their heated blow-up at Christmas. While he did not attack domestic violence campaigner Rosie Batty, he did say that after high-profile campaigns, including her own, the laws had become too onerous in stopping couples reconciling.

After his comments leaked, he was accused of denigrating Batty, which he argued was a misunderstanding of his remarks. 'This is dirty politics and this is wrong,' he said. 'I've got the utmost respect for Rosie Batty. It's sickening to me.'

Batty wanted to know what Setka meant when he suggested her work had led to men having fewer rights. 'If it means the right to harm, to threaten, to intimidate, to bully and use violence, then yes that's fair enough,' she said. 'I'm quite incredulous really that my name has been utilised in this way because I've never met the man. I've never heard his name and I didn't know who he was until this came about.'

For the recently elected Labor leader Anthony Albanese, the latest transgression of involving Batty – who had lost her only son to family violence in 2014 – was too much. He held a press conference confirming that his intention was to expel Setka from the Labor Party.

However, Setka remained defiant. 'Albo wants to expel me for that? Please. I've been elected by the union members. They are my bosses. If they want me to leave, I will step down tomorrow. But I am not going to stand down over innuendo and lies people have made up. This is dirty ALP politics.'

At first, the Labor Party argued that the move to expel Setka did not relate to the criminal charges. 'Of course, my actions don't relate to anything that is before the courts,' Albanese told the ABC's *7.30*. 'What they relate to is the views that Mr Setka has put forward on a range of issues that are, frankly, out of line – not just with the Labor Party, but out of line with mainstream Australian views.' Albanese also conceded he had no power to remove Setka from the CFMEU. 'Well, that's right. He's elected as the secretary of the union and that is a matter for the union. If he is not a member of the Labor Party he can't participate in any Labor Party forums. It is that clear.'

But after Setka pleaded guilty in June to one count of persistently breaching a family violence intervention order and one charge related to using a phone or carriage service to harass, Albanese formally added those offences to the long list of transgressions. 'We recognise that domestic violence is an issue in which excuses simply need to stop. We need to send messages that they are unacceptable, that there are consequences, and that society will say no to domestic violence. I'll continue to pursue Mr Setka's expulsion from the Labor Party.'

Setka's wife insisted that, while the text messages constituted family violence, he was never physically violent towards her. 'I was drinking too much to try and escape everything. Then I went, "I can't do this any longer," and that I'm not going insane. "This is wrong and it has to stop." I completely reject the characterisation of myself as the victim going back for more. I wouldn't have gone back to this relationship if I didn't think John could change.'

The Victorian branch of the CFMEU that Setka leads had donated $4 million to the ALP and the ACTU to fight the election.

But now Setka warned Labor that his union planned to stop bankrolling the party. 'What I said was no more money to the ALP. We are freezing everything. Not one more cent. The $12 million the ACTU spent, they might as well have gone down the racetrack and gone to the Crown casino and got a better return. It's pretty bad. They fucked it all.'

Finally, in October 2019, Setka agreed to resign from the party. He claimed that Albanese's support for the government's free-trade deals with Indonesia, Peru and Hong Kong were a trigger. Albanese naturally banked it as a victory. 'One of my first acts as leader of the Labor Party was to take action to suspend John Setka from membership of the Australian Labor Party,' he said. 'Australian Labor respects women. Australian Labor wants an industrial relations system that is orderly and treats people with respect.'

Albanese was a no-show for the Victorian ALP conference a month later, where a face-to-face clash with Setka was a real possibility. McManus did not resile from her calls for Setka to stand down from the union, particularly after crossbench senator Jacqui Lambie urged him to quit if the ALP wanted her vote on the Morrison Government's bill to crack down on unions, unveiled shortly after the election. The laws would have made it easier to deregister a union or union official. But Pauline Hanson shocked the government and even some Labor MPs when she voted down the laws with Lambie in late November. The CFMEU leadership in Queensland were among the lobbyists who convinced Hanson that the laws went too far. Once again, Setka survived.

17

THE BALLAD OF KAILA MURNAIN

She was hailed a trailblazer for women who could clean up the sleaze and corruption in the Labor Party. The NSW branch's first female secretary, Kaila Murnain, 32, promised to end a toxic, sexist, destructive culture she had been marinating in for years. She was appointed to the job amid a sex scandal involving her predecessor, Jamie Clements, who had an extramarital affair with a colleague before they broke it off and the woman accused him of harassment.

Murnain was expected to enter politics and was even promoted, somewhat preposterously, as having the potential of New Zealand Prime Minister Jacinda Ardern. But just days before Setka's exit from the ALP, Murnain resigned in disgrace from her job. Proof again that in politics, as in life, nothing lasts forever.

Murnain had worked for the ALP since she was a teenager. She was not a child, but she was hardly a wise old hand to put in charge of running the rotten borough of the NSW branch. Her work ethic was unquestionable, but she was quick to conflict – a character trait that had made her enemies. She struggled with feeling that she was not treated with the same respect as her male colleagues and that made her ruthless at times too. She had attended her first ALP conference at the age of just 15. By 19, she was running the ALP's office on the Central Coast while juggling university studies. By 29, she was running the ALP in NSW. Just four years later, her career in the ALP was over.

Every serious job she had ever had involved working for the NSW Right, including countless hours as a volunteer. But the ALP wasted little time in disposing of her – 'a broken person', according to NSW Labor leader Jodi McKay, who insisted she would never work in politics again.

Her enemies celebrated her demise with an enthusiasm that was brutal. In Roman times there was a name for it, *Damnatio ad bestias*, being mauled to death by wild animals in an amphitheatre. It was popular entertainment for the lower classes of Rome, and if the victim was particularly despised or the crime heinous, smaller animals were used to attack the victim and prolong the agony.

And so it was in the newsrooms across Sydney and in the privacy of Labor MPs' own offices, a 32-year-old woman's destruction was cheered on with a savagery that would have pleased Ancient Rome. Still, she was a difficult person to feel sympathetic for after the ALP leaked her salary. After she was suspended from her job in August, Murnain continued to have her $300,000-a-year wages deposited in her bank account for months. If the money seems ridiculous – and it was – consider the fate of her predecessors. Most had political careers that ended in scandal and disgrace. It was danger money.

Her crime was to keep a secret. Years earlier, she had learned that a banned Chinese billionaire, Huang Xiangmo, may have been responsible for a big donation to the ALP. The $100,000 donation had been unceremoniously dumped at NSW Labor's HQ in an Aldi bag during the tenure of her former boss Jamie Clements. The pair had a poisonous relationship. What did Murnain do about it when she found out? Certainly, she couldn't call Clements to discuss the issue. Her evidence to ICAC was that she did nothing, on the advice of a Labor lawyer. This was a big problem.

It was illegal for the NSW branch to accept the donation from a property developer. There was also a cap on individual donations. Which is why, according to evidence at ICAC, an elaborate conspiracy to find fake straw donors was developed. It was also why Murnain was so frightened. The Chinese Friends of Labor dinner in March 2015, where the $100,000 was pledged, was attended by Bill Shorten and NSW Labor leader Luke Foley. As was the established practice, the politicians were photographed grinning with the Chinese billionaire on the top table. While there was no prohibition on him donating to Shorten's campaign, it was completely illegal for him to donate to the state branch because of his property development links. Concerns he was running a Chinese foreign-influence operation targeting both sides of politics would emerge later.

The first hint of trouble arrived on 18 December 2018, when ICAC raided the NSW ALP's Sussex Street headquarters. Murnain and her staff were in Adelaide for the ALP conference – a carefully choreographed event designed to showcase Shorten as Australia's next prime minister. The news shocked delegates attending the conference. The steely and determined Murnain managed to smuggle herself out and avoid the cameras. Luckily, many of the assembled journalists wouldn't know what she looked like, if they weren't from NSW.

At the time, Murnain put out a public statement pledging co-operation. 'The donations in question were received in 2015 and have been fully investigated by the NSW Electoral Commission with the full co-operation of NSW Labor, including the provision of all relevant documents,' she said. It was months later that ICAC hauled her in to be interviewed under oath. But even during her first compulsory private examination by ICAC in July 2019, Murnain did not initially tell them everything she knew. This was a decision that could have dealt her serious legal consequences. After considering her options, she returned several weeks later and requested a second interview to tell the truth, before delivering her explosive evidence at public hearings in August.

On the first day of hearings, Counsel Assisting the Commission Scott Robertson revealed that Murnain had told ICAC she had reasons to believe the $100,000 donation at the centre of the raid was from a banned donor.

'Murnain said that Mr Wong [NSW Labor MLC Ernest Wong] told her that Mr Huang Xiangmo was the true source of the funds said to have been donated by that other person,' he said. 'Of course, Ms Murnain's statement as to what Mr Wong is said to have told her is not, of itself, conclusive proof that there were one or more "straw donors" or "pretend donors" associated with the Chinese Friends of Labor function in 2015, or that there was a scheme to conceal the fact that Mr Huang was the true source of funds deposited in NSW Labor and Country Labor's bank accounts.'

The hearings, where Murnain's career would spectacularly implode, were open to the public and the media. Outside, camera crews and journalists would gather in a scrum lobbing questions at witnesses as they arrived and departed. Inside, journalists were voluntarily quarantined to a media room, crammed around small tables and listening to the evidence on a big screen. It allowed reporters to file stories and make phone calls while they listened to the evidence.

For a while, Murnain held up under questioning. But eventually, as her voice cracked and it became clear she would cry, her laboured breathing broadcast into the media room with the volume turned up, one jaded reporter groaned in disgust. 'Here come the water works,' he announced. Murnain promptly sobbed in the witness box.

She seemed enthusiastic to inform ICAC about who had accompanied her to her first meeting with Huang. It was Labor's Treasury spokesman. 'Chris Bowen and others introduced me to Huang,' she said. 'Ernest Wong was there as well. We met at Huang's office.'

In her own evidence, she revealed that, on 16 September 2016, just days after Labor Senator Sam Dastyari had been forced to resign from the frontbench over links to Huang Xiangmo, she was called at short notice to a clandestine meeting. Prime Minister Malcolm Turnbull was calling for a ban on foreign donations. Concerns about foreign-influence operations targeting political parties were highly elevated and splashed across the nation's newspapers.

'Ernest [Wong] was quite distressed,' Murnain said. 'He sort of just blurted out that a donor who had said they'd given money to the Labor Party had not actually given money to the Labor Party. I just said, "Who donated the money?" And he said very quickly, "Mr Huang."' Murnain said she stepped back, in shock, as the magnitude of what she had just been told sunk in. 'What the shit?' she replied. But instead of reporting this 'shit' to the electoral authorities, she did nothing.

Wong's phone records confirm he made three calls after speaking to Murnain: to the alleged donor Huang Xiangmo, another Chinese property developer Jonathan Yee and an ALP official Kenrick Cheah, who had taken possession of the $100,000 when it was delivered to the ALP office in the bag. It was Yee who had told Wong the day before that the 'shit had hit the fan' and he couldn't lie about it anymore. Wong later gave evidence that Murnain put her hand up when Huang's name was mentioned as if to say, 'Don't tell me anymore.'

But she did tell someone. 'I called Sam Dastyari,' she told ICAC. When Murnain revealed that her first call was to the man dubbed 'Shanghai Sam' over his own Chinese donor links, audible gasps and laughter erupted in the media room at ICAC. It was an interesting choice. When Dastyari pulled up in his car to help Murnain with her 'freak out' about Huang Xiangmo that night in September 2016, it was just over a week after he'd been forced to resign from the frontbench.

Dastyari told ICAC that Murnain had called him in a panic. The pair drove around Sydney, Murnain crying. 'Kaila was shitting herself, right?' he said. 'She was very distressed, she was very upset. I recall that she specifically singled out Huang Xiangmo as someone she was concerned about.' Dastyari urged her to 'cover her arse' and go to the party's lawyers to sort it out.

According to Murnain, she headed straight to the offices of the ALP's lawyer Ian Robertson. At 7.18 pm, her phone records reveal she texted the managing partner of Holding Redlich, 'I'm at the top of the escalator.' Robertson had looked after Bob Hawke's affairs for years and was a trusted source of advice and wisdom. Murnain's evidence to ICAC was that the lawyer's advice was to stay quiet and forget what Wong had told her. If there was no hard evidence that what Wong said was correct, why overreact? Was it anything more than gossip?

'At the end of the conversation, Ian said to me, "There is no need to do anything from here,"' Murnain told ICAC. '"Don't record this meeting. Don't put it in your diary. Forget the conversation happened with Ernest. I won't be billing you for this either ... and don't tell anyone about it."'

This was a shocking allegation that drew gasps at the hearing. The managing partner of Holding Redlich said nothing on the day, leaving his evidence for the witness box. Later, his own lawyer Tony McInerney, SC dismissed this story as a 'pack of lies' designed to throw the lawyer under the bus to 'colloquially cover your own backside'. He confronted Murnain in a brutal cross-examination. 'They're fake tears, aren't they, Ms Murnain?' he said. 'They're not real.'

But here's the curious thing about that night and Murnain's tearful drive around the streets of Sydney. Dastyari's own evidence is that he never, ever asked her about it again. A mentor to Murnain, he took no further interest in the matter. Despite the fact that the pair were in daily contact, sometimes calling each other a dozen times a day.

For Dastyari, the donor saga had started in 2014, when he declared that the Yuhu Group – which was owned by Huang and was a big Labor donor – had paid his fees in a legal matter. Then, in August 2016, it was revealed that the Sydney-based Top Education Institute had repaid a debt on his behalf. A political fixer, Dastyari was used to finding solutions to problems. As the NSW ALP secretary, finding donors to fix little financial problems was part of the job description. It only dawned on him later this was a weird thing to do when you are a politician earning $200,000 a year. You don't get political donors to pay personal debts. Like his protégé Murnain, Dastyari had been marinating in the NSW Right's 'whatever it takes' culture for so long that he didn't seem to know right from wrong.

It also emerged that 'two bottles of wine' he'd been gifted by the Yuhu Group were actually Penfolds Grange. It was all declared properly to parliament, but it hardly passed the pub test.

Dastyari visited Huang Xiangmo in October 2016, just a few weeks after his drive around Sydney with Murnain during her 'freak out'. Exactly what was said in his final meeting with the billionaire at his Mosman mansion is unknown, but it was life-changing. Ultimately, it ended his political career and forced his resignation from parliament. Just a year after the drive with Murnain, he was gone from politics. Later, he was accused of providing counter-surveillance advice to Huang, warning him that his phone might be bugged. All of these discussions required a translator, because the billionaire did not speak English. So there was a witness to all of the exchanges.

'I reject any assertion that I did anything other than put to Mr Huang gossip being spread by journalists,' Dastyari said at the time. 'After the events of last year, I spoke to Mr Huang to tell him that I did not think it was appropriate that we have future contact. I thought it was a matter of common courtesy to say this face to face. I have never received a security-agency briefing, or received any classified information about any matter, ever. I've never passed on any protected information – I've never been in possession of any.'

But what else did he talk to the Chinese billionaire about in that meeting? Did he ask about the $100,000 donation? Sadly, this was not a question Dastyari was asked about at

ICAC or one that he answered as he arrived at the ICAC hearings, performing his lime-green share-bike vaudeville for the cameras.

This was one of the maddening elements of ICAC's investigation into Chinese donations. While evidence was drawn on the purpose of the donations, to buy influence within the ALP and the Liberal Party, it was not the focus of the inquiry. ICAC left many unanswered questions. Dastyari did tell the corruption inquiry in private evidence that he now accepted Huang Xiangmo may have been an 'agent of influence' for the Chinese government. His views are recorded in the transcript of his initial interview.

'In hindsight, I now have serious questions about whether or not he was, either directly or indirectly, an agent of influence for the Chinese government,' he said. 'He was a very big donor – probably, outside the trade-union movement, the biggest donor.'

In 2019, *Sydney Morning Herald* journalist Peter Hartcher wrote, in a *Quarterly Essay* on Chinese influence, that Murnain had called Labor's Defence spokesman Stephen Conroy on 17 June 2016 and complained, 'Steve, if you don't change your China position, we are going to lose $400,000.' It was reported that Conroy told Murnain in blunt terms he was not going to change his policy on matters of national security because of what a Chinese donor said.

Murnain herself expressly rejects this claim and insists that Hartcher never called her about it. 'The quote Peter Hartcher attributes to me in his *Quarterly Essay* is rubbish. I never said that.'

As communications minister, Conroy had already blocked China's Huawei from the NBN on national security agencies' advice. But he had become alive to what was regarded internally as a wholesale takeover of the NSW Labor Party by China's Communist Party during the debate over a free trade deal. It was a lengthy process after Tony Abbott and Chinese President Xi Jinping announced the conclusion of negotiations for the China–Australia Free Trade Agreement (ChAFTA) in 2014.

The NSW Right 'went nuts', according to Victorian MPs, about the prospect of not signing the China free trade agreement. The hardcore pressure from the NSW MPs who regarded the Chinese donations as precious was ferocious. Penny Wong and the Left were broadly supportive of signing the deal on policy grounds, while Shorten continued to negotiate a deal balancing the demands of the NSW Right, unions and Conroy's opposition. 'We didn't think they were stupid enough to take orders from Beijing,' a Labor figure said.

Former Labor MP Michael Danby later wrote that, at times, he felt he was one of the few who could see clearly that the rise of an aggressive China had many unforeseen consequences.

'Most New South Wales Labor MPs are patriots, with the dishonourable exception of a cabal from the NSW Right, led by their head of ideology Bob Carr, recently of Beijing's favourite think-tank – the Australia-China Research Institute,' he said. 'The NSW ICAC has shown these include people who would willingly take bungs from Beijing's influence-peddlers. Indeed, ICAC has rightly damned both sides of politics in NSW, where the spirit of the Rum Corps has inspired an ongoing tradition of malfeasance, with only its worst practitioners ending up in jail.'

But Danby maintains that Shorten and Conroy 'held the line' against the NSW Right. 'Together, they were a powerful counter against the mercenary instincts of some of our sleazy NSW colleagues, who at times seemed practically hypnotised by the shiny gold coins of Beijing's billionaire agents of influence.'

But back when Dastyari first cultivated Huang Xiangmo as a donor, it was hardly unusual to accept gifts from the billionaire. For example, in 2013 Scott Morrison had declared to parliament's register of members' interests that Huang had given him a Mont Blanc pen worth hundreds of dollars. Former Liberal MP and Trade Minister Andrew Robb was a big fan. In December 2013, he praised the billionaire as 'a visionary'. 'He's a very thoughtful, cerebral fellow. I've had many interesting conversations already with Mr Huang on an endless range of topics.'

These fascinating discussions were presumably with the assistance of an interpreter. After he quit politics, Robb went to work for another billionaire, Ye Chang, for $880,000 a year.

But Australia's spy agency, ASIO, had been trying to warn the major political parties for years. Director-General Duncan Lewis personally briefed former Liberal Federal Director Brian Loughnane and ALP Secretary George Wright in August 2015. He did not tell them to stop taking Chinese donations, but did want them to consider the risk of foreign influence operations. Despite that warning, Shorten would attend Huang's daughter's wedding in January 2016 and visit the billionaire at his home just a few months later, to obtain fundraising for the federal election. Around the same period, Murnain visited Huang at his North Sydney offices.

During the federal campaign, the Liberal Party's negative research unit effectively weaponised Shorten's attendance at the nuptials by sending photographs and video to journalists. John Macgowan, a former Liberal staffer seconded to the unit, confirmed that it was the Liberal Party that obtained the video of Shorten at the wedding.

'Remember, right at the beginning of the campaign, that donation scandal was sparking off?' said Macgowan. 'That night, we had video on TV of Huang Xiangmo's wedding with Shorten sitting there.' Where did they obtain the damning vision? From all the other Liberals who attended. 'There was a whole table of Liberals there,' he laughs. 'Stuff like that, we were trying to do that every day. The real fights happen down on the ground, but you don't want people turning on the 6 pm news seeing your guy getting smashed.'

Macgowan was a dirt-unit veteran, once accused of leaking NSW Labor leader Michael Daley's driving record to *The Sydney Morning Herald*. The newspaper had reported in February 2019 that Daley's staff phoned on a hotline used by MPs for constituents to inform Revenue NSW that his wife was driving his car at the time of a speeding offence. Daley referred the leak of private information to the police after it became clear that the journalist had been provided not only with Daley's information but that of dozens of other motorists.

Macgowan has confirmed his involvement with the leak of the Daley video that destroyed Labor's campaign during the March 2019 state election. The video featured the Labor leader at a 'Politics in the Pub' session in Wentworth Falls, in the Blue Mountains. It was filmed by an out-of-work journalist Daniel Pizzarro. In the video, Daley complained about Asians taking Australian kids' jobs.

'Our young children will flee and who are they being replaced with? They are being replaced by young people from typically Asia with PhDs,' Daley said in the video. The minute it was released, the Labor Party's support crashed.

'One of the kids in one of the ministers' offices – I don't know how he found it, but he made a meme,' Macgowan said. 'I rang him up and said, "How the fuck did you find that?" We found it when it had 40 views [on YouTube] and told everyone to take it.' But it was the story that almost got away because, according to Macgowan, the newspaper the Liberals dropped it to wasn't keen.

'I am 100 per cent serious. Here's how it happened. I dropped it to [*Daily Telegraph* journalist] Anna Caldwell. Unbeknownst to me, there's been a leadership meeting where [Liberal MP] Chris Stone shows [Liberal Treasurer] Dominic Perrottet the video. He gets the video and shows it to *The Daily Telegraph*'s Ben English and he doesn't reckon it's a yarn. Caldwell loses her mind. So they put it online about 8 pm. It got picked up on Chinese social media networks and it just went berserk.'

What Murnain also did not know was that the Chinese billionaire had recently delivered a cheeky $35,000 to the former NSW ALP Secretary James Clements for his 'legal fees' during a sexual harassment scandal that led to his departure and Murnain getting the job.

'He had a wine box and he [Huang] opened it,' said Clements. 'There was cash in it and he had a piece of paper handwritten in English that said, "For your legal fees." He closed the box, screwed the piece of paper up and we walked down and had a cup of tea.' Was Clements surprised to be given the money? 'Well, he paid Sam's [Dastyari] legal fees, so I suppose I wasn't.'

Clements revealed he had kept the money in a box at home to avoid upsetting his wife by putting it in their joint bank account, because she was already a bit annoyed about an extra-marital affair he'd had being all over the newspapers.

'I had a lot going on at the time,' he told ICAC. 'I had to face a police interview, I believed I was about to lose my job, I was told I'd been charged, I was just hit with an AVO, I admitted to my wife I'd had an affair … in the space of 24 to 48 hours.'

Time has not healed Clements' sense of betrayal in Shorten's own conduct during his downfall. After the ICAC hearings he offered to go through his text messages to collate the various examples of Shorten's conduct that he regarded as unreasonable.

It was Shorten's Chief of Staff, Cameron Milner, who was tasked with the job of telling Clements to resign. 'On the 14th of January 2016 I thought I was through my troubles,' Clements said. 'The day before, police had withdrawn my

AVO. I woke up to find my accuser had done a prearranged photo shoot with *The Daily Telegraph*. I was met at work by Sam Dastyari. He told me I was finished.'

The next day, the ALP President Mark Lennon told Clements that Bill Shorten was withdrawing his support.

'I told him that Bill would need to tell me that,' said Clements. 'An hour or so later, Cameron Milner called me. He skirted around the issue. I said, "Listen, mate, if you are calling me to ask me to resign, you can get fucked. I am not an MP. Bill was at my wedding 10 years ago. If he wants me to resign, he can call me himself." Bill called me a little while later. He started to softly dodge around the issue. I said, "Yeah, yeah, Bill, spare me the bullshit. If you want me to go, just say it." He confirmed he thought I needed to resign. I asked him to buy me some time to negotiate my payout, and he agreed. He went out and called for a report from Mark Lennon by the end of the day.

'Next thing I knew, journalists were reporting I told Cameron Milner to "Get fucked". They were leaking the details of my private phone conversations on live news. I quit that day, with a nice payout agreed. In the end I fell on my sword, for the good of the party.

'Bill called me the next day to smooth things over. I said, "I have known you for 15 years. You are the party leader and I served at your pleasure. I don't care that you called on me to go. But leaking my conversations while they were happening is unforgivable."

'I told him never to call me again. I'll never forget my mum ringing me in tears when Bill called on me to go. He had pulled her aside at my wedding, in 2005, and promised her he would always look after me. "How could he do this?" she said. "That's politics, Mum," I replied. The bloke in the focus group in Newcastle in 2014 was right. The only good thing about Bill Shorten being leader was that he can't stab himself in the back.'

Clements went to work for Huang after he lost his job in the ALP head office. Everyone knew he was working out of an office owned by Huang but he was mysterious about his employer. The extent of the largesse – a $4000 a week stipend – was not known until his appearance at ICAC. The general assumption within the ALP had been that he was working for the billionaire, however he only admitted to this at ICAC under oath.

But there were so many revelations. For example, on 7 April 2015, when he called Shorten to arrange the dinner with the billionaire as requested, Huang was sitting in Clements' office when he made the call to the Labor leader.

'Mr Huang said he would like to meet Bill Shorten – he would like to have a lunch or a dinner with Mr Shorten,' Clements told ICAC. 'Could I facilitate that? I said, "Yes, of course," and I gave Mr Shorten a call while Huang was sitting there.'

This was just days before the $100,000 in the Aldi bag was dumped at the ALP's NSW HQ. The cash was banked on 9 April 2015, two days after Huang's visit to organise a dinner with Shorten. ICAC's exhibits included WhatsApp messages from Shorten's Deputy Chief of Staff, Sarah Adams, organising the dinner in a private room at Master

Ken's Seafood, in Chinatown. 'I recall Shorten's staff were sitting there,' Clements told ICAC. 'Mr Shorten sent some glasses of Grange in for them.'

Clements told ICAC that Murnain 'hated his guts'. She explained how hard she had worked to improve governance at the head office. Murnain slammed what she described as the Labor Party's inability to grapple with its 'nasty culture of sexism'. When the sexual harassment scandal erupted that claimed Clements' job, Murnain had sided with the alleged victim and her partner. It was just another reason for the bad blood between them.

'The circumstances leading up to my election in 2016 were horrendous,' she told ICAC. 'Some of these events were reported in the media at the time, and some of these events have received more recent attention. There has been a lot said recently about the culture of the party. Over the past three years we have worked incredibly hard to improve that culture; however, it is clear more work needs to be done. I dedicated my entire life to Labor. I am devastated to leave. I'm sorry to have let you down.'

It was Murnain who had signed the misleading declaration to the NSW Electoral Commission. It demonstrated shocking judgement. It was also convenient to throw Murnain under the bus. Consider the long list of Labor figures who had sought Chinese donations or knew something about the $100,000 in the Aldi bag. They include Ernest Wong, who did not alert authorities, and Dastyari, who never followed the matter up. While he delighted the paparazzi by arriving at ICAC on the lime-green bike and cracking jokes in the witness box, it was Murnain who was sacked from her job.

Having caused the ruckus, Huang complained about being treated like a 'cash cow'.

'After they are elected, as there is no demand for "milk", there is no need to look after the interests of the Chinese community,' he said. 'If any of the past donations I made was deemed inappropriate by any political party or political figure, I again propose the option for them to duly return the amount donated without the need to pay any interest. The returned money will be then donated to Australian charitable organisations accordingly.'

Would you be surprised to learn that didn't happen?

It was all very perplexing, because there had been a simple solution to the donor problem from the outset. As Dastyari explained to ICAC, what happened left him 'flabbergasted'.

'To me, what's incomprehensible about this entire enquiry, to be honest, is that, if the series of events that have been purported are true, they could have just accepted the money into the federal campaign account, which is … how you normally take money from prohibited donors or people about the limits. The federal rules allow you to take that money. That was the bit that just shocked me about this whole thing, and as I heard reports around it … personally I was quite sceptical, because I thought, you can just take the money to the federal account?'

Dastyari's confusion is outlined in the transcript of his private interview, Exhibit 176 at ICAC's hearings.

'And that was your practice when you were general secretary, I take it?' Dastyari is asked.

'Of course, I mean, yeah, you, the rules, the rules are very, very clear. You take, they're not, let's be clear, prohibited state donors are not prohibited federal donors. You take the money, accept the money into the federal campaign account, and you fully disclose it.'

In other words, the NSW ALP had found its way around the pesky laws banning property-developer donors from the beginning. In politics, the cardinal rule is never let a good crisis go to waste. Labor leader Anthony Albanese adhered to the maxim and ordered a clean-out of the NSW branch. 'There is something fundamentally wrong when people running a political party office think it's normal to behave in this way,' he said.

18

ALBO'S DESTINY THING

Anthony Albanese was waiting in the wings as an alternative leader the entire time Bill Shorten led the Labor Party. Nobody was more acutely aware of this than his rival. After the election, Shorten admitted to friends that he spent six years 'looking over my shoulder'. But Albanese's self-identity rests on the idea he is a reluctant conscript. He does not regard himself as a politician driven by ego or ambition. 'I have never had a sense of destiny,' he said in an interview for this book. 'I never sat around in high school telling people that I'd be a politician, let alone that I would lead the Labor Party.' There is an implied criticism of Shorten's ambition contained within these remarks that is completely obvious to anyone who knows both men.

But the idea that he never had 'the destiny thing' is a personal mantra that Albanese has trotted out previously to make the point he is not a megalomaniac with a messiah complex. Once he had said it, his words landed with the dull thud of a practised soundbite. It proved irresistible to check how many times he had previously used the same formula. The answer was rather a lot.

Albanese has managed to insert the 'destiny thing' into just about every interview on leadership he has ever conducted. A simple Google search was enough to disgorge from the internet an exhaustive compendium of this. 'I don't have the "destiny" thing,' he declared when contesting the 2013 leadership ballot. 'You won't find anyone who says that I said to them, "I might be leader one day." Let alone, "I will be leader one day."' He also once told *The Sydney Morning Herald*, 'I don't have the "destiny" thing.' After the 2019 election, he rolled it out again. 'It certainly wasn't a lifetime ambition,' he said.

Shorten was never greatly comforted by Albanese's alleged lack of lifetime ambition. He remained deeply suspicious of his intentions. Albanese remains mildly offended that Shorten remained suspicious. He was never the sort of politician who spent his time endlessly leaking against the leader or leaking from cabinet. From this perspective, Albanese found criticism of him from Shorten's supporters unwarranted. The two men enjoy a relationship that is superficially functional and respectful, but marinating in deep distrust.

Loyalty is important to Albanese and the perception that he is not disloyal. For over a decade, he has excelled at the art of remaining close to leaders even if he was supporting the challenger. Albanese did not support the 2010 leadership coup against Kevin Rudd by Julia Gillard. Later, he told *Four Corners* that on the night of the challenge he spoke to the 'old Beazley group' – Wayne Swan, Stephen Smith, Stephen Conroy and Jenny Macklin – and warned that if Rudd was removed, 'We will kill two Labor prime ministers.' He was right about that. Rudd praised Albanese for acting as the loyal deputy that Gillard should have been.

When Rudd challenged Gillard to reclaim his prize in 2013, Albanese was the last to declare his support for the challenger in a tearful press conference where he sobbed that he just liked 'fighting Tories'. But really, everyone knew where he would land. There was never any doubt he would support Rudd.

'I have despaired in recent days as I have watched Labor's legacy in government be devalued,' he said. 'I have argued against this sort of action before, on the night of 23 June 2010. I believe the government's difficulties can be traced to that night.' Some would argue that Albanese's assessment is still true today, a decade after those traumatic events.

So, was Julia Gillard one of those politicians who harboured secret ambitions to lead the nation as a youngster? Did she have the 'destiny thing'? Yes is the answer. 'Are you kidding?' Albanese laughs when asked.

He knew her at university, in student politics. She was always ambitious. He does not offer this observation as a criticism – they are fond of each other. Albanese admires Gillard and always had a good relationship with her, despite his support for Rudd. There was mutual respect and affection. Together, they were an impressive double act.

It is not an exaggeration to say that the fate of the Gillard Government was sometimes in Albanese's hands. Any lack of discipline, any motion of no confidence, could have proved catastrophic. Labor and the Coalition each won 72 seats in the 150-seat House of Representatives at the 2013 election. It was the first hung Parliament since 1940, with six crossbench MPs holding the balance of power.

But despite the fragile numbers, Gillard and Albanese were a formidable team in securing the passage of substantial pieces of legislation. His skill as a tactician was universally respected and they never lost a substantive vote. Labor colleagues, including Penny Wong, credit him with saving the government. Albanese's failure to remain loyal to Gillard destroyed his relationship with Wayne Swan but his dealings with Gillard remained good.

The next prime minister, Tony Abbott, was a destiny man too. His mum, Fay, once joked on tuckshop duty that her young son would most likely become 'the Pope or prime minister'. Bob Hawke, who was quite possibly born wanting to be prime minister, was a big destiny man. Albanese noted this himself after Hawke's death.

'He towered in this place with the confidence of a man who'd always felt destined for it. Bob had long known that he wanted to be the prime minister of Australia. More importantly, he knew he would be. How could it be otherwise? Family legend always had it that when Bob's mother, Ellie, was pregnant with him her Bible fell open at Isaiah, chapter 9, verse 6: "For unto us a child is born, unto us a son is given; and the government shall be upon his shoulder."'

Albanese's absence of a God complex is refreshingly out of character for many of the nation's political leaders. But while you don't have to be an egomaniac to become prime minister, you do need to have a reason why you want to lead the country. In 2019, Paul Keating remarked on this during the 50th anniversary of his election to parliament with an interview with radio broadcaster Alan Jones.

'To do these jobs properly, you've really got to want to do them because they are so hard,' Keating said. 'And you have to have a framework. Because if you don't have a framework you are just a bit player on the scene, you know? We haven't had frameworks really since Bob and I left.' That's quite a reflection on the Rudd/Gillard governments. The question is, will it be Albanese's epitaph too?

Given his self-declared absence of a destiny complex, what does Albanese's past tell us? In his leadership pitch he talked about growing up in public housing with a single mum, on an invalid pension. 'Public housing down here in Camperdown. I know what it's like to do it tough,' he said.

His biography, *Albanese – Telling It Straight*, tells the story of a Sydney boy growing up with a mother he adored and the absence of a father he never knew. His mother had had a brief romance with his father, Carlos, on a cruise ship in the 1960s. As an adult, Albanese tracked him down to Italy and met him for the first time. Albanese agreed to co-operate for the book by journalist Karen Middleton, but it was not an authorised biography. It was published after the 2016 election, which would have been perfectly timed if he had challenged and become leader at that time. He didn't and the author confirms it wasn't planned to coincide with any leadership timetable.

Albanese was always the more experienced parliamentarian compared to Bill Shorten. He entered politics in 1996, the year that John Howard won office. At 56 when he became leader, he had served in parliament for 22 years. He had also served on Labor's frontbench for close to 20 years and as manager of government business during the Rudd and Gillard years. After Rudd returned to the leadership in 2013, Albanese served briefly as deputy prime minister.

However, apart from two years as a teller for the Commonwealth Bank, straight out of school, Albanese has never worked outside of politics. At the age of 26, he went to work at the NSW ALP head office as assistant secretary. What happens next has been told countless times. Albanese goes on holidays one year and, as some sort of office joke, the Right faction dismantles his corner office and reassembles it in the middle of the room, so everyone can observe him like a chimpanzee at the zoo. The idea is to reinforce the idea that the NSW Right runs the show. Albanese responds by getting some blokes from the manufacturing union to help him move it back when he returns from holidays.

By the time Shorten entered parliament in 2007, Albanese had been an MP for 11 years and was a senior member of shadow cabinet, while Shorten secured a junior parliamentary secretary role for disability and children's services. So there is something of the tortoise and the hare to the tale of Shorten and Albanese.

Speculation emerged of a possible leadership challenge at least three times during the six years Shorten served as opposition leader. The first threat emerged after Malcolm Turnbull rolled Tony Abbott in September 2015. Support for the Turnbull Government soared over the summer that followed. Concern about Shorten's leadership had even emerged in his own Victorian Right faction. Richard Marles, who had been best man at Shorten's wedding to his first wife, Debbie Beale, held talks with NSW Right faction leaders about whether Shorten should be replaced. Marles had also discussed his concerns with Labor MP Dave Feeney, who had been a groomsman at Shorten's wedding. As they say in the classics, if you want loyalty in politics, get a dog.

Sam Dastyari and senator and Treasury spokesman Chris Bowen warned Shorten he was at risk from leadership chatter in 2015. Bowen also confirms the leadership was in play over the summer of 2015/16. 'The general consensus was Turnbull would beat Bill. I wasn't wavering. But there was scuttlebutt around [that] he was under pressure, that there might be a challenge from Albo.'

Labor frontbencher Stephen Conroy also warned him face-to-face that the idea being circulated was: 'We can't win with Shorten against Turnbull.'

Albanese does not deny he was approached about the leadership or that he was in continuous discussions with the NSW Right, but argues there was never any counting or any serious prospect of a move because he made it clear he would not challenge.

'I made my position very clear from 2013 that I accepted the outcome of the leadership ballot and I would not challenge,' he said. Would he have accepted the job if Shorten could have been convinced to stand down? 'There was no vacancy and I did not see the circumstance being created in which Bill Shorten would create a vacancy.'

The second flare-up was in the lead-up to the 2016 election. It was expected that Shorten would lose and a leadership ballot would follow. But on election night it was clear that Shorten had exceeded expectations, coming close to winning government. As soon as the result was known, Bowen announced that he would not support a leadership change. 'On election night, I said, "Bill is safe and we should back him. You can't challenge him".' Tony Burke proved more difficult to convince and tried to persuade Albanese to run anyway.

Despite hailing from the Left faction, Albanese's supporters within shadow cabinet included members of the NSW Right and Victoria's Right. Burke, who hailed from the NSW Right, had voted for Shorten in 2013.

'The only time where I believed we should shift to Albo was immediately after the 2016 election,' he said. 'My view of the rules, and I wasn't mad keen when Kevin Rudd introduced them, was you can't change a leader mid-term. That's the advantage any leader gets under the new rules. But your clear run for three years is the one run you get. So that meant that once Bill had his three years and had not won, that was the moment leadership change should occur.'

'Paul Keating believed one of the great political strengths you have is to change leader and under these rules you can't do that anymore. I think Keating's assessment is correct. But at a federal level I don't think they will be abandoned.'

Burke has high praise for Albanese's political skills.

'He was always the leading parliamentary performer of his generation,' said Burke. 'We've seen how devastatingly effective he could be. I just believed he would be best. I put it to different people. People spoke about it in the NSW Right and it was shut down in 24 hours. Ultimately it was shut down when Albo said he wasn't going to run. He probably had a view, which was probably correct, that if he did contest it wouldn't be successful. Albo knew it was my view, Albo didn't challenge, and that was that.'

Asked if Albanese could have won the 2019 election, Burke said, 'Some things we would have been stronger and some weaker. It's just unknowable.'

Graham Richardson, who continued to play a role as a spiritual leader of the faction long after he quit politics, confirms the discussions. 'We all had concerns about Bill being unpopular. So yes, we had doubts. Bowen would have been worse. It's sad but the mob didn't like him. And then Bowen made it much worse [with franking credits]. So we were caught in one of these situations where you can't move.'

After the 2019 election, when Kevin Rudd popped up at the Canberra Writers' Festival slamming Shorten's election strategy, including franking credits, as 'nuts', he also confirmed that MPs did canvass the idea of switching leaders.

'Rightly or wrongly, the Australian people didn't warm to Bill, they didn't particularly like him and they didn't trust him,' he said. But, of course, the changes to the rules for leadership ballots that Rudd introduced made that tricky. 'Some of the caucus colleagues said to me, "Bugger you, Kevin, for bringing in the rule." From time to time they were thinking about it. That's where you require senior leadership in the party, after a certain period of time, to say to the leader, "We should think this through."'

As a member of the NSW Right, Bowen was always aware of the manoeuvrings within his own faction of those who wanted to replace Shorten. But he argues that Albanese was never the driving force of the NSW Right discussions. 'If there was any counting I wasn't aware of it. I am not critical of his behaviour.'

Albanese's provocative speech in his June 2018 Whitlam Oration fuelled the leadership speculation. It was a coded criticism of Shorten's leadership and was timed to send him a warning shot. Albanese urged closer links with business and warned it was not good enough for the Labor Party to expect voters to 'elect us because the other mob are useless'. And while he didn't specifically mention Shorten's 'top end of town' rhetoric, his criticism was hard to miss.

'Our job is not to sow discord,' he said. 'Labor doesn't have to agree with business on issues such as company tax rates, but we do have to engage constructively with business large and small. We respect and celebrate the importance of individual enterprise and the efforts and importance of the business community.'

Albanese also warned that Labor must appeal to workers who were not in unions, because 'this is not 1950'. 'Indeed, many people from working-class backgrounds are not members of unions because they were beneficiaries of Gough Whitlam's education reforms. They became the first people in their families to go to university, work in the professions and non-unionised industries, or start their own business. We cannot afford to ignore this demographic.'

His warning for Labor proved prescient. 'We must never make the mistake of hoping to slide into government off the back of our opponents' failures.'

Shorten later rang Albanese about the speech and the ideas he had raised. He was not one for ringing colleagues to read the riot act and was careful to adopt an inclusive style to avoid needless blow-ups. But Shorten knew what Albanese was up to.

Tanya Plibersek was sent out to respond to the media firestorm and told reporters she had not read the speech. It was a masterful exercise in subtle putdowns for Albanese.

'I was in Longman yesterday, I had a work function last night, I went to the gym this morning, I did the grocery shopping,' she said. 'I'll get around to it, don't worry. I've known him [Albanese] for a long time — I'm pretty clear on what he's probably got to say. It's probably what he says every day.'

But Albanese will not have a bar of any suggestion his speech was intended to cause trouble. 'The Whitlam Oration was consistent with other major speeches I had given over a long period of time and with the approach I implemented as a minister in the Rudd and Gillard governments,' he said. 'Every proposed amendment from Bill Shorten's office was incorporated into the speech which I had agreed to give on that date well in advance.'

This in itself was unusual. Albanese, unlike most other frontbenchers, did not generally run his speeches past Shorten's office. So, the fact he did this time underlined it would be a controversial speech and he didn't want to be accused of ambushing Shorten.

During this period the convenor of the NSW Right, Joel Fitzgibbon, held talks with Albanese before the July 2018 Super Saturday by-elections about him replacing Shorten if the results didn't go Labor's way. At the time, Fitzgibbon described Albanese to colleagues as 'ready to serve if asked'. Albanese argues he would have never challenged, only accepted the role if Shorten stood down.

Some MPs find that view questionable at best. The less diplomatic of MPs say it is a lie. If the seats of Longman in Queensland or Braddon in Tasmania were lost, there would be a challenge. There was a general view that if either was lost there would be a shift to Albanese. The view was if you couldn't hold seats in a by-election, you weren't much chance of picking up seats at a general election.

There had also been a serious blow-up over tax policy in the lead-up to the by-elections, after Shorten appeared to unilaterally announce a policy to repeal tax cuts for firms with a turnover of between $10 million and $50 million. The decision was approved by his budget razor gang but ran into turbulence from critics who complained it was stupid.

The idea of going to an election promising to repeal tax cuts that have already passed is rarely a great political strategy, because it creates an army of losers. Shorten had basically stuffed up, forgetting that the policy was yet to go through shadow cabinet and ALP caucus. He did not intend to announce the policy unilaterally or circumvent debate, but it was a sign that he did largely assume MPs' acquiescence. Shorten announced his compromise quickly. It involved keeping the tax cuts in place for businesses with a turnover of up to $50 million instead of $10 million.

'Our expenditure review committee made the decision to lift the threshold, to reduce the tax rate for companies between $2 million and $10 million,' he said. 'But what I have also said is that I have listened to all of the debate, spoken to colleagues, listened to business. I now accept that simply stopping at $10 million would have created more confusion and uncertainty and it was not the main game.'

The backdown ensured Labor would keep the tax rates for all companies with a $50 million turnover frozen at the current rate of 27.5 per cent. If elected, Labor would try to legislate to block any further scheduled reduction below 27.5 per cent. There were a lot of fed-up MPs in shadow cabinet and the ALP caucus, who were sick and tired of being presented with a fait accompli. If there was going to be a leadership challenge after the Super Saturday by-elections, this debacle would be a trigger point.

Retiring Labor MP Jenny Macklin warned her colleagues against pushing for a leadership ballot after the July by-elections. Shortly before she left politics, in an interview with the ABC's *Insiders* program, she urged the party not to change leaders again. 'I don't want to be particularly political today,' she said, 'but it certainly got through to our side of politics that unity is absolutely paramount, and I think the Australian people have actually made a really, really big shift over the last 20 years of my time in politics. It goes back much longer than the last 10 years, I'm sorry to say, and, well, if I'm just one example, I've learnt my lessons.'

She warned that voters expected a government that was united. 'I think we understand that the Australian people mark you down very heavily if you fight among yourselves, because they have an expectation of what we need to deliver to them.'

The intervention was significant for two reasons. Firstly, Macklin rarely commented on such matters, so it underlined the fact that the threat to Shorten's leadership was regarded as serious. Secondly, she was known to have a degree of scepticism about his capabilities and his policy agenda, given she was reluctant to embrace negative gearing or franking credits.

The by-elections, which posed the biggest risk so far for Shorten, had been sparked by the citizenship crisis. Multiple MPs were dragged into the saga over Section 44 of the Constitution, which states that any person who 'is under any acknowledgement of allegiance, obedience, or adherence to a foreign power, or is a subject or a citizen or entitled to the rights or privileges of a subject or citizen of a foreign power … shall be incapable of being chosen or of sitting as a senator or a member of the House of Representatives'.

In 2017, there were seven instances of a possible breach. Australian Greens Senators Scott Ludlam and Larissa Waters resigned, together with Liberal National Party Senator Matt Canavan, One Nation Senator Malcolm Roberts, Deputy Prime Minister and Nationals leader Barnaby Joyce, deputy leader of the Nationals and Senator Fiona Nash, and Nick Xenophon Team leader and Senator Nick Xenophon. Their cases were referred to the High Court.

At first, Shorten boasted that Section 44 was not an issue for his own MPs, a confidence that proved to be misplaced. After the Canavan case was decided by the High Court, Liberal Senator and President of the Senate Stephen Parry, Liberal MP John Alexander, Tasmanian Senator Jacqui Lambie and NXT Senator Skye Kakoschke-Moore also resigned after discovering that they held British citizenship by descent. And in December 2017, the House of Representatives referred Labor MP David Feeney to the High Court, as well as Labor Senator Katy Gallagher.

Shorten agrees that the greatest threat of a leadership challenge emerged in the lead-up to those by-elections. He knew that if he lost those contests, specifically in Longman in Queensland and Braddon in Tasmania, he was gone.

Shorten's office realised how vulnerable he was. Without direction from their leader, his staff were war-gaming and preparing for the prospect of a contest with Albanese – even drawing up a dirt file on him, featuring potential stories. The file included his decision to declare an investment property in Sydney, but not investment income from a second property he owned.

This was not an uncommon practice by politicians and not strictly against the rules, but something that might prove a negative story to drop to the newspapers, should the need arise. For example, the Labor Party had raised the Liberal MP John Alexander's failure to declare rental income in his disclosures to parliament during the Bennelong by-election in December 2017. He owned an eight-bedroom luxury property in the NSW Southern Highlands. At the time, newspaper reports noted that many other MPs chose to simply declare 'rental income' on the form in line with the request that you declare any other substantial forms of income. MPs who have done this in the past include Malcolm Turnbull, David Gillespie, Warren Entsch, Ian Goodenough and Barry O'Sullivan.

But Albanese clearly views the rules differently, because to this day he does not declare rental income to parliament. Despite owning several properties with his former wife, Carmel Tebbutt, he does not include any reference to investment income. It's a question of interpretation, of course, whether investment income is covered off by mentioning it's an investment property, but it isn't a caveat Labor was prepared to accept with Alexander.

After Albanese became Labor leader, tension continued to be evident between him and Shorten supporters. From the beginning of his leadership, Albanese privately accused them of leaking from cabinet and undermining him. It started with how Labor would approach the tax-cut legislation and went on from there.

In June, Albanese confronted the leakers face-to-face, complaining in shadow cabinet. He told his frontbench that 'they might have noticed the material for the meeting was distributed only an hour before the meeting', and he said there was a reason for that. Albanese complained that there had been more leaks in the previous three weeks – largely about shadow cabinet's position on the tax cuts – than in the past six years. He indicated that needed to stop. Shorten – leader during the six-year period Albanese referred to – had phoned in to the meeting because he was on holiday with his family in Bali. The entire exchange promptly leaked again, proving that asking anyone not to leak is usually not a great way to stop the leaks.

On 24 June 2019, The New Daily reported that the Labor Party was likely to land on a policy of waving through tax changes to deliver a 30-cents-in-the-dollar tax rate for all workers earning under $200,000. The strategy of amending the legislation, but not voting down the tax cuts if the amendments failed, was leaked weeks before it was formally announced.

Albanese indignantly denied the report at the time, before later confirming Labor would not block the tax cuts. The real pressure point was the government's refusal to pay out $1080 tax cuts for 10 million workers from 1 July unless Labor agreed to the entire package. Shadow cabinet also discussed bringing forward tax cuts due in 2022 to address the weakening economy.

The peace plan followed a warning from Labor frontbencher Joel Fitzgibbon at a shadow cabinet meeting earlier in June that the ALP should adopt a pragmatic approach. 'We've got to stop being a government in exile,' Fitzgibbon said. 'If John Howard hadn't won control of the Senate in 2004, WorkChoices would not have got through and he might still be the PM.'

At the same meeting, shadow Treasury spokesman Jim Chalmers had originally argued it would be 'offensive' for Labor to support a flat tax rate of 30 per cent for workers earning six figures. He was backed by the former Treasury spokesman Chris Bowen.

Unions remained sceptical, arguing Labor should not fold. 'We believe this reduces the progressive nature of the taxation system,' Sally McManus said. 'Someone on $50,000 will be paying the same tax as someone on $200,000.'

This pattern of capitulation on tax and national security rankled some Labor supporters. Albanese's response was to remind them of the simple reality that Labor had lost the election.

'I understand the disappointment that is out there,' he said. 'We have to examine things as they are, rather than as we would like them to be. For all those people who are disappointed – including myself and members of the caucus who looked at the Newspolls and looked at the commentary and thought we were destined to be in government – the fact is we have less seats now than we had before the election, the Coalition have more seats now and the Senate is more conservative, so it will be far more difficult to stop legislation.'

This is true, although it hardly precluded him from opposing bad legislation. As for the reason Labor lost an election it never expected to lose, Albanese accepted there were 'too many policies'.

'We got it wrong,' he said. 'Not everything was wrong, of course, but enough was. We lost an election, which, given the chaos on the other side, we should have won. The message to us is that too many people were confused, or even frightened, by our policies, or didn't trust us to implement them. We failed to present a clear and concise narrative that explained an optimistic sense of what our country could become.' Labor's largesse in policy development meant there was too much clutter for voters to recognise the good news. 'They didn't know that their childcare costs were going to be reduced substantially. They didn't know many of the benefits that we were proposing.'

This is an analysis that Shorten is on a unity ticket with. 'There were too many messages,' he said. 'And we should have offered people more in the way of income tax relief.'

But the danger for the Labor Party is that it becomes lost fighting the ghosts of previous elections. One lesson from Labor's failure to win is that fighting the last election is no way to win the current battle.

After the election, Albanese was fond of telling journalists he planned to 'hasten slowly' in the job. It was a famous saying of the first Roman emperor, Augustus Caesar. 'Hasten slowly,' he said. 'Better a safe commander than a bold'. And 'That which has been done well has been done quickly enough.'

It's good advice, although it's questionable how much time Albanese has. It's highly unlikely Labor will allow him another go if he makes it to the next election and loses. He's got one chance to remain as Labor leader and it involves not only surviving in the job long enough to fight an election, but winning it.

Drawing on the collective wisdom of his 92 years, Queensland union leader Bill Ludwig doesn't think Albanese is much chop and predicts Labor frontbencher Jim Chalmers is a better option in the long term. 'I think he's the only hope we've got, quite frankly,' he said. 'He comes across well. He's got a presence on the television and he's from Queensland.'

Just six months after the election, Scott Morrison's supposed Midas touch as prime minister was already dented. He was lashed for going on holidays to Hawaii during the bushfire crisis. It was the first time since the election that he had sustained any genuine national criticism. When he returned home, he was heckled by bushfire survivors in the town of Cobargo, on the NSW South Coast, an exchange that made international news. A firefighter in nearby Quaama, who'd lost his own home, declined to shake his hand. Predictions that Morrison would command unprecedented authority after his upset election win, or that he had perfect political judgement, suddenly seemed premature. Albanese again proved cautious, not rushing to criticise the prime minister, but also not interrupting his enemies making mistakes. He left the question of which policies Labor would dump, and which ones it would keep, open until closer to the election.

It remains unknown whether Albanese has the personal popularity to get Labor over the line. As his friend Labor frontbencher Mark Butler notes, the ALP has won only three victories over Liberal governments since World War II and all have involved an immensely popular leader, a compelling national vision and a superior campaign. The vision thing might work, and the superior campaign Labor can work on, but an immensely popular leader? There's no evidence to date of that. The danger is that the ALP will again – to quote Butler – get its 'arse handed to it on a plate by *The Muppet Show*'.

So Albanese's road map is essentially in the mould of John Howard's 1996 victory. Howard won with a small-target strategy. He was not regarded as a hugely charismatic leader at the time; in fact, he was dismissed as an electoral loser. But he was a known quantity. He was assisted by an unpopular leader, Paul Keating, who was lucky to win in 1993. Could history repeat itself?

Kerry Packer once said that you only get one Alan Bond in your life and Keating was lucky to get one John Hewson. As it turned out, Scott Morrison was incredibly lucky to get Bill Shorten and Chris Bowen's franking-credits policy. The Liberal Party won a supposedly unwinnable election with a threadbare book of policies. But as any student of history can tell you, it would be premature to write Labor off. Events have a habit of intervening in unpredictable ways that change the political landscape. And this is the lesson that even Howard takes from the ALP's bitter defeat. 'The Labor Party is not dead,' he said. 'The Labor Party will come back fighting again. Deep down, we should never imagine that we are immune from hubris, that we are never going to lose an election.'

ACKNOWLEDGEMENTS

This book was an idea that grew out of a conversation in the leafy and sometimes treacherous wisteria patio at my home with two journalists I've known since I arrived in Canberra in 1998, Annabel Crabb and Jim Middleton. The former I have known for even longer and she has been parenting me with mixed success since I was teenager. Thank you for your wise advice and guidance. I would like to thank my publisher Meredith Curnow and lovely editor Patrick Mangan for all of their tireless work and patience with a book novice. My editors and colleagues at The New Daily have also been a delight to work with and I would like to thank them all for their support, in particular Neil Frankland, Patrick Elligett and the fabulous Zona Black.

Several journalists I admire agreed to read extracts of this book and provide advice. I am grateful to the legendary Laurie Oakes, David Speers, Matt Cunningham, Nick Leys and Louise Milligan for their thoughts and friendship. A Labor MP who shall remain nameless also provided this service – thank you also for your guidance, it was excellent. I have relied on the work of many journalists in researching this book – as much as possible I have tried to reference this in my book, but thank you all. I would also like to thank Amy Remeikis, James Campbell, Niki Savva and Sharri Markson for their sharp political analysis and advice, and Mel Bell, Beelah Bleakley and Sally Rugg for being wonderful in general. Mostly, I would like to thank all of the political animals that spoke to me for this project, the politicians, staff and pollsters who were so generous with their time and guidance. I enjoyed all of our conversations. Without your assistance I would never have written this book. Many times during these months, after being bundled out of the house again by their dad, Tim, my children Bill, Ned and Matilda have returned home asking me, 'Have you finished the book yet, Mum?' Thank you for being smart, wonderful and extremely patient and the best children ever invented. I love you.

Samantha Maiden is the political editor for The New Daily. She has covered federal politics from the Canberra press gallery for 21 years, including the rise and fall of six prime ministers, seven elections and multiple leadership challenges. She is a regular panellist on *The Project*.